JavaScript®

How to Order:

For information on quantity discounts contact the publisher: Prima Publishing, P.O. Box 1260BK, Rocklin, CA 95677-1260; (916) 632-4400. On your letterhead include information concerning the intended use of the books and the number of books you wish to purchase. For individual orders, turn to the back of this book for more information.

JavaScript®

Paul Kooros
Michele DeWolfe

PRIMA PUBLISHING

Publisher:
Don Roche, Jr.

Associate Publisher:
Ray Robinson

Managing Editor:
Heather Kaufman Urschel

Senior Acquisitions Editor:
Alan Harris

Project Editor:
Anne Owen

Technical Reviewer:
Jim O'Donnell

Indexer:
Sherry Massey

P ™

is a trademark of Prima Publishing, a division of Prima Communications, Inc.

Prima Publishing™ is a trademark of Prima Communications, Inc.

Prima Publishing, Rocklin, California 95677.

ISBN: 0-7615-0685-3
Library of Congress Catalog Card Number: 96-68062
Printed in the United States of America

96 97 98 99   DD   10 9 8 7 6 5 4 3 2 1

Contents at a Glance

Table of Contents

Chapter 4
The JavaScript Object Model
87

Chapter 5
Creating and Using JavaScript Objects
97

Chapter 6
JavaScript Events
109

Chapter 7
JavaScript Objects

127

Chapter 8
JavaScript Methods   201

Chapter 9
JavaScript Properties 277

Introduction

Welcome to JavaScript! JavaScript is one of many exciting new developments on the frontier of the World Wide Web (WWW). JavaScript, along with Java, Microsoft's ActiveX, and Virtual Reality Modeling Language (VRML), has changed the way we look at and interact with the Internet. These programming tools have taken a medium designed for simple text documents and turned the Web into an interactive experience. JavaScript is a "C++-like" programming language designed to be included directly in HTML documents. JavaScript programs execute on the Web browser computer. This gives Web pages the new capability to control the browser's behavior. JavaScript bridges the gap between HTML and Java.

Some of the cool uses of JavaScript programs include checking the user's input on an HTML form. Also, it's now possible to do simple animations as well as communicate with Java applets. There are many more uses of JavaScript in the examples throughout this book. The important thing to remember, as you will soon see, is that JavaScript is *much* easier to learn and use than Java.

This is an exciting time to witness the evolution of the Internet and the World Wide Web. Many of these Web interactivity programming tools are currently under development, and what you see today is just a shadow of what you're going to see tomorrow.

This is certainly the case with JavaScript, which will continue to evolve as user needs are better understood.

Chapter 1, "Introducing JavaScript," is a high level introduction to JavaScript that covers its strengths and weaknesses and leads you through writing your first JavaScript program.

Chapter 2, "Getting Started: JavaScript Basics," covers the basics of JavaScript, the small parts or building blocks of the language. Many of these basics will be familiar if you know Java, C, or C++. However, even if you're a Java expert, be sure to read through this section. JavaScript is quite different from Java, and we'll point out significant differences where they occur.

It's a lot easier to learn a new language when you see its use demonstrated. Therefore, JavaScript code examples are provided throughout this book. Because of programming dependencies, some parts of JavaScript may be used before they have been defined. Please bear with us and have faith that everything will be explained soon! .We use this as a way to tie together the elements of JavaScript. Chapter 2 also introduces the object model of JavaScript; however, the object model is covered in more detail in Chapter 4.

Chapter 3, "HTML Overview and Primer," is a review of the HTML code and concepts with which the user should already be familiar. An understanding of HTML is vital to coding in JavaScript because many JavaScript objects are created by using HTML. This chapter examines the structure of HTML forms and documents. It also introduces the relationship between HTML elements and JavaScript elements such as properties.

Chapter 4, "The JavaScript Object Model," introduces the JavaScript object model. JavaScript is object based, not object oriented. This chapter compares JavaScript structure to that of Java, C++, and other object-oriented, nonprocedural languages. Finally, it introduces terms and concepts used in object-oriented design and programming.

Chapter 5, "Creating and Using JavaScript Objects," puts JavaScript Objects to use. This chapter also discusses arrays as a special kind of object.

Chapter 6, "JavaScript Events," is an introduction to events. It can be said that object-oriented programming is nonprocedural because it is event driven. This chapter introduces the terminology and structure associated with events and event handling. JavaScript contains special properties that are designed to notify an object that an event has occurred, which in turn triggers other actions. This chapter also gives examples of event usage.

Chapter 7, "JavaScript Objects," Chapter 8, "JavaScript Methods," and Chapter 9, "JavaScript Properties," are reference sections that detail the use of JavaScript objects and methods. Chapter 7 covers each JavaScript object in detail. Chapter 8 describes JavaScript methods organized by object type. These two chapters list alphabetically all of the methods associated with an object. Chapter 9 lists JavaScript properties in alphabetical order. Be sure to refer to the specific method or property if you have questions about what is happening in the examples.

Appendix A, "Colors," is a detailed list of JavaScript default colors and instructions on how to create your own colors. And finally, the "Glossary" lists the terms introduced in this book.

We had a lot of fun coming up with examples that demonstrate the power and usage of JavaScript. We hope that you try the examples out for yourself. The power of JavaScript will become evident when you try programming in it on your own to bring your HTML pages to life. And programming is a lot more fun than reading lines of code!

Chapter 1

Introducing JavaScript

World Wide Web usage is on the brink of an explosion. The history of computing technology shows that user needs drive the development of tools, and tools present users with ideas for more needs. Think of the current Internet as a primordial soup, a fertile ground in which endless variations occur and vie for superiority, a high-velocity natural selection. In this case, the ability to survive is measured in cost and usefulness to the user, as well as adaptability to new technical demands and changing environments.

We believe that JavaScript has a fighting chance to rise above the "soup" and find its niche of utility. It bridges HTML (HyperText Markup Language), which is a ubiquitous "standard" for the World Wide Web, and Java, an extremely powerful, general-purpose language. The Microsoft Explorer 3.0 Web Browser now supports both Java and JavaScript. Netscape got JavaScript off the ground and proved the usefulness of bridging the gap between HTML and Java with a flexible browser control language. This has certainly contributed to Microsoft buying into JavaScript, and the domination of Netscape in the browser market hasn't dampened Microsoft's interest, either.

Java is designed to bring object-oriented concepts to the Web and may be used as a full-blown application language. However, in its initial implementations, it was used to construct applets for the World Wide Web. Because Java's class structures are loaded separately, it's perfectly modularized for network distributed applications.

Unlike Java, which is a compiled language, JavaScript is a scripted language. In other words, the language exists only in source text form. A compiled language is translated into a binary executable format by the programmer. This binary executable can then be directly run by the computer. A script, on the other hand, is interpreted by a program (interpreter) directly from its source code. The JavaScript program is executed directly by the JavaScript interpreter built into the Web browser.

The terminology "script" comes from the Internet's UNIX heritage, where command interpreter (shell) batch files are called "shell scripts." Other scripted languages include Perl, TCL, and AWK.

JavaScript is not Java. JavaScript is intended to fill the gap between HTML, CGI (Common Gateway Interface), and Java, and implements some of the concepts of object-oriented languages, but not all. This is both a blessing and a curse. For example, JavaScript is easier to learn and apply because it is loosely typed. However, because it lacks the type-checking features of strongly typed languages, such as Java, the dependency is on the programmer for correctness. Java enforces a strict structure on Java programs, greatly complicating the construction of even the simplest program. JavaScript, on the other hand, substantially reduces or eliminates Java's red tape.

Because JavaScript is easy to learn, we feel that at the end of this book, you'll be a competent JavaScript programmer with many useful examples under your belt.

Although JavaScript is simple to learn, it has its limitations. JavaScript's current incarnation is restricted to the domain of the browser. (This is the curse part.) JavaScript limitations include the inability to open remote files or network connections, lack of direct graphics, and lack of support for exceptions.

Nonetheless, JavaScript supplies the tools to solve many user-interface problems that are very common to the Web. JavaScript empowers HTML documents to be self-sustained and independent of CGI programming restrictions. JavaScript also enables HTML pages to be interactive. Finally, JavaScript enables programming of documents to be more modular. In other words, JavaScript code embedded in HTML documents is reusable, one of the hallmarks of object-oriented programming.

Past and Future of JavaScript

JavaScript started out as LiveScript, which was developed by Netscape in 1995. This development effort was undergone at the same time Sun Microsystems was bringing Java to the market. Netscape and Sun decided to team up to tackle different aspects of Internet applications. Sun brought out Java to cover full-blown applications that use the Web as a giant network. Netscape developed LiveScript to jazz up and make interactive Web pages, and to allow them to process data and control browser behavior. LiveScript was also meant to be a precursor to an integrated, object-oriented Web authoring system.

LiveScript was renamed JavaScript when Netscape and Sun announced their collaboration to the world. This was meant to emphasize the complementary nature of the two languages.

One of the common misconceptions that has arisen based on the similarities of the names Java and JavaScript is that one is a subset of the other. Another misconception is that learning JavaScript will prepare a programmer for Java. While they both share a common syntax heritage from C and C++, Java and JavaScript are substantially different languages; learning one will not prepare you much for learning the other.

The future of JavaScript is to add features and fix bugs. Netscape 2.0 was full of bugs; although Netscape 2.01 is much better, it's still full of bugs. New Netscape releases are perpetually imminent; therefore, JavaScript will evolve along with Netscape. Because it's very early in the JavaScript product life cycle, we anticipate that it will become more feature rich and bug free as time goes on.

What's Missing in JavaScript

There are some language features that are not currently supported by JavaScript. Even without these features, JavaScript is a robust Internet programming tool. However, here are some features that would be convenient to have in future incarnations of JavaScript:

- Network communications

- Disk I/O of some form

- Persistent local data storage, beyond HTTP cookies

- Access to the user's local environment variables

- Table object support

- Threads

- Method of overriding security for local application with user consent

- Read-only property for use with output objects

- Capability to create new events in JavaScript

- Addition of richer set of properties to browser objects, such as history and anchors

This list is not comprehensive; the limitations of JavaScript will become better known as it's more widely used. As these limitations are overcome, JavaScript will become a richer language.

We anticipate that Netscape will meet these demands. Netscape has done well in their market due to their responsiveness to the user, and we have no reason to believe that will change.

The Nuts and Bolts of Creating JavaScript

One of the best features of JavaScript, as opposed to Java or even CGI programming, is that the only tools the programmer needs are a JavaScript-capable Web browser and a plain text editor. This is in contrast to Java, which requires a compiler and an ability to manage a somewhat complex development environment. Web CGI programming is no cakewalk, either, as access to the server directories and configuration is needed. The delicacies of developing and debugging CGI or Java programs should *not* be underestimated.

Therefore, JavaScript development can be managed in a low-budget, relatively low-complexity environment. The Web browser can be any JavaScript-aware browser, such as Netscape Navigator Microsoft Explorer. JavaScript-incapable browsers will happily ignore JavaScript programs. This allows CGI-based Web pages to be augmented with JavaScript while still maintaining backward compatibility.

Creating a JavaScript Program

Creating and running a JavaScript program is easy. Simply create a file with the program in it and then load the file into the browser. All of the examples in this book have been created and tested in this way.

Use a plain text editor, not a word processor, to create the HTML file containing the JavaScript program. The native document formats of most word processors are unusual binary formats, not suitable for producing an HTML document. Plain vanilla editors, like the MS-DOS program EDIT, the MS Windows program NOTEPAD, or UNIX programs like *vi* and *emacs*, will do just fine. If you use an HTML editor, you can continue to do so. Just make sure it allows manual entry of unrecognized HTML tags.

The following example uses the MS Windows program NOTEPAD to create an HTML file named first.html:

```
<HTML>
<HEAD>
<TITLE>My First JavaScript Program</TITLE>
<SCRIPT LANGUAGE="JavaScript">
    document.writeln("Hello there, wide world of
JavaScript!<BR>");
</SCRIPT>
</HEAD>
<BODY>
This is the body of my first JavaScript program's HTML
➥document.<BR>
<SCRIPT LANGUAGE="JavaScript">
    document.writeln("Arivederci!<BR>");
</SCRIPT>
</BODY>
</HTML>
```

After you create this simple text file, you can ask Netscape to read it in and then process it. Use the File | Open File pull-down menu to tell Netscape to read in a file.

That's all it takes. Now you're ready to learn the elements and structure of JavaScript.

Chapter 2

Getting Started: JavaScript Basics

This chapter covers the elements of JavaScript, the building blocks of the language. Many of these basics of JavaScript will be familiar to those of you who know Java, C, or C++. However, even if you are a Java expert, be sure to read through this chapter.

The components of JavaScript covered in this chapter are: data types and values, variables, literals, arrays, expressions, operators, statements, blocks, control flow structures, and functions. You need to be familiar with these concepts to be able to program in JavaScript; mastery of them is essential. The rest of the book builds upon these concepts and shows their power and usage.

The first thing you need to understand is the structure of JavaScript in the context of HTML; therefore, the next section offers a review of HTML as it relates to JavaScript. Once again, please read the next section even if you are an HTML expert because there may be a few surprises for you.

JavaScript and HTML

JavaScript is integrated into, acts on, and produces HTML (HyperText Markup Language). It would be very difficult to work with JavaScript without a working knowledge of HTML. There are plenty of books available on just about every aspect of HTML. If you have trouble with this chapter, take a look at some books on HTML and refer to Chapter 3, "An HTML Overview and Primer."

It's important to at least be familiar with basic HTML and HTML forms because JavaScript currently exists only as part of an HTML document. In effect, JavaScript extends the functionality of HTML. JavaScript also provides a bridge between Java, the browser, and HTML, allowing manipulation of browsers and document components. This purpose of JavaScript will become evident through the examples in the rest of this book and especially in Chapter 3, "An HTML Overview and Primer."

JavaScript programs cannot perform anything without residing within an HTML document. HTML carries JavaScript code within it as an HTML comment to prevent JavaScript-incapable browsers from seeing and displaying JavaScript code. This allows HTML documents that carry JavaScript code to be backward compatible with non-JavaScript enabled browsers.

JavaScript programs are typically located in the <HEAD> section of an HTML document. See the example in the next section if this structure is unfamiliar. The JavaScript within an HTML document is processed as the browser receives the document.

Using a JavaScript function before it has been defined results in an error. Therefore, it's recommended practice to put all function definitions and initializations in the <HEAD> section of the document, where they will be processed before the browser renders any part of the page.

Generating Output

JavaScript programs can use three mechanisms to generate output: with a pop-up window containing an error warning message or confirmation; by manipulation of browser and document components, such as making a message appear in a form's text input box; and finally, by actually generating HTML and having the browser render its output as a document.

In addition to these explicit or direct ways of producing output, JavaScript can also indirectly produce output by manipulating browser objects.

JavaScript's Context within HTML

As you probably are aware, HTML tags are instructions to the browser. They are distinguished from text to be printed by being surrounded by angle brackets < and >. Immediately following the opening angle bracket is the name of the tag. Tags may contain parameters, called *attributes*, which influence the tag's behavior. Attributes reside within the angle brackets with the tag and have the form

```
<NAME = VALUE>
```

All JavaScript code begins with the HTML tag

```
<SCRIPT Language="JavaScript">
```

and ends with the tag

```
</SCRIPT>
```

This tells the browser that it can find a JavaScript program between these script tags. For example:

```
<HTML>
<HEAD>
<TITLE>Use of script tags</TITLE>
<SCRIPT Language="JavaScript">
<!- HTML comment hiding the JavaScript program from old
➡browsers
//the body of the JavaScript program goes here...
//end hiding from JavaScript-incapable browsers: ->
</SCRIPT>
</HEAD>
<BODY>
This page doesn't do much.
</BODY>
</HTML>
```

Of course, this program doesn't do much. It just shows the layout of a JavaScript program within an HTML document.

Another item of interest you may have noticed in the example is `<!–`. This begins an HTML comment, extending from the `<!–` up through the `–>`. This is how JavaScript tricks JavaScript-incapable browsers into ignoring JavaScript code.

The HTML spec requires browsers to disregard unknown tags. A browser incapable of dealing with JavaScript will ignore the `<SCRIPT LANGUAGE="JavaScript">` and `</SCRIPT>` tags. If the JavaScript program text itself is enclosed in HTML comment tags, the JavaScript-incapable browser will also ignore the entire program. However, JavaScript-capable browsers are smart enough to disregard the HTML comment and process the program.

Many existing HTML tags have had their definitions extended to include new attributes that influence the behavior of JavaScript programs. For example, form elements can have an `onClick` attribute that defines the JavaScript code that runs when the element is clicked on.

Other currently defined HTML attributes are used by JavaScript's object model to make documents accessible from programs. For example, an HTML form's `<INPUT>` elements are all accessible via their `NAME` attribute's value. This enables a JavaScript program to do range checking on form input, for example. The following section discusses JavaScript's object model.

A Little about the JavaScript Object Model

The JavaScript *object model* is covered in detail in Chapter 4, "The JavaScript Object Model." It's introduced here to make it easier to understand the relationship between the browser and JavaScript.

JavaScript allows access to components of documents via an *object hierarchy*. JavaScript's object model is hierarchical, as is a directory tree, genealogical tree, or an organizational chart. This means that elements may have sub-components or may be sub-components of other elements. For example, `<FORM>` may contain several `<INPUT>` or `<SELECT>` sub-components. The same `<FORM>` is itself a sub-component of an HTML document.

The object model allows JavaScript programs to access and manipulate browser objects in the same manner that a directory tree allows a user to manipulate and access files. The following example shows a

JavaScript program called from an HTML document (remember that HTML is not case sensitive):

```
<HTML>
<BODY>
<FORM NAME="mystuff">
<INPUT TYPE="text" NAME="foom" VALUE = "The Text">
</FORM>
</SCRIPT LANGUAGE="JavaScript">
alert(window.document.mystuff.foom.value);
</SCRIPT>
</BODY>
</HTML>
```

This code prints the text contents of the input box in a pop-up window. Pop-up windows are created by a call to `alert`. Objects such as form elements or browser objects are accessible to JavaScript programs via this object hierarchy. In this example, `value` is a sub-object (known as a *property*) of the text-input box `foom`. `foom`, in turn, is a sub-object of the form `mystuff`, which is a sub-object of `document`. A *property* is an object that has a real value. The concept of *property* is similar to the HTML *attribute* concept.

Objects are structurally analogous to directories, and properties are the equivalent of files. Objects (directories) may have sub-objects (subdirectories), as well as properties (files). Properties (files) have values (file contents) of several types (file formats). The preceding example's conceptual equivalent path would be /window/document/mystuff/foom/value, which would contain the text as its file contents. The only difference here is that file contents actually correspond to the real-life state of browser components.

The Building Blocks of JavaScript

JavaScript has a much simpler structure than Java, C, or C++, which are full-featured languages. As of this writing, JavaScript cannot support a standalone application. JavaScript programs run only within the browser. Java and C++ are object-oriented, but JavaScript is object-based. JavaScript has little notion of classes, inheritance, encapsulation, or data hiding. All of these concepts are explained later, but we want you to begin to become familiar with these terms.

Before discussing how to put together a JavaScript program, it's necessary to first understand the language's individual component nuts and bolts. These components can then be assembled into programs that put JavaScript to work.

The components of JavaScript include *comments*, *statements*, *literals*, *expressions*, *operators*, *variables*, *control structures*, and *functions*. Use this chapter as a reference for Chapter 4, which puts these pieces to use. The rest of this chapter is devoted to explaining these elements.

Comments and Programming Style

JavaScript *comments* serve the same purpose as comments within any other computer language: they're used for program readability and maintainability. The interpreter ignores text within comments. Just because something is difficult to code shouldn't mean that it should be difficult to maintain—use comments!

Comments in JavaScript are defined the same as in Java and C++: they're delimited by /* and */ or //. A tag comment begins with the comment delimiter // and extends through the end of the line. Traditional C style block comments begin with a /* and extend through the first */. In JavaScript, you cannot nest block style comments. All characters within a block comment, including a second /*, are ignored by JavaScript.

Here is an example of a complete HTML document demonstrating the use of JavaScript comments:

```
<HTML>
<HEAD>
<TITLE>Program that does nothing</TITLE>
<SCRIPT Language="JavaScript">
<!- HTML comment hiding the JavaScript program from old browsers
➥/* This is a comment */

// This is a one-line comment.

// A one-line comment is terminated by the end of the current
➥line.

/* This is a
    multi-line comment */

/*
```

```
**   A typical use of multi-line comments
**   is to format successive lines with a column
**   of *s, forming a vertical bar,
**   visually indicating the extent of the comment.
*/

// This ends the HTML comment:  ->

</SCRIPT>
</HEAD>
<BODY>
The JavaScript program in this HTML document does nothing.
</BODY>
</HTML>
```

Strive to maximize clarity with comments. Comments are meant to be read by other programmers who may need to modify a given JavaScript program. Comments may also be read by the program's author who may not remember how the program written six months ago behaves.

Comments should be useful. Here is an example of a useless comment:

```
i = i + 6;              // Add 6 to i and store back into i
```

The comment does nothing but repeat what is already said succinctly by the code. Here is a better comment:

```
i = i + 6;              // Advance the array index to the next
data set.
```

This comment tells the reader the intention of the code and describes the part it plays in the program. Consider the following JavaScript function:

```
function alert_props(obj, str) {
    var acc = "";
    for (var i in obj) {
        acc = acc + str + "." + i + " = " + obj.i + "\n";
```

```
    }
    alert(acc);
}
```

Compare it to this JavaScript function, which is identical except for comments and variable names:

```
/*
**   alert_props  — Display an object's properties in an alert
➥pop-up
**      Arguments: obj        The object
**                 obj_name   The object's name (str)
*/
function alert_props(obj, obj_name) {
    // result accumulates the string to send to alert()
    var result = "";

    // For each property of the object 'obj'
    for (var prop in obj) {
        // Add the current object's name and value onto end of
➥'result'
        result = result + obj_name + "." + prop + " = " +
➥obj.prop + "\n";
    }

    alert(result);
}
```

The second function is more easily reusable because someone looking at the code can simply read the header comment to know the function's use. Ideally, those reading the code should not even need to know JavaScript to understand the program if the comments are descriptive enough.

JavaScript is a free-form language. This means that, generally, the JavaScript interpreter disregards whitespace, such as spaces, tabs, and newlines put between language elements. If JavaScript doesn't find a full command on one line, it continues on to subsequent lines until it does. For example, this program

```
var i=2;while(i<8){if(i>3){alert(i);}i++;}
```

and this program

```
var i = 2;
while (i < 8) {
    if (i > 3) {
        alert(i);
    }
    i++;
}
```

appear identical to the interpreter, because they differ only in the way white space has been used to separate the various program elements.

An advantage of being free-form is that the appearance of the program can correspond to the actual program structure. Indenting the program text to show the membership of a statement in an enclosing block of code makes the program text appearance correspond to its actual structure. JavaScript has inherited its programming style from C and C++. Because the interpreter doesn't care about white space, you can choose your own style. Try to remember that someone else may need to modify the program someday. Following an established style will help ease other programmers' understanding of the code.

Notice also that the variables in the preceding `alert-props` code are named differently than those in the second program. Using descriptive variable names can help a program to be more self-documenting, eliminating the need for obvious comments. For example, compare the following two statements:

```
nw++;            // Increment the count of the number
➥of widgets
num_widgets++;   // Much more descriptive - no comment needed!!!
```

Of course, these suggestions are just good programming practice.

Variable Names

A *variable* is an object in the computer's memory that holds data. As stated earlier, JavaScript variables keep track of what type of data they contain, as well as remembering the actual value.

Variable names are used to reference variables. It makes life a lot easier for both the program writer and maintainer if variable names are as explicit and descriptive as possible. Variable names can be any length (which some operating systems may have trouble digesting) and are case sensitive. They can begin with an alphabetic character or under-score, and subsequent characters can be alphabetic, numeric, or underscore.

Variables

Variables are the containers for values in memory. Each variable holds a single item in memory in a place referenced by the variable name. When a variable is associated with an object, it's known as a *property*.

It's unnecessary to declare variable types. Simply assign a value to a valid variable name. A run-time error results when you use the value of a variable before an assignment has been made to it.

When assigning a value to a variable for the first time, you can pre-cede the assignment with the optional keyword `var`. This signifies your intention to create the variable, which is good programming practice as it enhances the readability of the code by humans. You can use the keyword `var` to restrict the *scope* of a variable (*variable scope* is discussed in the next section). This allows the creation of a local instance of a variable, possibly with the same name as another variable.

Valid variable names all begin with an alphabetic character or underscore, possibly followed by additional alphabetic or numeric characters; other characters are not legal in variable names. JavaScript variables cannot have keywords as their names. JavaScript variable names are also case sensitive. The following lists some examples of legal variable names:

```
a

sensor34z

abracadabra

this_is_my_variable

_z

a1b2c3

inaWhile

maximum_velocity

myvar
```

Examples of illegal variable names include the following:

```
14themoney

$abc

rate%

while

maximum velocity

"myvar"

000_destruct_0

del-ete
```

Variable Scope.   JavaScript supports static variable scoping, which allows for a basic form of *encapsulation*. Encapsulation helps facilitate code reusability by eliminating the interaction of variables in functions with global variables. In other words, *scope* provides boundaries within which a variable is recognized. A local variable is a variable defined only within a function. The ability to create a local variable within a function allows the programmer to write functions without worrying about accidentally messing up other variables within the program. Functions written using only local variables may therefore be reused in any program without worry.

The `var` declaration of a variable within a function restricts the scope, or range, of that variable to the enclosing function. Regrettably, this is the current extent of scoping support in JavaScript; a variable is either local to a function, or global. Thus, this code:

```
var i = 5;     //declare a global variable named i
function foo() {
    var i = 6;     //declare another variable named i
                   //which is local only within foo
    document.writeln("Value of i in foo = " + i);
}
foo();     //call to function foo
document.writeln("Value of global i = " + i);
```

produces the output:

```
Value of i in foo = 6
Value of global i = 5
```

There are two variables named i in this code fragment. The first variable i is not affected by what happens to the other variable i within the function block delimiters. Keep variable scope in mind when modifying variables, otherwise the wrong instance of a variable might inadvertently be modified.

At first glance, it may seem insane to even allow two distinctly different variables to have the same name. However, the concept of variable scoping usefully supports code modularity. The programmer should be able to make use of a library of standard functions without variables in the imported code stomping all over the programmer's own variables. Variable scope allows program modularity by restricting a variable's stomping zone to one particular function.

JavaScript Keywords

JavaScript has reserved words, or *keywords*, that should not be used as variable, property, function, method, or object names. Because JavaScript is case-sensitive, reserved words are recognized only in lowercase. It is allowable to use these words for other than their intended use if they're in mixed or uppercase, but why do it? Then you're asking for debugging and maintenance trouble. Glance over the following list of reserved words to avoid future pain.

Data declaration keywords:

var

Loop keywords:

while	for	break	continue
if	else	switch	in

Value keywords:

true	false	null

Object definition keywords:

this	with	new

Function definition keywords:

function   return

Reserved, unused words, currently undefined:

byte	int	float	char	double
throw	throws	try	catch	
class	extends	interface	implements	
public	private	protected		
abstract	Boolean	case	const	default
do	final	finally	goto	import
instanceof	long	native	package	short
static	super	synchronized	transient	void

The last group of keywords is reserved, even though they are not being used in JavaScript. These words may be used in future versions of the language.

Data Types and Values

JavaScript is a loosely typed language. This means that JavaScript does not require declaration of a variable type. When a valid variable name is assigned a value for the first time, memory space for that variable is automatically allocated. This brings the variable into existence.

There are basic data types supported by JavaScript: *numeric (integer* and *floating-point)*, *Boolean*, and *string*. When a variable is assigned a value, JavaScript remembers both its value and its type.

This example shows five variables being assigned different data types:

```
mystring1  = "Buffy Dog";        // A string of 9 characters
mystring2  = "37";               // Also a string, 2 characters
mynumber   = 74;                 // An integer number
myfloatnum = 49.58;              // A floating-point number
myBoolean  = true;               // A Boolean
```

If the statement

```
address = stringname2 + " Washington Park";
```

were to be executed, the variable `address` would be assigned the string value `"37 Washington Park"`.

A *loosely typed* programming language has advantages and disadvantages. Typing in a program is more convenient because you don't have to spend time writing declarations. It also decreases programmer worries about converting data between different types because JavaScript automatically takes care of data type conversion. JavaScript also allows a variable's data type to change during its lifetime.

On the other hand, many serious programmers consider these conveniences to be harmful because they eliminate the computer's capability to automatically check program correctness. In *strongly typed* languages where every variable is declared and every data conversion must be explicitly requested, the computer can be assured that no action is occurring without being explicitly requested by the programmer. For example, if the programmer mistakenly assigns a value to a misspelled variable, a strongly typed language, such as Java, will complain. A loosely typed language, such as JavaScript, will silently create a new misspelled variable. Being loosely typed puts more of the responsibility of assuring program correctness on the programmer.

Data Type Conversion.   When several different data types are involved in an expression, JavaScript performs conversion operations on the data to make the types compatible. Generally, if either operand is a string, JavaScript converts the other operand into a string. Consider the following statements with this idea in mind :

```
mynumber = 101.1;
mystring = "91.7";
mystring2 = mynumber + mystring;
mynumber2 = mynumber + parseFloat(mystring);
```

The first expression's first argument is `mynumber`, a number; the second operand is `mystring`, a string. Because one of the operands is a string, JavaScript will convert `mynumber` into a string. In the first computation, this results in `mystring2` being assigned the value `"101.191.7"`, the concatenation of the two strings. In the second computation, we use the built-in JavaScript function `parseFloat` to explicitly convert `mystring` into a number. The result of the second computation is the number 192.8.

```
mystring2 = "37";
mynumber  = 74;
mynumber2 = mystring2 + mynumber;
```

This expression's first argument is `mystring2`, a string. JavaScript then converts `mynumber` from the number 74 into the string `"74"`. Because the + operator concatenates (joins) strings, `mynumber2` now has the value `"3774"`.

Besides the function `parseFloat`, we could have used the built-in function `parseInt` to transform a string into an integer number. As they scan through their string argument, both `parseInt` and `parseFloat` stop scanning at the first character inconsistent with the standard appearance of that type of numeric literal. Conveniently, `parseInt` can convert strings representing numbers of bases other than 10 into JavaScript numbers. See Chapter 8, "JavaScript Methods," for more details.

```
mystring1 = "SpotDog";
mynumber  = 74;
testme = mynumber + mystring1;
```

In this example, JavaScript evaluates `mynumber` to a number and attempts to convert `mystring1` to a number. The contents of `mystring1`, the string `"SpotDog"`, cannot be evaluated to a numeric value. Rather than generating an error, JavaScript converts the number to a string and concatenates it to the following string.

A simple method of converting a number into a string is by adding the number to the null string, the string with no characters in it. Remember that the JavaScript + opertor associates (operates) from left to right. Here is an example of a data conversion that might have unexpected results if you are not careful:

```
myvar1 = 8;
myvar2 = 16;
myvar3 = " Washington Park";
string1 = myvar1 + myvar2 + myvar3;
string2 = "" + myvar1 + myvar2 + myvar3;
```

The desired value for `string1` is `"816 Washington Park"`. Instead, this expression will produce an undesirable result. The value for `myvar1` is numeric, and `myvar2` is then successfully converted to a number and added, resulting in the number 24. `myvar3` is a string and causes the value 24 to be converted to a string, resulting in the string `"24 Washington Park"`. `string2` has the null string up front, converting the numeric values that follow in the operation to string values. In this case, the value of `string2` is `"816 Washington Park"`, as desired. Once again, be careful with the "dark side" of automatic data conversion in loosely typed languages.

Valid conversions supported by JavaScript between data types are represented in Table 2.1. Find the type to be converted *from* in the left column and the type to be converted *to* across the top of the table.

Table 2.1.
Datatype
Conversion.

	Converted to Data Type				
Data Type	function	object	number	Boolean	string
object	error		error	true	toString
Null object	funobj OK		0	false	"null"
number(non-zero)		Number		true	toString
0		null		false	"0"
Error (NaN)	error	Number		false	"Nan"
+infinity		Number		true	" +Infinity"
-infinity		Number		true	"-Infinity"
Boolean:false	Boolean	0		"false"	
true	error	Boolean	1		"true"
string(non-nul)	funstr OK	String	numstr OK	true	
null string	error	String	error	false	

Literals

Literals are literal representations of data values. Look at the following statements:

```
count = 5;
gpa   = 3.68;
name  = "Huckleberry Hound";
```

In these examples, 5 is the literal representation of the integer with value 5, 3.68 is the literal representation of the floating-point number with the value 3.68, and `"Huckleberry Hound"` is the literal representation of the string value `"Huckleberry Hound"`.

Literals are not variables; they are actual instances of particular data values. Where a variable is the abstract, symbolic representation of a value, a literal is a concrete, explicit representation. Every variable consists of a value and a data type. Data types are information about the variable, while literals are values entered explicitly into the code.

JavaScript literals may be of the following types:

integer

floating-point

Boolean

string

Some examples of literals include the following:

```
375

22.8

-15

6.02e23

"z"

true

.8

"Lagavulin is a fine single malt."
```

Any of these could be used to fill appropriate variables in a JavaScript program.

Numeric Literals.   *Numeric literals* are either of type *integer* or *floating-point*. This is a fancy way of saying that numeric literals are number values. JavaScript distinguishes between integer and floating-point simply because computers store them differently internally. In this statement

```
x = 3;
```

3 is the literal value, and x is the variable.

Integer Literals.   Integers are positive or negative whole numbers. Unlike Java, JavaScript integers are not typed by size. Where Java uses integer types `byte`, `short`, `int`, and `long` to decide the size of memory to allocate to a variable, all JavaScript integers are stored as 32-bit integers.

As in Java, JavaScript integers can be represented as decimal (base 10), octal (base 8), or hexadecimal (base 16). JavaScript knows the base of the variable by the leading characters. Decimal values may not have a leading zero. Octal values have a leading zero. Hexadecimal values have a leading 0x or 0X and may also include the letters *a-f* (or *A-F*) as "digits." See the following example for clarification:

```
myvar1 = 12;        //value is decimal 12
myvar2 = 012;       //value is octal 12, or decimal 10
myvar3 = 0x12;      //value is hexadecimal 12, or decimal 18
```

Numeric values are always stored in binary internally. It doesn't matter whether numeric literal values are written as decimal, octal, or hexadecimal.

Floating-Point Literals.   A *floatint-point* number is a number with some fractional part represented in decimal form, as in 52.80. There is no such thing as either single- or double-precision floating-point literals in JavaScript, another difference between Java and JavaScript. JavaScript does not distinguish between floating-point number sizes. Floating-point numbers are stored as *double* precision internally. JavaScript standardizes the sizes of its various datatypes on different platforms.

Floating-point literals may be either positive or negative. Floating-point literals must have at least one digit, plus a decimal point. For example, the following lines of code show the assignmet of floating-point values to variables:

```
var4 = 19.85;

var5 = -19.85;
```

Floating-point numbers allow for the representation of numbers in scientific notation. When writing the number, simply use the letter *e* in the number, which can be read in English as "times 10 to the power of." The *e* is not case sensitive. For example, the value 2.1e3 is a representation of the value 2100. Other examples of floating-point literals are

```
var6 = 6.02e23;     // 6.02 times 10 to the power of 23,
Avogadro's Number

var7 = 3E-5;        // 3 times 10 to the power of -5
```

String Literals. *String literals* are a sequence of characters enclosed in double or single quotes, such as

```
stringLit_A = "This is an example of a string literal";

stringLit_B = 'This is another example of a string literal';
```

A string literal could be `"Islay Malt"` or even `""` for a null character string, which is a string consisting of no characters. Do not confuse a *null string* with the special object null.

String delimiter quotation marks must be the same on both ends of the string. It is illegal to have

```
stringLit = "Be careful of your typing and not do this';
```

String literals cannot span more than one line in definition within the code. They can, however, contain multiple lines by using the special character `\n to denote a line break.`

The backslash character (\) is used to help users type characters into strings that would normally not appear plainly. If the character following the backslash is not special, the \ gives the character special meaning; if the character is special, the \ takes away its special meaning. The escape sequence \ and the following character(s) always translate into a single character. Here are the special characters and their functions:

Character	Escape Sequence
Backspace	\b
Form Feed	\f
New Line	\n
Carriage Return	\r
Tab	\t
Double Quote	\"
Backslash	\\

An example of usage with special characters is

```
document.write("Function\tCharacter");
```

The output would look like this:

```
Function        Character
```

String literal values can be concatenated with the JavaScript + operator. If one string literal contained the value `"Islay Single Malts "` and another contained `"tend to be smooth and slightly smokey."`, then they could be concatenated together like this:

```
"Islay Single Malts " + "tend to be smooth and slightly
➡smokey."
```

Boolean Literals.   *Boolean literals* operate exactly the same in JavaScript as they do in Java. They contain either the value `true` or `false`. This is different from other languages in which the value for Booleans is a numeric 0 or 1. Booleans are used in program control flow logic, which determines whether certain instructions should be executed or not. Boolean literals may be converted to other types; refer to the previous conversion.

Expressions

Expressions are JavaScript formulas or equations intended to perform some computation. Expressions consist of operators and operands. The effect of performing the operations indicated in the expression is a resulting value, along with any side effects those operations may have caused. Almost every aspect of JavaScript involves an expression. Expressions are made up of operands such as literals, variables, and function calls, the input values to the computation; and operators, which order the computation to be performed based on the operands.

One kind of JavaScript expression is the *assignment* expression. This not only performs the indicated calculation, it also has the side effect of performing an assignment, creating the variable if it did not exist previously. The following are all examples of assignment expressions:

```
x = 29;

y = z - 25;

z = "Highland Single Malts";

{
```

```
compound = x + (y - 10);

second_one = "Saturn";

}
```

The Conditional Operator.   One of the more obscure yet
interesting operators is the ternary (three operand) conditional operator `?:`. The conditional operator returns one of two values,
depending on whether a condition evaluates to true or false. The
syntax is

```
condition ? expression1 : expression2;
```

Because expressions are composed by using operators, the next section enumerates the JavaScript operators and explains their use.

Statements and Blocks

JavaScript *statements* are expressions that either compute something
or do something. A semicolon (;) terminates a statement just as in
Java, C, and C++. However, semicolons are not required, although
they are recommended. The term *statement* in this book describes a
syntactically correct executable unit that the JavaScript interpreter
is capable of running.

A *block* is a group of statements that has been surrounded by curly
braces, { and }, to form a single *compound statement*. Blocks logically
group statements for program flow and readability, as well as for
correct syntax.

An example of a single simple statement is

```
x = 5 + 7;
```

The expression 5+7 is computed, and the resulting value of 12 is
assigned to variable x. It's also possible to build compound statements, such as

```
{x = 3 * 4; y = 2 + 5; }
```

Compound statements must be enclosed by curly braces and separated by semicolons. Think of compound statements as groupings of
multiple single statements. A compound statement can be used anywhere a single simple statement is used, including inside another
compound statement.

Compound statements are very useful because most control structures operate only on a single statement. For example, the `while` loop structure expects `statement` to be a single statement:

```
while (condition) statement;
```

It's necessary to "trick" JavaScript in situations where multiple statements are necessary. A block is used in that case. See the following statement:

```
while (count < 10) {
    i = i + 1;
    document.write("Counting: " + count);
}
```

Statements do other things besides computation. Statements can also call *functions*. When a function is called, the processor makes a note of where the program is in execution. The processor then goes off to execute the instructions defined by the function and its declaration. When it has completed those instructions, processing resumes executing at the spot it left off in the original program. An example of a *function statement* is

```
alert("Bogus Data");
```

Print statements are *function calls* that perform a `print` or `write` to the browser window. (Function calls are covered in detail at the end of this chapter in the section "Using Functions." They are introduced here to illustrate the point that these calls are another form of statement.) An example of a print statement is:

```
document.write("hello world");
```

This function call writes HTML text to the browser display area within the current window or frame.

Control flow statements are pieces of code that control whether and when statements will be executed. Control logic tends to use compound statements to accomplish its goal. For example, the `if` statement may perform several statements based on true or false outcomes. These statements are enclosed in curly braces { } because they are compound statements. It is advisable to use the curly braces to group multiple logically connected statements into a block to assure predictable program execution.

Another type of statement is an *expression*. Expressions typically perform some kind of computation based on input data. This input data may be *literal*, as in 7.35, *symbolic*, as in the value of the variable x, or the *result* of some other function, as in the function call mycomputation(123.45).

Here are some examples of expressions:

```
1 + 1

(count * 5 + 1) / 2.4

(F - 32) * (5 / 9)

(C * 9 / 5) + 32
```

Operators

Every expression computes a value. *Operators* specify the calculation operations to be performed on the input variables, literals, and function calls. JavaScript operators are quite similar to operators in Java, C, and C++, with a couple of differences.

It's not necessary to have spaces on either side of an operator, as long as the JavaScript interpreter can figure out what the programmer intended. However, white space may have to be inserted in order to make the code unambiguous.

Unary Operators.   There are six types of JavaScript operators: *unary, assignment, bitwise, logical, comparison,* and *conditional*.

An operator that operates on a single value is called a *unary operator*. *Binary operators* act upon two values, and the ternary operator (?:) operates on three values. A common unary operator is the *unary negation* [-] operator. It multiplies its operand by -1, in effect reversing the sign of an integer. For example:

```
Negative = -4.3;
Positive = -Negative;
```

The variable Negative is operated on by the unary operator -, which returns the negative of its operand. Thus, after the two previous statements, Positive contains the value 4.3.

Certain unary operators have side effects on their operand that modify the operand's value. For example, the ++ unary operator adds one to (increments) its operand:

```
increment_me = 5;
increment_me++            //adds one to increment_me.
```

`increment_me` has a value of 6 at the end of the operation. *Incrementing* and *decrementing* are examples of unary operations that change the value of the original variable.

The unary operators are listed in Table 2.2.

Operator	Operation
++	Increment
—	Decrement
-	Unary Negation
~	Bitwise Complement
!	Not

Table 2.2.
Unary Operators.

Decrement decreases the value by one, as in

```
downer—;              //downer is now decremented by 1
```

The ++ and – operators can be used either in a prefix position, before their operand, or after their operand in a postfix position. There is a subtle yet important distinction between these two uses:

```
a = 7;
b = 7;
x = ++a;              // Afterwards: a=8, x=8  "Pre-increment"
y = b++;              // Afterwards: b=8, y=7  "Post-increment"
```

After the preceding code executes, both a and b are 8; however, x and y differ. The ++ operator in the prefix position first increments a, then returns the value of a after the increment, 8. In the postfix position, the value of b was returned before the increment, making b 7. The – operator operates exactly the same way. In either the prefix or postfix position, its operand is decremented. In the prefix position, its return value is the value after the decremen;, in the postfix position, the return value is the operand's value before the decrement.

Just think of it this way: if the ++ is before the operand, the operation occurs first, then the value is returned; if the ++ is after the operand, the value is returned, then the operation is performed. Only the ++ and – unary operators modify their operand's value.

The *Not* (!) logical unary operator is the Boolean equivalent of the unary negation operator. It returns the Boolean value `true` if its operand is `false`, and returns `false` if its operand is `true`. The following two statements accomplish the same thing:

```
if (!(a>3)) {...              //if a is not greater than 3

if (a <=3) {...               //if a is less than or equal to 3
```

The bitwise unary operator ~ performs the same logic on binary values. Because JavaScript stores integers as plain binary values internally, the ~ operator operates on an integer number. The not operation, as described earlier, is performed on each bit within the number individually. For example:

```
myNum = 10;          // myNum  in binary is 0000...001010
newNum = ~myNum;     // newNum in binary is 1111...110101
```

Every bit that was a 1 has been flipped to 0; every 0 has been flipped to 1.

Arithmetic Operators.   The simplest operators, common to programming languages since Fortran IV, are the arithmetic operators for addition (+), subtraction (-), multiplication (*) and division (/). Like most of the other binary (two operand) operators, the arithmetic operators operate from left to right. Multiplications and divisions in a given expression will occur first, followed by additions and subtractions. For example, consider this expression:

```
3 + 7 * 4 + 1
```

The 7 is first multiplied by 4, giving 28. Then 3 is added to 28, giving 31, added to 1 gives 32.

In order to perform the operations in a different order, the programmer may always use parentheses to group operations. All operations within parentheses must complete before the parenthesized expression's value is used in an operation. Modifying the preceding example:

```
(3 + 7) * (4 + 1)
```

The parentheses now force the addition of 3 to 7 and 4 to 1 to occur before the multiplication, which now results in 50, not 32 as before. Since it does no harm to use parentheses, use them whenever uncertain of operator precedence.

JavaScript has inherited an additional arithmetic operator from C and C++, the *modulo operator* (%). The modulo operation returns the remainder resulting from an integer division. For example, 26 divided by 7 is 3, remainder 5. Thus the expression

```
26 % 7
```

returns the result 5.

The arithmetic operator + operates on strings, in addition to numbers. Given string operands, the + operator concatenates (joins) instead of adding. Should the + operator be given one string operand and one numeric operand, it determines its behavior from the left operand. For example, if the left operand is a number, the right operand will be converted into a number if it is not one already, and a numeric addition will occur. On the other hand, if the left operand of + is a string, the right operand will be converted into a string if it is not one already, and a concatenation will occur.

Assignment Operators.   *Assignment operators* are used to modify the value of a variable, placing (assigning) a new value to the variable. There are six assignment operators in JavaScript, which are listed in Table 2.3.

Table 2.3.
Assignment
Operators.

=
+=
-=
*=
/=
%=
&=
|=
^=
<<=
>>=
>>>=

Consider the example a = b. Implicitly, the operand on the left side of an assignment is the variable to be modified (called the L-value). The expression on the right side of the = is evaluated, the result of which is assigned to the L-value. Thus, the value of b is assigned to a.

Just as in Java, C, and C++, the assignment operation itself is just an expression with a side effect. Thus, assignments may be cascaded like this:

```
a = b = c = 5;
```

The value 5 is first assigned to c. The assignment expression returns the value assigned, 5, which is then assigned to b. The assignment to b returns the value assigned, 5, which is then assigned to a.

As operators, assignment operators are right-associative, making them different from the other JavaScript operators. Where the other binary (two operand) operators operate from left to right, assignment operators operate from right to left. Assignment operands have a very low precedence, higher only than the comma operator, making the assigment the last operation (usually) to occurs.

The programmers who designed the C programming language noticed that a very common form of assignment involved the same variable in both the L-value and the expression on the right side of the =. For example:

```
x = x + 1;
```

1 is added to the old value of x, which is then placed back in x. Because these same people wanted to save time typing, they came up with a shorthand operator:

```
x += 1;
```

Because they also noticed that it was rather common to add or subtract one to and from things, they implemented a further shorthand, the unary operators ++ and −. Similar shorthand assignment operators exist for all the normal binary operators, including the following bitwise operators. All of these shorthand assignment operators are constructed simply by following the operator by an equal sign.

Consider the following operations:

```
h -= 1;        //assigns to h the result of h - 1
b *= 2;        //assigns to b the result of b * 2
d &= 0x1f;     //same as d = d & 0x1f
z /= 3;        //same as z = z / 3
g %= 4         //assigns to h the result ofsame as g = g % 4
```

As the + operator, described previously, operates on strings, concatenating (joining) them, the assignment operator += also works with strings. This is shown in the following example:

```
stringa  = "Lagavulin";
stringa += " is an Islay malt";
```

The value of stringa is now "Lagavulin is an Islay malt". This is a shorthand way of using the more verbose statement

```
stringa = "Lagavulin";
stringa = stringa + " is an Islay malt";
```

Bitwise Operators.   *Bitwise operators* are used for manipulating the binary bits within integer-valued quantities. The original numbers are converted to a 32-bit integer before being operated on. Bitwise operators are either *logical operators* or *shift operators*. The logical operators compare two numbers, one bit at a time, and construct a value based on the operator used. For example, if the bitwise AND operator is used

```
result = a & b;
```

bit 0 of a is ANDed with bit 0 of b, and the result is placed in bit 0 of result. The same thing happens for bit 1, bit 2, and so on. The bitwise logical operators are listed in Table 2.4.

Table 2.4.
Bitwise Logical
Operators.

Logical Operation	Operator	Description
AND	&	Returns a one bit if both operands are one.
OR	|	Returns a one bit if either operand is one.
XOR	^	Returns a one bit if one but not both operands are one.
NOT	~	Returns a one bit if operand is zero; zero if operand is one.

Here are examples of bitwise logical operators:

```
a = 5;              // 5  is ...00000101 in binary
b = 3;              // 3  is ...00000011 in binary
```

```
resultAND = a & b;      // result:...00000001 in binary
resultOR  = a ! b;      // result:...00000111 in binary
resultXOR = a ^ b;      // result:...00000110 in binary
resultNOT = ~a;         // result:...11111010 in binary
```

Bitwise *shift operators* move their operand left or right the number of bit positions specified. The operands are converted to 32-bit numbers, then the bits are moved right or left. Bits may be shifted off the end of the 32-bit word and discarded. The bitwise shift operators are listed in Table 2.5.

Operator	Operator Name
<<	**Left Shift**
>>	**Sign-Propagating Right Shift**
>>>	**Zero-Fill Right Shift**

Table 2.5. Bitwise Shift Operators.

Left shift (<<) shifts the first operand the specified number of bits to the left. Excess bits shifted off to the left are discarded. Zero bits fill in on the right to complete the 32 bits. An example of left shift is

```
a = 7;              // 7  is  ...00000111 in binary
z = a << 2;         // result:...00011100.  The bits have
➥moved left 2 places
```

Sign-propagating right shift (>>) shifts the first operand the specified number of bits to the right. Excess bits shifted off to the right are discarded. The leftmost bit, called the *sign bit*, is propagated to the left to fill in the 32 bits. An example of sign-propagating right shift is

```
a = -6;             // -6 is ...11111000 in binary
z = a >> 2;         // result:...11111110.  The bits have
➥moved right 2 places
```

Zero-fill right shift (>>>) shifts the first operand the specified number of bits to the right. Excess bits shifted off to the right are discarded. Zero bits fill in from the left to complete the 32 bits. An example of zero-fill right shift is

```
a = 48;             // 48 is  ...00011000 in binary
z = a >>> 1;        // result:...00001100.  The bits have
➥moved right 1 place
```

If the *sign bit*, the most significant bit, is 0, >> and >>> have identical results.

Logical Operators.   *Logical operators* operate on two expressions and return either true or false. This is different from the *comparison operators* in that two values are not being compared to see if one is greater than the other, or equal to each other. Instead, two expressions are examined to see if each is true or false. Then, based on the operator, the expression will return true or false. When thinking of logical operators, think of truth tables.

The logical operators are listed in Table 2.6.

Table 2.6.
Logical Operators.

Operator	Operator Name
&&	AND
||	OR
!	NOT

AND (&&) returns true if both of the expressions tested are true. If either of them is not true, or both are not true, the value returned is false. Usage of && is as follows:

expression1 && *expression2*

For example:

```
if ((age > 12) && (age < 20))
    document.writeln("Teenager");
```

OR (||) returns true if either of the two expressions tested are true. It returns false if both of the expressions are false. Usage of || is as follows:

expression1 || *expression2*;

For example:

```
if ((age <= 12) || (age >= 20))
    document.writeln("Human");
```

The || and && operators have an important behavior called *short circuit evaluation*. An || expression is true if either of its operands is true. In the previous example, if age is 6, then the first operand of || is true. Thus, JavaScript knows the result of the || operation to be true, regardless of the value of the right operand (age >= 20).

Because evaluating the right operand is a waste of CPU cycles, JavaScript *guarantees* that it will not proceed in an || expression after it finds a true value, "short circuiting" the expression. In the same way, at the first sign of a false value, an && expression will short circuit, not evaluating any further.

Short circuit behavior has uses beyond just increasing computational efficiency. In the following example, a division by zero error is avoided in case NumGoats is zero:

```
if ((NumGoats != 0) && (NumDogs/NumGoats < 0.13)) {
    document.write("There are not enough dogs.");
}
```

If NumGoats is zero, the first operand of && will be false, thus causing the expression evaluation to terminate (short circuit), avoiding the division by zero. && and || expressions always evaluate strictly from left to right.

NOT (!) was discussed earlier as a unary operator. It returns true if an expression is false and false if an expression is true. In other words, it returns the opposite Boolean value of the expression. Usage of ! is as follows:

```
!expression
```

For example:

```
if ( ! ((age > 12) && (age < 20)))
    document.writeln("Human");
```

Comparison Operators.　*Comparison operators* evaluate the values on each side of the operator and make comparisons of those values based on the operator. The value returned is true or false. Table 2.7 lists the comparison operators.

Table 2.7.
Comparison
Operators.

Operand	Returns/Description	Example
==	True if both operands are equal	x == y
!=	True if operands are not equal	x != y
>	True if left operand is greater	x > y
>=	True if left operand is greater or equal	x >= y
<	True if left operand is less	x < y
<=	True if left operand is less or equal	x <= y

These operands may be used to compare both numeric values and string values. The comparisons of string values are based on alphabetical order (ASCII order, actually). See the following example:

```
stringa = "aardvark";
stringb = "arizona";
if (stringa > stringb)
    document.writeln(stringa + "comes after" + stringb);
else
    document.writeln(stringa + "comes before" + stringb);
```

If the condition expression evaluates to the Boolean value true, the expression returns the value of the expression *expression1*. Otherwise, it evaluates and returns the value of *expression2*. For example, consider the following expression:

```
able_to_drive = (aged >= 16) ? "ready" : "not ready";
```

If aged is greater than or equal to **16**, able_to_drive will be assigned the string value "ready". If not, able_to_drive will be assigned the string value "not ready". Although at first glance it may seem too cryptic, the conditional operator can be powerfully concise. Consider this statement, which computes the absolute value of the variable x, placing the result in the variable ax:

```
ax = x<0 ? -x : x;
```

If x is negative, -x (a positive value) is returned; if x is positive, x is returned. The equivalent if statement would have taken several lines.

Comma Operator.   The *comma operator* is a seldom used binary operator, seldom enough even that Java chose not to borrow this C and C++ operator at all. As binary operators go, it behaves rather stupidly, simply discarding its left operand's value after evaluating it, and returning the result of the evaluation of its right operand. For example, the useless expression

```
myvar = (4, 9, 6);
```

simply discards (in order) 4, then 6, finally returning the value 6 to be assigned to myvar. This makes the comma operator really useful only in expressions that involve side effects:

```
x = ( y=5, y*y );
```

which assigns 5 to y, then promptly forgets the value 5, going on to calculate y times y, returning that value to be assigned to x. Note that the comma operator has a lower precedence than even the assignment operator, thus requiring the parentheses. The preceding code could have been more clearly shown in two separate statements:

```
y = 5;
x = y * y;
```

The comma operator is really necessary only in situations that require a single expression, such as while loop conditional expressions.

Operator Precedence

JavaScript performs operations of highest precedence first, determining the order in which the operations are executed. Table 2.8 shows the order of precedence from highest to lowest. Among equal precedence operators, JavaScript evaluates operators from left to right. If all levels of operator precedence in an expression are the same, the expression is strictly evaluated from left to right.

Table 2.8.
Operator Precedence, from Highest to Lowest.

++	—	!	~
*	/	%	
+	-		
<<	>>	>>>	
<	>	<=	>=
==	!=		
&			
^			
&&			
||			
?:			
=			
,			

Left to right order of evaluation is preempted by separators. Grouping expressions with the separators [ ] and ( ) override precedence. Parentheses ( ) may be used anywhere, including when calling functions. Brackets [ ] may be used only where you intend to access an array element or object property. Everything within these separators is computed before going outside them. Once again, this evaluation is from left to right. See the following example for clarification:

```
FigureItOut = (2 * 3 + 4) + (6 + 10 / 5);
```

The resulting value of `FigureItOut` is 18. Multiplication and division are of a higher precedence than addition and subtraction. The order of evaluation is to complete the computation within the first set of parentheses by its order of precedence: `2 * 3` is 6, then 4 is added for a total of 10. Then the second set of parentheses is evaluated. `10 / 5` is 2, then 6 is added for a total of 8. `10 + 8` is 18.

JavaScript operator precedence is generally the same as for Java, C, and C++. It's a good idea to become familiar with operator precedence for more predictable results in complex computational statements. Always remember that using parentheses overrides operator precedence and clearly establishes the order of operations. It doesn't do any harm to use parentheses and be explicit.

Control Flow Structures

Up to this point, we have been talking about the basic JavaScript elements. These elements include expressions, statements, variables, operators, and so on. Expressions and operators work together to manipulate data in a variety of ways. The only thing missing is the capability to make decisions within the program. The programming instructions that tell the program how to decide what to do next are called *control flow structures*. These instructions allow the program to choose between alternative sets of statements to execute. They also allow the program to repeatedly execute a given list of statements while a specified condition remains true. Generally speaking, a control flow structure is any statement that influences the sequence of instructions to be executed.

The keywords used to control program flow are `for`, `if`, and `while`. JavaScript control keywords are a subset of Java. Java, however, includes the `do` structure while JavaScript does not.

***if...else* Conditional.**   `If...else` is the easiest control flow logic to understand. Each of us makes dozens of `if...else` decisions every day. Here is an example of an `if...else` decision process. Your humble authors live in Colorado and like to climb mountains. Most mountains here are taller than tree-line, the altitude at which trees can grow. Also, there tend to be thunderstorms just about every afternoon in the summer. Where there is thunder, there is lightning, which tends to strike the taller objects around. If a hiker is above tree-line, she may be the tallest thing around. Therefore, it is a good idea to reach the summit and return to tree-line by early afternoon and beat the lightning. The big decision is what time to get up and going on the hike to reach a summit miles away in distance and perhaps with a significant altitude gain. Keep in mind that the hiker is usally leaving a snug sleeping-bag to go out in the predawn chill to achieve this objective. The logic looks like this:

```
if (weather == fair) {
    if (time < 4:00 am) {
        rise_and_shine = "most likely";
    } else {
        rise_and shine = "too late to start anyway, get more
➥sleep";}
} else {
    rise_and_shine = "rainy weather, stay in bed"
}
```

A simpler decision to break out logically is

```
if (high_altitude_oxygen_deprived == true {
    hikers = "silly";
}  else {
    hikers = "sensible";
}
```

This is fairly easy to follow. The first statement is performed if the answer is true, and the second statement is performed if it is not. This is always the case with if logic.

The else clause of the if statement is optional. The syntax of the simple if statement is as follows:

```
if (expression) statement;
```

The syntax of a simple if statement, with block, is

```
if (expression) {
    statements;

}
```

The parentheses around the condition expression are required in both of the above cases. Finally, if the option else clause is used, the statement looks like this:

```
if (expression) {
    statements;
}
else {
    statements
}
```

`if` statements may be as complex as desired and may be nested an unlimited number of levels deep. However, good programming practice is to keep this logic as simple as possible.If an `else` clause is used, it will correspond to the closest previous `if` statement. Should an `else` need to correspond with some farther `if`, blocks should be used to force correct syntactic interpretation.

It's not necessary to have an `else` statement. Program execution falls through the code if the first statement is false. This is demonstrated in the following code fragment:

```
if (name_value == "") {
    document.write(name_value);
}
    document.write("If null, the previous statement was
➥skipped.")
```

`name_value` is evaluated, and, if null, execution continues on the line following the `if` statement. If `name_value` is other than null, everything within the `if` statement is performed, and then execution continues on the line following the `if` statement.

***while* Loop.**   A construct that continues to execute a block of code until a certain termination condition has been met is the `while` loop. The `while` loop's logic is to perform actions *while* a condition is true.

The `while` loop is very similar to the `for` loop, discussed in the next section. The condition expression is tested for truth before the block of code is executed.

The syntax of the `while` loop is as follows:

```
while (expression) statement;
```

or

```
while (expression) {
    statements;
}
```

The *expression* is a conditional statement that evaluates to true or false. The block of code within the curly braces is executed only if the expression evaluates to true. As long as the condition expression remains true, the statements within the while loop are repeatedly executed. If the expression is false, execution resumes at the first statement following the while block. The expression test is always the first action within the while loop. Therefore, if the expression evaluates to false on the first time through the loop, the block is never executed.

It's possible for the while loop to continue execution forever if the condition expression never evaluates to false. This is an example of an infinite loop. Always check the code to make sure that at some time, the expression has the possibility of evaluating to false. Even if the condition expression is always true, it is possible to exit an infinite loop by using the break statement, described later.

In this simple example of a while loop, statements inside the loop's block are executed as long as the value of i is less than or equal to 10. The while loop computes 10 factorial (the numbers 1 though 10, all multiplied together) by initializing i to 1 and increasing i by 1 in every loop execution. This assures that the loop will terminate when the value in i is increased to 11. Note that the loop will not execute when i has the value 11:

```
i = 1;
product = 1;
while (i <= 10) {
    product *= i;
    i++;
}

document.writeln("10 factorial = " + product);    // Show
➡Result
```

***for* Loop.**   Because `while` loops that repeat for a given count are common programming structures, like the previous example, the `for` loop is provided as a simple shorthand. Just like `while` loops, `for` loops repeatedly execute a block of code until a Boolean expression evaluates to false. The syntax of a `for` loop is as follows:

```
for (initializing-expression; continuation condition;
➥update-expression) {

      statements...

   }
```

Following the `for` keyword is a required pair of parentheses, containing exactly three expressions, separated by semicolons. These three expressions are known as the *initialization expression*, the *continuation condition*, and the *update expression*. Following the required parentheses containing the three expressions is the statement or block to be executed as the body of the loop.

The initialization expression is executed once before any other action occurs in the `for` loop. It provides an explicit way to initialize a *loop variable*. A loop variable is a variable that changes its value in each iteration (repetition) of a loop. In the `while` loop section's example, earlier, the variable `i` was used as the loop variable. It's also possible to declare a local variable with the `var` keyword. This initial expression is optional within the `for` loop's required parentheses.

The continuation condition is the expression that contains the test that determines if block execution will continue. If it evaluates to true, then repeated execution of the body of the loop continues. If false, execution resumes following the `for` loop block. The continuation condition is tested at the beginning of every loop, exactly like the `while` loop.

An update expression allows the programmer to specify a statement to be executed after the body of each loop iteration completes. Typically, an update expression changes the value of the variable tested in the condition. The most common form of update is to increment the variable. The update expression is optional. Be careful in omitting the update expression, as an infinite loop may be created.

Program statements making up the body of the loop are executed after the continuation condition is evaluated and found to be true. This program execution continues until the expression evaluates to false. Execution continues forever if the expression never evaluates to false. This is, once again, the dreaded infinite loop. A common cause of this loop is to forget to update the loop variable. If the variable never changes, it always evaluates to the same value, and an infinite loop results.

One common usage of `for` loops is to perform something a preset number of times. In the following code fragment, the value of the loop variable i is displayed in the document:

```
for (var i = 0; i < 5; i++) {
    document.write(i);
}
```

The variable i is initialized to 0 the first time through the loop. A test is performed to make sure that i is less than 5. The current value of i is displayed in the browser document, then i is incremented by one, completing one full loop through the block.

The next round through the loop begins with a test of i to make sure that it is less than 5. Once again, the value of i (which is 1) is displayed. Finally, i is incremented by 1. This continues until i is 5, whereupon i will no longer be less than 5. The execution then continues on the first line following the `for` loop block.

It's not necessary to initialize the test variable in the `for` loop. The variable i must have been given a value previously in the code in the following example. An error will occur if i has not been given a value before the loop executes.

```
for ( ; i < 5; i++) {
    document.write(i);
}
```

In any case, the `for` loop's parentheses must contain exactly two semicolons.

The `for` loop is really just a special case of the `while` loop, a sort of shorthand for a common form of loop. The `for` loop

```
for ( A ; B ; C ) {
        D ;
}
```

where *A*, *B*, and *C* are expressions, and *D* is the body of the loop (any number of statements), is equivalent to the `while` loop

```
   A   ;
while (   B   ) {
        D   ;
        C   ;
}
```

An exception to the preceding equivalence is that the `continue` statement, described later, will not skip *C* in the `for` loop. Here is a `for` loop that computes 10 `factorial`:

```
product = 1;

for (i=1; i <= 10; i++) {
    product *= i;
}

document.writeln("10 factorial = " + product);
```

Compare it to the equivalent `while` loop above. The `for` loop provides a simple, quick method to set up an iterative loop.

It's possible to omit the condition test. If omitted, the continuation condition always evaluates as true, resulting in an infinite loop. The statement

```
for (;;) {
    statements;
}
```

is known as a "forever" loop. The only way to exit an infinite loop is by using the `break` statement, described next.

***break* Statement.**   The `break` statement is used to break out of `while` and `for` loops. Execution resumes at the first statement following the current loop. `break` can be used to interrupt execution in case of an unexpected input, in order to avoid error or to exit a loop when a normal termination condition has occurred. For example, this loop calculates 10 `factorial` in a different way than earlier examples:

```
i = 1;
product = 1;
```

```
while ( true ) {
    if (i > 10)
        break;
    product *= i;
    i++;
}
document.writeln("10 factorial = " + product);
```

Ordinarily, a `while` loop with the condition `true` would repeat forever. In this case, the `break` statement is executed inside the loop as soon as the value of `i` goes over 10. The loop is then terminated, and processing continues on to execute the `document.writeln()` method.

continue Statement.   The `continue` statement is similar to `break` in that it interrupts execution of a `for` or `while` loop. While `break` exits the loop entirely, `continue` simply skips the remainder of the current iteration. When `continue` occurs in a `while` loop, it jumps back to the condition expression at the beginning of the loop. In a `for` loop, the same thing happens, except that the update expression at the beginning of the loop is not skipped.

One use of `continue` may be to skip code in a loop. Let's return to the document example. Suppose that an array of numbers called `mydata` is to be summed up, except array elements with negative values should be skipped. Here's a `while` loop that does just that by using the `continue` statement:

```
i = 0;
while ( i <= 20 ) {
    if (mydata[i] < 0)              // don't sum if value is
➥negative
        continue;                   // skip remainder of this
➥iteration
    sum += mydata[i];
    i++;
}


document.writeln("Sum = " + sum);
```

for...in Statement.   The `for...in` statement allows iteration over all properties of an object. If an object has 10 properties, the loop will execute 10 times, each time setting the *loop variable* to the current property name. The syntax for the use of `for...in` is

```
for (variable in object) {
    statements;
}
```

The following example shows a sample for...in loop:

```
for (prop in document) {
    i++;
}
```

The for...in loop can be used to enumerate object properties, like this:

```
<HTML>
<BODY>
<FORM NAME="CoolForm" METHOD="GET" ACTION=
➡"http://www.foo.com/cgi-bin/form1">
Please type your Full Name:
<INPUT TYPE="TEXT" NAME="FullName" VALUE="M. Snerd" SIZE="25"
➡MAXLENGTH="40">
</FORM>
<SCRIPT LANGUAGE="JavaScript">
    for ( prop in document.CoolForm.FullName) {
        document.writeln("Properties of FullName object are " +
        prop  + "<BR>");
    }
</SCRIPT>
</BODY>
</HTML>
```

This example also shows the HTML code that brings the referenced form object into existence. For each property of the FullName object, the writeln method will be called to print each of the property names and associated values.

Functions

Abstraction is one of the most important capabilities a programming language can offer. In procedural languages, functions support this capability. Functions allow the programmer to extend the set of instructions that the language recognizes, adding new instructions. This section discusses the mechanics of defining and using functions.

In other object-oriented languages, such as Java and C++, functions are typically directly associated with objects. When a function is defined and associated with an object, it is called a *method*. Where Java automatically associates functions with objects in this way, in JavaScript the programmer must make the association manually.

Functions are familiar to anyone who has coded in any procedural language. Functions are a group of statements that perform a certain task. The idea is that the programmer solves a given task once and from then on, only needs to refer back to the previous solution. This avoids having to repeat all the statements necessary to solve the problem. Functions can be called from anywhere within the current program.

Think of a function as a way to group a block of code together and then refer to it by name. It's much easier to write code to do something once and then just refer to it by name throughout the program. This saves a lot of coding.

A *method* is a function that has been associated with a class. Because JavaScript's built-in methods are a vital part of the object-based methodology of JavaScript, they deserve their own chapter. Methods are examined in detail in Chapter 8, "JavaScript Methods."

Defining Functions.   Functions can be more useful if they can accept and use data inputs, called *arguments*, and return a data output, called the *return value*. The loosely typed nature of JavaScript is reflected in the syntax of function declarations. There is no need to define the return type of a function or to define the types of its arguments, as is necessary in Java or C++. The syntax for a function is

```
function function_name (argument_list ) {
    statements
}
```

Arguments, also called *parameters*, are input values that are passed to the function when it is called. These parameters may be manipulated by the function. The arguments to a function consist simply of a comma-separated list of variable names. When the function is used, those variables will be initialized to contain whatever values were supplied in the function call. For example, here we declare a function to average three numbers:

```
function avgThree(first, second, third)
{
```

```
    var sum = first + second + third;
    return (sum / 3);
}
```

After this function declaration has been made, we can then use (call) the function to average the three numbers 7.5, 2, and the value of z (5):

```
z = 5;
x = avgThree(7.5, 2, z);
```

When the function is called, the variable first will be assigned the value 7.5, second will be 2, and third will be 5. Once the average is computed, the return statement orders the function to exit and return the computed value as the value of the function. This value is then assigned to the variable x.

Using Functions.   Functions may return a value or just perform work. A JavaScript function that performs work but does not return a value is similar to a Java or C++ method declared type void. The following example is a function that does not return a value; it simply performs a print to the browser document.

```
function print_me(string_in) {
    document.write("Display information " + string_in);
}
```

string_in is an argument passed to the function. This argument receives its value before the function is called. See the following code fragment:

```
string_in = "passing information";
print_me(string_in);
```

Functions can perform manipulations and return a value. The value to be returned to the calling code is designated by the return keyword.

JavaScript passes its parameters by value, just like C. The function parameter variables are local variables, just as in Java, C, and C++. A local variable is a personal copy of a variable known only to that function. The function may choose to alter any local variable, and no change will occur to any variable by that name within the main program.

Variables used within a function may be local. A local variable is a variable that exists only within a particular function. A variable used within a function for the first time will be local if it is preceeded by the keyword `var`. Variables used within a function may also be global. Changing a global variable within a function changes the value of a variable that is accessible throughout the program. If the `var` keyword is not used within a function when a variable is first used, it will be global. (Refer to the section "Variable Scope" if this is confusing.) The following example demonstrates the use of `return` and the *scope* of variables within a function:

```
function return_me(string_in) {
    var string_end = " added on the end.";
    string_in += string_end;
    document.write(string_in + "  <from function>");
    return string_in;
}
```

```
...
```

```
string_in = "Show information";
string_end = "I am not changed.";
print_me(string_in);          //call the function defined above;
➥perform display
document.write(string_in);    //show the value of string_in is
➥changed
document.write(string_end);   //print out the current value of
➥string_end
...
Output to the browser is:
    Show information added on the end.  <from function>
    Show information added on the end.
    I am not changed.
```

Even though the value of `string_end` is changed within the function, the program that called the function will not reflect this change because the keyword `var` was used when first using the variable, making it local to the function. It's important to be aware of the scope of variables within functions when writing code.

Functions can also call themselves *recursively*, meaning that a function may call itself. For example, you can implement the factorial program using a recursive function:

```
function factorial( n ) {
    if ( n == 0 ) {
        return 1;
    } else {
        return(n * factorial(n - 1));
    }
}
document.writeln("10 Factorial is " + factorial(10));
```

An important characteristic of recursive functions is that every time it calls itself, it reduces the size of its task. The first time it is called, it reduces its problem to computing factorial(9), which it can multiply by 10 to obtain factorial(10). As long as the problem it repeatedly hands itself becomes increasingly smaller, it eventually is able to solve the problem directly. In this case, it knows directly that factorial(0) is 1. Many types of programming problems are handily solved with recursive functions. The capability to write recursive functions adds yet another tool to the programmer's tool belt.

Arrays

The *array* is a data structure common to many programming languages. Arrays are simply named, ordered lists of items the component items of which are accessible via their *index* or *subscript*. The index, or subscript, is a number (or name) that corresponds to the item's place in the list. For example, the item TestArray[1] is element number one of the array. JavaScript also allows names to be used as an element's "selector" into the array, as in TestArray[one].

Think of a line of mailboxes at the end of a country road. The mailboxes are numbered 0, 1, 2, and so on to the end of the line. (We start with zero because, in their simplest form, JavaScript arrays do.) Each mailbox may contain something, hopefully not fruitcake. The contents of the third mailbox in the line may be accessed by using the name "MailBox[2]". A fruitcake may be placed in the seventh mailbox by the command

```
MailBox[6] = "A Fruitcake";
```

Anything that may be put into a variable may be put into an array element. After all, an array is simply a way of grouping similar variables together and making it easier to access them iteratively.

It is important to keep a mental image of an array in mind if this is a new concept to you. Whether it be the line of mailboxes, children in a line, or items on a grocery list, find an analogy that works for you. Arrays are a very powerful programming tool.

Arrays are created by using the new operator, which requires a constructor function to be supplied when calling it. Constructor functions are discussed in Chapter 5, "Creating and Using JavaScript Objects."

```
function newarrayfunc {      //array definition
...
}
myarray = new newarrayfunc(); // create an object, initialized
➡by  newarrayfunc
```

You can use the constructor function to initialize elements in the array. After you create the array myarray, you can insert elements into the array, as in the following:

```
myarray[0] = 1;
myarray[1] = 123;
myarray[7] = 111;
myarray[5] = 2.71828;
myarray[42] = "Life, the Universe, and Everything";
```

These statements create five elements in the array myarray, with indexes 0, 1, 5, 7, and 42. Again, *indexes*, also known as *subscripts*, are used to identify the element of interest in the list. JavaScript arrays automatically increase their size as needed. They do not have to be preallocated as in many languages. It is only necessary to assign a new element to have the array size expand.

The subscript must always be enclosed in rectangular brackets. Also notice in the preceding example that the indexes do not need to be sequential. Array references may be used in any expression wherever a variable can be used, as in the following:

```
total = myarray[7] + myarray[1] - 1;
```

which sets total to the value 111 + 123 -1, or 233.

Array names have the same rules and restrictions as normal variable names. Note that elements need not have the same type.

Arrays are intimately related to objects. In fact, arrays and objects are one and the same. Chapter 5, "Creating and Using JavaScript Objects," fully explores objects. At this point, just remember that arrays are useful for creating lists of data items.

The following example shows the use of an array to keep track of donut consumption at XYZ Corp. as part of a new health program. The array is indexed by employee badge number:

```javascript
function newarrayfunc {

...

}

donuts = new newarrayfunc();
donuts[1] = 14;          // BOB, company founder
donuts[2] = 6;           // Ed,  company VP
donuts[4] = 0;           // Nancy, company dietician
donuts[6] = 22;          // Fenton, Nigel's supervisor
donuts[18] = 9;          // Nigel, Ralph's supervisor
donuts[15] = 3;          // Ralph, worker

...

donuts[6] = donuts[6] + 1;    // Fenton eats yet another donut
```

A nice feature of JavaScript which makes it completely different from Java, C, and C++ is that JavaScript arrays can have *string subscripts* as well as numeric subscripts. The following example uses string subscripts in place of numeric subscripts. This program is equivalent to the preceding program:

```javascript
function newarrayfunc {

...

}


donuts = new newarrayfunc();


donuts["BOB"] = 14;             // BOB, company founder
donuts["Ed"] = 6;               // Ed,  company VP
donuts["Nancy"] = 0;            // Nancy, company dietician
donuts["Fenton"] = 22;          // Fenton, Nigel's supervisor
```

```
donuts["Nigel"] = 9;              // Nigel, Ralph's supervisor
donuts["Ralph"] = 3;              // Ralph, worker
...
donuts["Fenton"] = donuts["Fenton"] + 1;     // Fenton eats yet
➥another donut
```

Because arrays are implemented by using JavaScript objects, array elements that have not been defined will not exist. Accessing an undefined element will result in a run-time error. JavaScript array elements are accessible via the `for...in` loop construct, just like JavaScript objects, as discussed in the earlier section "Control Flow Structures."

Functions with a Variable Number of Arguments.

Programmers may pass arguments to functions without listing them explicitly as formal parameters in the function declaration. Whenever a function is called, JavaScript automatically creates an array object called `arguments` containing the list of parameters the function was called with. The array `arguments` is a property of its own function, has elements sequentially numbered from zero, and has a length property, just like other arrays. The `arguments` array allows the programmer to write functions that accept a variable number of arguments. For example, the following function finds the maximum value in an arbitrarily long list of items:

```
function maximum() {
        var max = 0;
        for (var i=0; i < maximum.arguments.length; i++) {
                if (maximum.arguments[i] > max) {
                        max = maximum.arguments[i];
                }
        }
        return (max);
}
```

To make the code more readable, it is often convenient to substitute a local variable. For C-related historical reasons, many people choose to use the local variables `argv` (argument vector) and `argc` (argument count) to access the arguments array. By rewriting the preceding function

```
function maximum() {
    var argv = maximum.arguments;             // Argument vector
```

```
(array)
    var argc = maximum.arguments.length;   // Argument count
    var max = 0;
    for (var i=0; i < argc; i++) {
        if (argv[i] > max) {
            max = argv[i];
        }
    }
    return (max);
}
```

the function may then be used like this:

```
x = maximum(7, 5);                      // Returns 7
y = maximum(1.7, 3.9, 2.8);             // Returns 3.9
z = maximum(7, 2, 1, 11, 5, 14, 3);   // Returns 14
```

Summary

This chapter introduced you to the basics of JavaScript. Just as one must crawl before walking, it's necessary to understand the building blocks of the language. You should at this point be at a good walking stride. You have learned the basic structures of JavaScript and how JavaScript relates to HTML. At this time, JavaScript cannot exist without HTML. JavaScript code is usually located in the <HEAD> block of an HTML document.

You have also learned about the language components available in JavaScript: comments, expressions, statements, and control flow structures. Comments are used in JavaScript to help the programmer decipher code. Statements are commands in JavaScript.

JavaScript variables may be declared by the keyword var, but are not otherwise typed. Literals are values that may be assigned to variables. JavaScript is a *loosely typed* language, which means that variable type may change on the fly, and type conversion is automatic. The four data types available in JavaScript are integer, string, Boolean, and floating-point.

JavaScript operators manipulate numeric and string data. It is important to understand operator precedence in order to create code that performs as expected. Operator precedence is very similar to that of C, C++, and Java.

Control flow allows decision making logic in JavaScript programs. The control flow structures are if, while, and for.

Finally, *functions* are blocks of code that can be used many times throughout a program simply by being called. They provide a key reusability structure within JavaScript.

The next step in this learning process is to build powerful, flexible applications using these building blocks.

Chapter 3

An HTML Overview and Primer

Browser/client side JavaScript currently cannot exist without HTML. HTML is used to create objects that JavaScript can later control. Of course, the HTML file carries the actual JavaScript program as well as specifies event handlers for the various objects. This chapter covers some HTML basics, as well as new features of HTML as associated with JavaScript. It is in not intended as a replacement for a book that is a comprehensive tutorial or reference for HTML. This chapter is intended to be a refresher for those readers familiar with HTML and an introduction for readers new to HTML.

A Little about HTML

HTML stands for *HyperText Markup Language*; it is the backbone of the World Wide Web. HTML establishes the links and formats the displays seen on Web pages the world over.

HTML is derived from *Standard Generalized Markup Language (SGML)*. SGML has long been used in the publishing industry, and many companies still use it for technical writing tasks. HTML is defined as an application of SGML. HTML has undergone steady development since the Web started exploding in 1994, particularly in the World Wide Web Consortium (W3.ORG) standards track and via corporate leadership and innovation. Netscape has played a leading role in extending HTML. Netscape has continued to incorporate access to the new technologies it puts in its browsers via HTML.

HTML allows the assignment of characteristics to text, such as font size, style, and type. It also allows the creation of new structural elements such as objects and the definition of characteristics of those objects. According to the HTML 3.0 specifications, HTML was guided by the following principles:

- **Lingua Franca.** HTML was meant to be a common language that could be used to tie together information from widely different sources.

- **Simplicity.** HTML was meant to be simple for both HTML authors and programmers to use.

- **Scalability.** HTML was meant to accommodate technological and social changes in the way people use the Web.

- **Platform Independence.** HTML was meant to provide platform-independent rendered content.

HTML follows the general philosophy of the Web, which is to "be conservative in what is produced and liberal in what is accepted." This means that servers try to maximize the correctness and conformance of the HTML they output and that Web browsers strive to make sense out of what the server sends.

One example of this philosophy is what the browsers are required to do when faced with unfamiliar *tags*, or commands. The browser does not abort in most cases; it ignores what is unfamiliar and tries to go on as best it can to interpret what has been sent. This is helpful in making browsers and HTML pages both forward and backward compatible. This is also how browsers approach JavaScript. A browser that is not JavaScript compatible ignores the JavaScript components within the HTML document and carries on as best it can.

This philosophy allows companies such as Netscape to extend their browser to accept new HTML tags. Older browsers continue operating even though they're unfamiliar with the new extensions. A Netscape browser correctly interprets a form with the new extensions, while the older browsers simply ignore the new extension tags. In this way, the HTML page remains usable across many more browsers than it would be otherwise.

Creating HTML Tags

HTML was originally designed for basic presentation of document content to users. It simply consisted, and still consists of, the text to be displayed interspersed with *markup tags*, indicating the way in which the text around them should appear. Over time, additional tags have been added to HTML to extend the scope and functionality of structures that can be defined. HTML tags can be used for the following:

- To describe text appearance, style and layout

- To display images and provide links between pages

- To define forms and tables

- To influence browser structural layout and behavior in the platform window system

HTML tags are commands to the browser. The commands do everything from setting up text format to pointing to images to be retrieved and displayed.

Each HTML tag begins with a < and ends with a >. The angle bracket symbols differentiate commands from the surrounding test. The opening < is followed immediately by the name of the tag. Some examples of tags are

```
<I>

<BLOCKQUOTE>

<DL>

<BODY>
```

The tags are not case sensitive, but in this book we have chosen to use the convention of all capitals for HTML tags to differentiate them from JavaScript commands and other HTML document text.

Some tags have counterparts, called *container tags,* that serve to enclose the HTML text between them. The tags <B> and </B> enclose text that is to be printed in bold font. Tags <DL> and </DL> enclose a definition list. Here are a few other examples:

```
<CENTER> </CENTER>

<HEAD> </HEAD>

<TITLE> </TITLE>

<UL> </UL>

<A> </A>

<TT> </TT>
```

Some tags have counterparts that are optional. The <P> tag, for example, is almost never used with its matching </P> tag. This is a reflection of the browser being "liberal" in what is accepted. It's best in practice to follow the conventions as much as possible for predictable, cross-browser results.

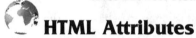 HTML Attributes

Between the opening <*tagname* and the closing >, there may also be attributes. An *attribute* is additional data associated with the object the tag represents. An attribute can be thought of as either an argument to the tag or as a specification of some characteristic of the tag. Attribute names are separated from the tag name by spaces.

Attributes may or may not have values associated with them. Unknown attributes are ignored by the browser, even while it recognizes the associated tag. Also, an attribute's keywords are not case sensitive. The values associated with an attribute, however, have their case preserved.

Attribute values are designated by the equal sign (=), as in the following:

```
<IMG SRC="picture.gif" ISMAP>
```

This HTML statement directs the browser to load an image. It has an SRC attribute that contains the value `picture.gif`. This statement also has an ISMAP attribute. The SRC attribute tells the browser the location of the image and to go ahead and load it. The ISMAP attribute tells the browser that the image is to be treated as an image map.

Following are more examples of tags that contain attributes:

```
<FORM NAME="InforForm" METHOD="POST" ACTION="/cgi-bin/handleform">

<A HREF="http://www.w3.org/">

<FRAME SRC="page1.html" NORESIZE>
```

Attribute values may be enclosed in double quotes, single quotes, or nothing. Double quotes are preferred by convention. Quotation marks must be used if any spaces or unusual characters are in the value. Additionally, in the event that quotation marks are to be preserved, double quotes may enclose a string with single quotes in it, and vice versa.

White space around tag and attribute elements is ignored by the browser. The HTML code may put as many spaces, tabs, and newlines between attributes as desired, even around the = between the attribute name and value. Unless specifically told to do so by tags, the browser ignores HTML source spacing and formation.

Please note that HTML tag attributes are one way of setting the values of JavaScript properties.

HTML Document Structure

An HTML *document* is the contents of a single HTML file. Every HTML document is divided into two sections: a *HEAD* and a *BODY*. Therefore, the basic skeleton for an HTML document is

```
<HTML>
<HEAD>
</HEAD>
<BODY>
</BODY>
</HTML>
```

Most browsers assume HTML code is inside the `<BODY>` if this skeleton is not followed strictly.

HTML *<HEAD>* Section

Only certain HTML tags are valid in the document `<HEAD>` section. This area of the document is reserved for general information that pertains to the complete document.

One of these tags is the `<TITLE>` tag, which sets the document title. The document title appears in the window title bar.

Another tag that may be located in the `<HEAD>` section is `<SCRIPT>`. Recognition of the `<SCRIPT>` tag is currently specific only to the more recent releases of the Netscape Navigator (2.0 or later) and Microsoft Internet Explorer (3.0 or later) browsers. JavaScript code is located between the `<SCRIPT>` and `</SCRIPT>` delimiters. An HTML file may contain any number of `<SCRIPT></SCRIPT>` blocks.

Other tags can be in the `<HEAD>` section of an HTML document. Please see a good HTML reference book for other tags.

HTML *<BODY>* Section

The `<BODY>` section of an HTML document, described by the text and HTML markup tags, contains the information that is to be displayed in the browser document.

HTML tags in the `<BODY>` section control many aspects of the browser's rendering of the document, including the following:

- Font size

- Font style

- Font color

- Text layout control

- Image display

- Anchor display

- Form rendering

Many HTML objects rendered by the browser, such as form elements, implicitly create JavaScript objects that allow the programmer to query and manipulate those objects.

<*BODY*> Attributes.   The <BODY> tag has several important attributes associated with setting up the initial document and displaying it in the browser. One of the attributes controls the background color. Another attribute tells the browser what to do in case of an event such as loading or unloading the page.

This is an example of a <BODY> tag using all available attributes:

```
<BODY BACKGROUND="image.gif" BGCOLOR="#0A1B2C"
TEXT="#987654" LINK="green" ALINK="magenta"
onLoad="alert('Page was loaded');" onUnload"alert('Page was
➥unloaded');" >
```

Possible <BODY> attributes are described in the following list. All of these attributes are optional. All of the attributes of <BODY>, with the exception of BACKGROUND, have been originated by Netscape. Other browsers may or may not recognize them.

- ⊙ **BACKGROUND.** Specifies an image to be used to tile on the document background. Do not use with BGCOLOR.

- ⊙ **BGCOLOR.** Specifies a solid color to be used for the document background. See Appendix A, "Colors," for allowable color values. The corresponding JavaScript property is document.bgColor. Do not use with BACKGROUND.

- ⊙ **TEXT.** Specifies the text color. Text is black by default. The corresponding JavaScript property is document.fgColor.

- ⊙ **LINK.** Specifies the hypertext link color. The default color for the hypertext link color is light blue. The corresponding JavaScript property is document.linkColor.

- ⊙ **ALINK.** Specifies the "activated" hypertext link color. The default is red. The link changes to this color when the mouse button clicks on the link and *before* the mouse button is released. The corresponding JavaScript property is document.alinkColor.

- ⊙ **VLINK.** Specifies the "visited" hypertext link color. The default is dark purple. This is the color that indicates that the link has been previously visited. The corresponding JavaScript property is document.vlinkColor.

- ⊙ **onLoad.** Specifies JavaScript code to be executed when the document is loaded, or entered. Loading a document is an event recognized by JavaScript. Chapter 6, "JavaScript Events," has more information on the onLoad event handler.

🌎 onUnload. Specifies JavaScript code to be executed when the document is unloaded, or exited. Unloading a document is an event recognized by JavaScript. Once again, Chapter 6 has more information on the onUnload event handler.

<BODY> Tags.   This section describes some tags that may be contained in the <BODY> section. As stated earlier, the exciting things that an HTML document does are generated by HTML markup in the <BODY> section. Of course, there are many, many tags available for use in the <BODY> section. Please see a good HTML reference work for a complete list. The tags listed here are particularly useful in documents that contain JavaScript.

🌎 <A>. The anchor tag builds a hyperlink.

🌎 <FORM>. Defines a form.

🌎 <INPUT>. Defines form sub-objects, such as text input boxes, radio buttons, checkboxes, pushbuttons, and other input areas within a document.

🌎 <TEXTAREA>. Creates a multi-line text input box within a form.

🌎 <SELECT>. Identifies a selection list or a multiple selection scrolling list within a form.

🌎 <FRAMESET>. Defines a subdivision of the browser window into rectangular subregions called *frames*. These subregions may divide the browser window vertically into columns or horizontally into rows.

🌎 <FRAME>. Defines the document to be displayed in a frame.

Once again, this is but a small subset of tags available in HTML; however, they are very important to the discussion of the structure and interaction between HTML and JavaScript. Other HTML tags that control document presentation also have JavaScript counterparts. These HTML counterparts are noted in the JavaScript description. The following remainder of this chapter discusses the usage of these tags in greater detail.

HTML Tags and JavaScript Properties

Some HTML tag attributes and JavaScript properties are intimately related. The use of certain HTML tags results in the automatic creation of corresponding JavaScript objects. HTML attributes, which describe characteristics of their tags, implicitly set the equivalent properties in the corresponding JavaScript object.

The word *property* is used here in the sense of traits, characteristics, attributes, or qualities of an object. A JavaScript property is characteristic information about an object. For example, imagine the following form has been created by using HTML:

```
<FORM NAME="InfoForm" METHOD="GET" ACTION="/cgi-bin/info.pl"
➥TARGET="Lwin">
<INPUT TYPE="TEXT" NAME="username" VALUE="Bob Jones">
</FORM>
```

Implicitly, a JavaScript form object is created, called `InfoForm`. `InfoForm` is automatically initialized with the property `METHOD`, having the value `GET`, the property `ACTION` having the value `"/cgi[ms]bin/infoform.pl"`, and the property `TARGET` having the value `Lwin`. JavaScript code may then access these properties by using the notation *object.property*.

Just as properties may be values, properties may also be objects themselves. The `InfoForm` object in the preceding would actually be a property of the `document` object, which is the parent of objects within the browser frame. The form is then accessible to the programmer as the object `document.InfoForm`, and the `TARGET` attribute is `document.InfoForm.target`.

In this example, if the form's target property is `Lwin`, some action is taken:

```
if (document.InfoForm.target == "Lwin") {
    // Do something!
}
```

The following sections cover certain tags and their corresponding JavaScript object properties. The JavaScript object model's properties are discussed in detail in Chapter 9, "JavaScript Properties."

`<A>`—Anchor Tag

The anchor tag `<A>` is used to build a hypertext link, also called a *hyperlink*. Anchor elements are used to specify a link between a specific image or piece of text and another document or resource. By default, anchor text is shown in the browser as blue, underlined text, while an anchor image is shown with a blue border. The user clicks on the text or image, and the associated object is loaded into a window.

The following attributes are supported for the anchor tag <A>:

- HREF
- NAME
- REL
- REV
- TITLE
- CLASS
- ID
- LANG
- —
- SHAPE

Consider this scenario as an example of the use of <A>. The following statement in a document allows a user to bring up additional information on trees:

```
Do you want <A HREF="url"> information on trees?</A>
```

This prints to the screen the text "information on trees" which is in blue and underlined. The listed URL is loaded into the current browser window when the user clicks their mouse on the blue text.

```
Do you want <A HREF="url" TARGET="windowName"> information on
trees?</A>
```

This statement does something slightly different. When the user clicks on the blue text, the URL is loaded into the *windowName* frame or window. The original window is not overwritten unless it is named *windowName*. If the window *windowName* does not exist, a new browser window is created with that name.

JavaScript Anchors Arrays.   JavaScript automatically creates an array, document.anchors, which contains one element for each anchor in the current document, as long it has declared the NAME attribute. The JavaScript properties for the document.anchors array are:

- `document.anchors.length`: The number of elements in the array

- `document.anchors[n]`: The *n*-th anchor

This is a feature within JavaScript that is apparently not fully implemented. `document.anchors[n]` always returns `null` and is not very useful; however, it may be more useful in the future if access to the `NAME` attribute is provided. Anchor tags that include an `HREF` attribute are known as *links*. JavaScript automatically creates an entry in another JavaScript array, the `document.links` array, corresponding to each link in the document.

The JavaScript properties for the `document.links` array are

- `document.links.length`: The number of elements in the array

- `document.links[n]`: The *n*-th anchor

Each `document.links` array object is a JavaScript location object, allowing access through its own properties to that link's `HREF` information.

<FORM>—Form Tag

The `<FORM>` tag is used to define a form. Every form resides in, is owned by, and is a sub-component of a parent document. JavaScript can access the form object via its name. If the form name is `myForm`, the form object name is `document.myForm`.

A form is terminated by a `</FORM>` tag. Forms may contain most of the other HTML elements and text. Tags `<INPUT>`, `<SELECT>`, and `<TEXTAREA>` can exist only inside forms.

The `<FORM>` syntax is:

```
<FORM NAME="formName" TARGET="WindowOrFrameName"
➥ACTION="CGIServerUrl"
METHOD="HTTPmethod" ENCTYPE="encoding"
onSubmit="EventHandlerJavaScript" >
```

For example, here is a simple form:

```
<FORM NAME="NameForm" TARGET="ResultWin" ACTION="/cgi-
➥bin/uname.pl"
METHOD="GET" ENCTYPE="application/x-www-form-urlencoded"
onSubmit="alert('Sent Data');" >
```

```
<INPUT TYPE="TEXT" SIZE="20" NAME="UserName"> Your Username
</FORM>
```

NAME specifies the name by which the form will be known in the JavaScript object hierarchy. Use only legal JavaScript identifier names for your form name.

TARGET specifies the name of the frame or window for displaying the results returned after submitting the form.

ACTION specifies the destination URL to which information entered into the form is to be sent when the form is submitted.

METHOD specifies the HTTP method to be used to communicate the form data to the server specified in the ACTION attribute URL. Currently, this is either GET or POST.

ENCTYPE specifies the MIME encoding type to use when transmitting the form data specified by the ACTION attribute. The default is application/x-www-form-urlencoded. Use this attribute *only* if it is necessary to transmit a file to the server from the browser machine using the form input <INPUT TYPE="FILE"> tag along with other form data. Consult RFC-1867 for further information. RFCs are the IETF (Internet Engineering Task Force) standards documents. RFC-1867 is available at the URL http://ds.internic.net/rfc/rfc1867.txt.

onSubmit specifies JavaScript code to be executed when the form is submitted. This code can check over form data, and if it is deficient, prevent the submission from continuing by returning a false value. Any other return, including null, results in the specified ACTION being taken, transmitting the form data.

<INPUT>—**Input Tag**

The <INPUT> tag is used to define form sub-objects, such as text input boxes, radio buttons, checkboxes, pushbuttons, and others. Form input elements allow user interaction with Web pages. A JavaScript program can access the properties of input elements via the form object of which they are members.

The type of input object is defined by the TYPE attribute of <INPUT>. Permitted values for the TYPE attribute include the following:

- TEXT

- PASSWORD

- CHECKBOX

- HIDDEN

- RADIO

- BUTTON

- RESET

- SUBMIT

The FILE input type is currently legal in Netscape, but its interface is not yet enabled in JavaScript.

The general syntax for <INPUT> is

```
<INPUT TYPE="inputType" NAME="elementName" VALUE =
➡"initialValue">
```

inputType is one of the input types listed earlier. *elementName* is the name given to the input element. *initialValue* is the initial value assigned to the input element. Each particular input type adds its own specific attributes.

NAME Attribute.   Every input element should be given a name that is set with the NAME attribute. The input element name should be a legal JavaScript identifier.

Text Type.   The TEXT input type creates a one-line text input box, suitable for prompting for any text.

HTML Syntax.   <INPUT TYPE="TEXT" NAME="textName" SIZE="length" MAXLENGTH="maxlength">

textName is the name of the text input element passed to the server. *length* is the width in characters of the text input box. *maxlength* is the maximum number of characters the text input box will accept.

JavaScript Syntax.   JavaScript program access to the text object and its properties is via the form object:

```
document.myForm.textName.name
document.myForm.textName.type
document.myForm.textName.value
document.myForm.textName.defaultValue
```

The JavaScript event handlers are

```
document.myForm.textName.onChange
document.myForm.textName.onFocus
document.myForm.textName.onBlur
document.myForm.textName.onSelect
```

Password Type.　The PASSWORD input type is identical to the TEXT input type except that text typed into the box appears as * to mask the actual input. Please keep in mind that although PASSWORD does not appear on the screen when typed, it is actually *not* encrypted when it is communicated to the form handler specified in the ACTION URL. Therefore, the password can be spied upon easily on the network.

HTML Syntax.　`<INPUT TYPE="PASSWORD" NAME="passwdName" SIZE="length" MAXLENGTH="maxlength">`

passwdName is the name of the password element passed to the server. *length* is the width in characters of the text input box. *maxlength* is the maximum number of characters the text input box will accept.

JavaScript Syntax.　JavaScript program access to the password object and its properties is via the form object:

```
document.myForm.passwdName.name
document.myForm.passwdName.type
document.myForm.passwdName.value
document.myForm.passwdName.defaultValue
```

The JavaScript event handlers are:

```
document.myForm.passwdName.onChange
document.myForm.passwdName.onFocus
document.myForm.passwdName.onBlur
document.myForm.passwdName.onSelect
```

CHECKBOX Type.　The CHECKBOX input type allows the user to make a nonexclusive binary selection. In other words, the user can choose any or all of the "yes-or-no" selections.

The name of the checkbox should be unique within the form. The VALUE attribute specifies the value to be returned if the checkbox is checked. This corresponds to the JavaScript value property. If not

checked, the checkbox returns no value. The CHECKED attribute specifies that the box should be checked by default. CHECKED corresponds
to the JavaScript defaultChecked property. The JavaScript property
checked allows read/write access to the current state of the checkbox.

HTML Syntax. <INPUT TYPE="CHECKBOX" NAME="*checkboxName*"
VALUE="*value*" CHECKED>

checkboxName is the name given to the checkbox element *value* is the
value returned to the server if the checkbox is checked.

JavaScript Syntax. JavaScript program access to the checkbox
object and its properties is via the form object:

document.*myForm*.checkboxName.name

document.*myForm*.checkboxName.type

document.*myForm*.checkboxName.value

document.*myForm*.checkboxName.defaultChecked

document.*myForm*.checkboxName.checked

The JavaScript event is

document.myForm.checkboxName.onClick

RADIO Type. The RADIO input type allows the user to make
an exclusive selection; in other words, the user can choose *only one* of
the selections. The term "radio" alludes to the similarity of the old-
fashioned car radio selector buttons. Pressing one button popped
out the last button that was pressed in.

The name of all dependent radio buttons of the same group have the
same name. Just as in CHECKBOX, the VALUE attribute sets the value to
be returned if the button is selected. The CHECKED attribute also
works to select the default selection, which is the JavaScript property
defaultChecked. Because all radio buttons of the same group have
the same name, their individual elements may be accessed from
JavaScript via an array. The *n*th radio button element of the group
named *radioName* is accessed by document.*myForm*.*radioName*[*n*].
These elements are numbered from 0.

HTML Syntax. <INPUT TYPE="RADIO" NAME="*radioName*" CHECKED>

radioName is the name given to the radio element.

JavaScript Syntax. JavaScript program access to the radio object
and its properties is via the form object:

```
document.myForm.radioName.length
document.myForm.radioName.name
document.myForm.radioName.type
document.myForm.radioName[n].value
document.myForm.radioName[n].defaultChecked
document.myForm.radioName[n].checked
```

The JavaScript event is

```
document.myForm.radioName[n].onClick
```

HIDDEN Type.   HIDDEN input type is not an interactive input mechanism; it simply sets a value that cannot be altered by the user to be sent with the form data to the ACTION URL. This is useful to provide state information for dynamically generated forms. HIDDEN can also be used to differentiate between multiple forms that will be processed by the same ACTION URL.

For example, imagine two forms that are concerned with insurance quotations. One form gives a quotation for cars, and one quotes boats. The specified ACTION is the same URL. The form handler script at that URL might have to deal with different data on each form, yet it knows what action to take. The form handler checks the value of a *hidden* variable that identifies the form that was filled out.

HIDDEN has only two attributes: NAME and VALUE.

HTML Syntax.   `<INPUT TYPE="HIDDEN" NAME="secretName">`

`secretName` is the name given to the hidden element.

JavaScript Syntax.   `document.myForm.secretName.name`
```
document.myForm.secretName.type
document.myForm.secretName.value
```

BUTTON Type.   The BUTTON input type creates a pushbutton that generates a Click event. Its VALUE attribute simply determines the text that appears on the face of the button.

HTML Syntax.   `<INPUT TYPE="BUTTON" NAME="buttonName">`

buttonName is the name given to the button element.

JavaScript Syntax.   `document.myForm.buttonName.name`

```
document.myForm.buttonName.type
document.myForm.buttonName.value
```

The JavaScript event is:

```
document.myForm.buttonName.onClick
```

RESET Type.   The RESET input type is identical to type BUTTON, except that pressing it has the additional side-effect of setting all form elements back to their default values and states. The default values are determined from the property defaultValue, and the default states are determined from the property defaultChecked.

The onClick event handler can be used to prevent the reset button from performing the reset if the event handler returns the Boolean value false.

HTML Syntax.   `<INPUT TYPE="RESET" NAME="resetName">`

resetName is the name of the reset element.

JavaScript Syntax.   document.myForm.resetName.name
document.myForm.resetName.type
document.myForm.resetName.value

SUBMIT Type.   The SUBMIT input type is identical to type BUTTON, except that pressing it also encodes and transmits the form data to the URL given in the form's ACTION attribute. A SUBMIT object is a special form of BUTTON. SUBMIT also loads whatever page is returned by that URL into the window or frame named by the form's TARGET attribute. If no TARGET is specified in the <FORM> tag or in the document's <BASE> tag, the resulting document will load into the current browser window.

Traditionally, the URL is a server-based CGI script that processes the form's data and returns a resulting page. Now a JavaScript-enhanced document can be used for many of the same applications.

The specified onClick event handler is called before performing the SUBMIT operation. It can prevent the form from being submitted if it returns the Boolean value false. To validate the contents of the form and possibly abort the submission, you may also use the <FORM> tag's onSubmit event handler.

This feature is useful to "pre-approve" the form data by checking the ranges of legal values. This can significantly offload processing in server-based CGI form processing situations, especially if there is a non-trivial chance of data that must be corrected. This offloading of processing is a significant example of JavaScript rebalancing the client-server relationship.

HTML Syntax.   `<INPUT TYPE="SUBMIT" NAME="submitName">`

`mySubmit` is the name of the submit button element.

JavaScript Syntax.   `document.myForm.submitName.name`

`document.myForm.submitName.type`

`document.myForm.submitName.value`

<TEXTAREA>—Textarea Tag

The `TEXTAREA` tag causes the browser to create a multi-line text input box. `TEXTAREA` is a peer to `<INPUT TYPE="TEXT">`, allowing free-form user input to be captured.

The size of the `TEXTAREA` box is `ROWS` rows by `COLS` columns. `ROWS` and `COLS` are attributes of `TEXTAREA`. Text appearing between the delimiter tags `<TEXTAREA>` and `</TEXTAREA>` is used to initialize the contents of the `TEXTAREA` text input box.

`WRAP` is an additional attribute used to set text wrap to the next line. `WRAP` may be set to `PHYSICAL` for enforced automatic line wrapping at the box boundary. The browser automatically inserts carriage returns into the text when the user types beyond the right margin of the textarea. `WRAP` may be set to `VIRTUAL` to wrap the browser display while not altering data. Finally, `WRAP` may be set to `OFF` to not force line wrapping.

The syntax for `TEXTAREA` is

`<TEXTAREA NAME="myTextarea" ROWS="n" COLS="n" WRAP="PHYSICAL">`

The corresponding JavaScript properties are

`document.myForm.myTextarea.name`

`document.myForm.myTextarea.value`

The JavaScript events are

`document.myForm.myTextarea.onBlur`

`document.myForm.myTextarea.onFocus`

```
document.myForm.myTextarea.onChange
document.myForm.myTextarea.onSelect
```

<SELECT>—Select Tag

The <SELECT> tag identifies a selection list or a multiple selection. The <SELECT> tag is a tool that has similar functionality to radio buttons. <SELECT> allows selection of a single item from a list of possible selections.

The attribute MULTIPLE signifies that the list should allow multiple items to be selected. This behavior allows any and all items to be selected and is similar to checkboxes.

The attribute SIZE specifies the appearance size of the list as a number of items. The list is manifested in the browser as a pull-down selection list widget, or as a scrolling list widget for multiple selection.

The select list is constructed by inserting <OPTION> tags and text between the select delimiters, <SELECT> and </SELECT>. An <OPTION> tag may include the attribute SELECTED to select that specified option by default. The value returned is specified by the VALUE attribute in the selected <OPTION> tag within the <SELECT> block. The value returned if no VALUE attribute is present is the text string that follows the selected <OPTION> tag.

The syntax for <SELECT> is

```
<SELECT NAME="selectName" MULTIPLE>
```

The corresponding JavaScript <SELECT> properties are

```
document.myForm.selectName.name
document.myForm.selectName.type
document.myForm.selectName.length
document.myForm.selectName.options[n]
document.myForm.selectName.selectedIndex
```

The corresponding JavaScript <OPTION> properties are

```
document.myForm.selectName.options[n].length
document.myForm.selectName.options[n].defaultSelected
document.myForm.selectName.options[n].selected
document.myForm.selectName.options[n].value
document.myForm.selectName.options[n].text
```

The JavaScript events are

```
document.myForm.selectName.onBlur
document.myForm.selectName.onFocus
document.myForm.selectName.onChange
```

<FORM> Tags

Whenever an element is created in a form object using `<INPUT>`, `<SELECT>`, or `<TEXTAREA>`, JavaScript automatically creates a reference to that object in the array `elements`, as a property of that form. Given the following HTML form definition:

```
<FORM NAME="myForm" METHOD="GET" ACTION="/cgi-bin/infoform.pl"
➡TARGET="Lwin">
<INPUT TYPE="TEXT" NAME="username" VALUE="Bob Jones">
<INPUT TYPE="TEXT" NAME="cityname" VALUE="Denver">
</FORM>
```

The value of the `username` input is accessible identically via `document.myForm.username.value` and `document.myForm.elements[0].value`.

The value of the `cityname` input is accessible identically via `document.myForm.cityname.value` and `document.myForm.elements[1].value`.

The elements of the `elements` array are created starting with element 0 and are created in the same numerical order in which they were defined in the HTML document. The number of elements in the array is stored in the property `elements.length`. Each `<INPUT>` or `<TEXTAREA>` tag creates a new element in the `elements` array. This means that each radio button will be a separate element in the `elements` array, even though they are normally accessed through another array of their own. Each `<SELECT>` tag, however, creates just a single element in the `elements` array.

Frames and Framesets

Here is a quick review of the HTML hierarchy:

- The largest unit of an HTML display is the window.

- Windows are *parent objects* of document objects.

- A document is a sub-object of a window.

◑ It could be said that a document is the *child* of a window.

◑ Forms are *children* of a document.

◑ Form elements are *children* of forms.

Although many fine Web pages occupy a single window, Web pages can be made more dynamic and user-friendly with *frames*. *Frames* divide a window into several separate sub-windows, and each of these frames is capable of displaying a document. The structural information needed to construct a Web page with frames is contained within the <FRAMESET> HTML tag. A *frameset* defines a set of rectangular strip areas, arranged either in vertical columns or in horizontal rows. FRAMESETs contain specifications of what to fill into those rectangular strips, either FRAMEs or other nested FRAMESETs.

FRAMESET attributes also define JavaScript event handlers for the Load and Unload events. Also, each document containing FRAMESETs automatically creates an array of frame objects named frames. The notation frames[n] refers to the *n*th child frame within the current window. The notation is

```
window.frames[n]
```

or for framesets in document already in frames, it is

```
myFrameName.frames[i]
```

A good example of framesets and frames is the on-line documentation for JavaScript, found at

```
http://home.netscape.com/comprod/products/navigator/version_2.0
➦/script
```

The documentation has multiple frames within a window that can each be manipulated separately.

<FRAMESET>—Frameset Tag

The <FRAMESET> tag defines a subdivision of the browser window into rows and columns. The ROWS attribute arranges the sub-windows, or frames, from top to bottom. The COLS attribute arranges the frames from left to right. The value of the ROWS and COLS attributes is a string representing the vertical width of each frame in sequence. The values are a comma-separated list. Each value may list either number of pixels, a percentage of the size of the parent window, or * to indicate the remaining space left over in the parent window. The last two types of values change size if the parent window is resized.

<FRAME> tags indicate which files to load into each of the frames. These statements are gathered together within <FRAMESET> tags. The following example separates a window into three frames. The first frame is 40 pixels tall, the second is 50 percent of the window height, and the last frame is the size of any leftover space.

```
<FRAMESET ROWS="40,50%,*">
  <FRAME SRC="top.html" NAME="high">
  <FRAME SRC="middle.html" NAME="mid">
  <FRAME SRC="bottom.html" NAME="low">
</FRAMESET>
```

The top sub-window is named "high" and will have the file "top.html" loaded into it. The middle frame is named "mid" and will have the file "middle.html" loaded into it. The bottom frame is named "low" and will have "bottom.html" loaded into it. Note that four separate HTML files make up this example. One defines the frameset, and three fill in the three frames.

<FRAME>—Frame Tag

The previous example showed the FRAME attributes SRC and NAME. FRAME has several other useful attributes that control the appearance and behavior of a frame.

SCROLLING Frame Attribute. A scrollbar automatically appears and disappears within a frame, according to the space taken up by the document within the frame, by default. The scrollbar disappears if there is enough space to view the whole document. If not, the scrollbar appears to allow the user to scroll to obscured parts of the document.

The default scrolling characteristics of a frame may be overridden by setting the SCROLLING attribute to NO for permanent disabling and YES for permanent enabling. AUTO is the default. There are known bugs with the SCROLLING attribute working as advertised in Netscape 2.0.

Syntax of Frame *SCROLLING*. `<FRAME SRC="myfile.html"`
`NAME="myName" NORESIZE SCROLLING="NO|YES|AUTO">`

Examples of Frame *SCROLLING*. `<FRAME SRC="myfile1.html"`
`NAME="myName1" SCROLLING="NO">     //Never scrolls`

```
<FRAME SRC="myfile2.html" NAME="myName2" SCROLLING="YES">
➥//Always scrolls
<FRAME SRC="myfile3.html" NAME="myName3" SCROLLING="AUTO">
➥//Automatic scrollbar
```

NORESIZE Frame Attribute.

Frames may be resized by using the mouse to drag the border between frames by default. This characteristic of frames may be disabled by placing the NORESIZE attribute in the <FRAME> tag.

Syntax of Frame NORESIZE.

```
FRAME SRC="myfile.html"
NAME="myName" NORESIZE SCROLLING="NO|YES|AUTO">
```

Examples of Frame NORESIZE.

```
<FRAME SRC="myfile1.html"
NAME="myName1" SCROLLING="NO">      //Does Resize

<FRAME SRC="myfile2.html" NAME="myName2" RESIZE SCROLLING="NO">
➥//Does NOT Resize
```

MARGINWIDTH and MARGINHEIGHT Frame Attributes.

Frame attributes MARGINWIDTH and MARGINHEIGHT may be used to set the number of pixels desired for margin width and height.

Example of Frame MARGINWIDTH and MARGINHEIGHT.

```
<FRAMESET ROWS="40,50%,*">
  <FRAME SRC="top.html" NAME="high" NORESIZE SCROLLING="NO">
  <FRAME SRC="middle.html" NAME="mid" SCROLLING="YES">
  <FRAME SRC="bottom.html" NAME="low" SCROLLING="AUTO">
</FRAMESET>
```

The top frame is fixed at 40 pixels tall, never scrolls, and will not resize. The middle frame is 50 percent of the width of the browser, always has a scroll bar, and can be resized with the mouse. The bottom frame is the remainder of the window, can be resized by the user, and its scroll bar appears and disappears according to necessity.

Summary

Those of you who are new to document creation should have gleaned enough HTML from this chapter to begin to program in HTML and JavaScript. Those of you who are already very familiar with HTML will have learned of the changes to HTML through its extensions of HTML for JavaScript.

This chapter covered the structure of an HTML document: its HEAD and BODY. Many of the tags, or commands, in HTML were presented. Any changes to HTML or Navigator 2.0 specific attributes were noted. Finally, the link between HTML attributes and JavaScript properties were demonstrated.

We hope this chapter has given you enough HTML to be dangerous. The information given here is certainly not intended to be a substitute for a complete manual of HTML or taking a class. Its intention is to place JavaScript and HTML relationships in perspective.

Chapter 4

The JavaScript Object Model

An understanding of the use of objects is crucial to an understanding of the flexibility and power of JavaScript. Previous chapters introduced the component pieces of JavaScript, such as datatypes, literals, variables, and control-flow logic. You've also seen the HTML framework in which JavaScript must reside. Now it's time to begin to use these pieces as part of a total application. This is where objects come into the picture.

There are several good books available that explore object-oriented analysis and design, as well as the foundations of object-oriented programming (OOP). We recommend that you take a look at them if this is your first try at OOP. A thorough knowledge of OOP is not necessary for use of JavaScript, but the more you know about it, the better your applications will be.

Quick Review of Object-Oriented Concepts

Two of the main concepts within object-oriented programming are *non-proceduralness* and *code reusability*. Non-proceduralness means that the applications are event-driven. Code reusability is the ability to break the language down into small pieces of code that may be stored separately and used by multiple programs and applications. Different languages use different tools to accomplish these goals, which are intended to speed up application development.

Objects, Properties, Methods, and Events

This chapter introduces the concepts of object-oriented programming: *abstraction*, *encapsulation*, *hierarchy*, and *polymorphism*.

JavaScript does not have language elements to fully support all of these concepts, so we'll show you how to use the tools at hand to come close. The JavaScript tools are its *objects*, *properties*, *methods*, and *events*. These tools are discussed in detail later in this chapter and in Chapters 5 through 9 of this book. Chapter 5, "Creating and Using JavaScript Objects," shows how to create and make use of JavaScript objects; Chapter 6, "JavaScript Events," discusses events; and Chapters 7 through 9 provide a listing of all objects, methods, and properties. Use this section to understand their functions and the relationships between them.

An *object* is an abstract, conceptual entity intended to correspond with a concrete, physical counterpart. An object can remember the characteristics and expected behaviors of the concrete counterpart. *Car* could be used as an object.

The object can remember its characteristics. The car object could have associated with it "maximum speed," "color," "horsepower," "gas mileage," and "current speed." These remembered characteristics are called *properties*. Objects may have any number of properties.

The object can remember procedures. These procedures can be used to command the object to perform some operation, such as "stop," "accelerate to 55 MPH," "break down," "fill tank with gas," and "have accident with this other car object." These procedures are called *methods*. Methods are directly known to the object. The object would know what to do if the programmer asked the object to perform any of them. The object may remember any number of methods.

The object may also remember what to do in case of some event. If the car's ignition is turned on, the car knows to start. The object's knowledge of what to do in case of an *event* is called an *event handler*.

The basic characteristics that define an object are its set of properties, methods, and event handlers. The complete object includes everything it needs to exist and function properly. An object also defines the way in which it expects other objects to use it. This concept is known as *encapsulation*, which is discussed in greater detail later in the chapter.

Advantages of Object-Oriented Programming

The reason object-oriented programming is considered desirable is that it addresses the fundamental software engineering problems of modular design and maintainability. Software definitions of objects can be isolated into independent modules of code. This characteristic is called *modularity*. The code can then be re-used in other projects. If a car object was needed in another program, it would already exist.

Well-designed objects allow programmers to create related objects by derivation or composition. If a *minivan* object were needed, its code could be written much more quickly because its definition can be derived from *car*. Likewise, if an *engine* object exists, it can be used to simplify the problem of building the original car object.

Each object definition is basically its own independent system with well-defined properties and methods. The code for an object can be modified without affecting the remainder of the program, just as long as the way it allows other objects to use it remains the same. Object encapsulation makes the task of writing a program easy to divide into manageable chunks among several programmers. Once the program is written, it becomes easier to maintain.

In years past, Computer Science was much more of an art than a science. Maintainability of systems was a serious problem. There are famous cases of multi-hundred-thousand line programs that were simply abandoned because they were unmaintainable. Use of object-oriented techniques has made substantial progress in reducing the fundamental organizational complexity of programs, thus greatly improving maintainability.

Abstraction, Encapsulation, Hierarchy, and Polymorphism

Classic object-oriented languages provide mechanisms for building and using objects easily and reliably. Certain terms are often cited in the description of object oriented programming: *abstraction, encapsulation, hierarchy*, and *polymorphism*.

Abstraction allows the programmer to define a new object or process in terms that have already been defined. Think of our car example. We can define a function called *start* that does all the steps of starting a car. These steps could include "press gas," "gear shift to neutral," "clutch pressed," and "turn ignition." After this function definition, *start* is the only step we need to ask our car to do. This greatly simplifies our programming task. Rather than enumerating the minutiae of steps needed to start the car object every time, it's possible to call the function.

C++ and Java abstraction provide support for the capability to define a function (*method*) with a well-defined set of inputs (*arguments*) and outputs (*return values*). The fundamental efficiency that abstraction supports is the ability to never have to write the same code twice.

Encapsulation is the conceptual act of unifying properties, methods and event handlers together into a single unit, an *object*. The object is self contained, with the conceptual and software engineering benefits explained earlier.

An *object* is the union of properties, methods, and event handlers. *Encapsulation* is the philosophy that certain language elements should be dealt with as a unit. Objects are JavaScript's attempt at encapsulation.

C++ and Java allow the creation of objects by specifying formal definitions of objects, called *classes*. The class allows the language to enforce restrictions on access to internal data. The object permits only data that is defined as *public* to be accessed. Data that is not public is *private*, or *protected*, and unknown to outside objects. This concept is known as *data hiding*.

C++ and Java also allow for the provision of *constructor* methods, which bring an instance of the class into existence. Unfortunately, JavaScript does *not* support constructor methods.

JavaScript allows for the creation of objects without a formal definition such as class. JavaScript requires the programmer to enforce access restrictions by manual inspection of the program. This increases the difficulty of maintenance but is usually practical with JavaScript programs because they are necessarily on the small side.

However, JavaScript does have an equivalent to the constructor method. This might be called a *constructor function*, meant to be used to initialize objects. Again, JavaScript requires the programmer to enforce type checking in the constructor function because JavaScript doesn't check type.

Hierarchy is the building of family trees of objects. The car object might be the basis for a truck object. In C++ and Java, this is directly supported in the class definition. A Java applet can automatically avoid all the work done to build the car object simply by saying "class truck extends car." This idea is known as *inheritance*.

JavaScript does not directly support classes, nor does it support inheritance. As will be shown, JavaScript objects are created with constructor functions. It's possible to include a constructor function for another object within a newly created function. The properties set by the new function include the properties set by the old function plus whatever new properties are needed. In other words, these various object definitions can be cascaded into one another. This is JavaScript's way of simulating inheritance.

JavaScript has no direct line of class derivation. However, it does support basic object hierarchy by allowing one object to be a property of another. Hierarchy is the concept that allows for abstraction of objects and the construction of more complex objects from component objects within JavaScript. Enforcement of access restrictions is again left to the programmer.

Polymorphism allows for continuity of behavior via the provision of standard methods in a hierarchy of classes. For example, a standard method called *shutdown* might be a method in every object in our car hierarchy. Polymorphism means that the *shutdown* method does the same sort of thing, and has the same meaning, for every object in the hierarchy. C++ and Java both support polymorphism via the data hiding mechanism inherent in their access control.

JavaScript does not support data hiding; therefore, there can be only one method with a particular name. Support of polymorphism is limited to those cases where objects are not derived but are included. Once again, object hierarchy is used to simulate traditional polymorphism.

This means that instead of creating an object *car* that is a superset of *engine*, an object *car* is created that includes an *engine* object as *one of its properties*. Polymorphism simplifies the overall design of a complex program by making the component objects more intuitively simple.

JavaScript Is Object-Oriented, After All

Even without these supporting mechanisms, programmers can still program in an object-oriented way. A programmer could write an object-oriented program in Pascal or Assembly Language, but the responsibility of ensuring the correctness of the program is on the programmer. The programmer would have to keep track of each object's properties, methods, and event handlers. The MIT X Window System toolkit (Xt) is written in C, which does not have many mechanisms supporting object-oriented programming but is object-oriented. Many programmers programming in non-object-oriented languages simulate object-oriented systems using state-machines. *State-machines* are abstract theoretical models of representing (modeling) the behavior of object-oriented systems.

Objects can be almost anything. The smallest logical unit of JavaScript is the object. A button on a browser window is an object. The button has an appearance and set of actions associated with it. It can be used in more than one window, needing only to change its label. In fact, buttons are one of the pre-defined objects available for programming use in JavaScript. Buttons and other pre-defined objects will be discussed in Chapter 7, "JavaScript Objects." It's also possible to create new, application-specific objects. We will show you how to do this in Chapter 5, "Creating and Using JavaScript Objects."

Nonproceduralness.   Obviously, other languages are capable of taking a series of events and reducing them to machine code. The difference between COBOL or BASIC and Java is that Java and other object-oriented languages allow events to proceed in a non-procedural manner.

Being *non-procedural* means that the program remembers the state it is in not by the loop in which it is spinning at the moment, but through state variables. Instead of coding state-holding loops, the programmer defines when the state should change and the action to take when that change occurs.

Object-oriented programming is intended to reduce the effort required to develop new applications by reusing code. Reusability becomes very easy if the application is already broken up into callable modules of code. Code reusability is a nice by-product of the *non-proceduralness* of Java, C++, SmallTalk, Eiffel, and other object-oriented languages.

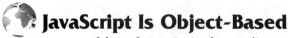 JavaScript Is Object-Based

Although JavaScript has rudimentary support for object-oriented programming, many of the convenient features of object-oriented programming such as inheritance, abstraction, exceptions, and encapsulation are lacking in JavaScript. This is the reason that JavaScript is called *object-based* rather than *object-oriented*.

JavaScript can use objects, but it's not as full featured a language as true object-oriented languages; however, it's a much easier language to learn and use. Java can be used to create applets, which are specific to Web pages and browsers, and applications, which are full featured, standalone programs. However, JavaScript can be used only in conjunction with HTML documents.

JavaScript is a language intended to allow manipulation of browser objects and sub-objects. To do this, the programmer must have some way of identifying what characteristic of which object is to be manipulated. For this purpose, JavaScript provides an *object hierarchy*, which is discussed next.

The JavaScript Object Hierarchy

Object hierarchy is notation, or syntax, that precisely denotes the specific object. JavaScript object hierarchy proceeds from least to most specific: the least-specific object is the document; next is the form, if used; after that is the property of the form, which is the equivalent of the FORM attribute in HTML; and finally, any values that are assigned to the property. Some of these objects may be elements within an array, such as document or anchor arrays. Arrays are discussed in the next chapter.

Following is a generic example of the JavaScript object hierarchy:

```
document.form.property.value
```

Here is an actual statement example:

```
myhouse.neighbor.paintcolor
```

It's easier to understand concepts through examples than through endless explanation. The next section shows the building of an object hierarchy, as well as how to access and assign object values.

An Example of the JavaScript Object Hierarchy

This example uses the postal system to explain the JavaScript object hierarchy. The postal system divides the population of our planet into a hierarchy based on geographic location. The largest unit of location is country. A Country is a very large location and, as a default, all letters can be assumed to originate from it. Usually, the only time country needs to be explicitly noted is when the letter goes outside the country of origin.

The United States is divided up into states, which are then subdivided into city, street, house or apartment building number, perhaps apartment number, and finally occupant within the residence. Everyone in this country is locatable with just five or six items of information.

For this example, we will ignore ZIP codes. ZIP codes are actually a redundant piece of information, duplicating state and city. ZIP codes help pinpoint the exact location of the post office for sorting mail and are not really necessary to define a geographical location (state and city are enough).

Use this information for the example:

```
John R. Brown
123 Juniper Lane
Boulder, CO
```

The period or dot is used in JavaScript to denote the levels of specificity within the hierarchy. By using this *dot notation*, the address is denoted in JavaScript as follows:

```
CO.Boulder.JuniperLane.123.JohnRBrown
```

This object follows the hierarchy:

```
State.City.Street.HouseNumber.Occupant
```

Another object has this hierarchy:

```
State.City.Street.AptAddress.Apartment.Occupant
```

This object could have the following value:

```
CO.Denver.Ogden.1984.5.NRice
```

The preceding structure allows individual objects to be accessed from a document. This is the basic structure used in all object manipulation.

An Example of Manipulating Objects within a Hierarchy.
Now that the basic object hierarchy structure has been explained, it's time to add values to an already existing object. Object creation comes in the next chapter. Values are initially assigned to an object by the equal sign assignment operator (=).

In the following example, an object named myHouse has a property name houseColor, and houseColor is given the value of green.

```
myHouse.houseColor = "green";
```

The property houseColor is a characteristic or attribute of myHouse. A property is created when it is assigned a value.

Another object is yourHouse, which has a completely different and independent value. If the house next door is yourHouse, this is represented by the following statement:

```
myHouse.neighbor = yourHouse;
```

After this relationship is established, it's possible to access the color of your house by this statement:

```
myHouse.neighbor.houseColor
```

Properties may themselves be objects. It's possible to build a hierarchy of objects and sub-objects through dot notation. The next chapter gives many examples of this concept.

Summary

The object model for JavaScript is particularly important because JavaScript is not a full featured, object-oriented language. It must simulate through its hierarchy many of the language features that support object-oriented programming found in C++ and Java.

The main attraction of object-oriented languages is that it *should* be faster to bring applications to completion than through procedural languages, such as COBOL or BASIC. Object-orientation is faster because it is both non-procedural by design and allows for great flexibility in code reusability and maintainability. Applications are, in reality, groups of object code. These code groups can be mixed and matched to create new applications. Code groups can also be modified without affecting other objects.

An object is just about anything a programmer wants it to be. It is usually a representation of a concrete entity, its characteristics and its expected actions. An object may also be a definition of something that may be reused later. Encapsulation is the "binding together" of these aspects of an object.

JavaScript uses objects, methods, properties and events as its tools to implement object-oriented applications. Methods are functions that perform activities for an object. Properties are characteristics or attributes of the object. Events are situations that the object recognizes and causes the object to take responsive action.

JavaScript does not have the direct language support to implement the full features of the concepts of abstraction, encapsulation, and polymorphism. It uses its object hierarchy to simulate these concepts. Other languages have tools in place to make sure that the programmer's attempt to implement these object-oriented concepts is correct. JavaScript is much more free-form. JavaScript does not do consistency checking, among other things. Therefore, the burden is on the programmer when trying to ensure the correctness of the program when concretely implementing these concepts.

This chapter discussed the advantages of object-orientation and the JavaScript object hierarchy. The next chapter discusses in detail the process of creating JavaScript objects.

The final version of the Moving Worlds specification should appear sometime during the summer of 1996. Until then, new drafts will be posted periodically. You'll find notes—generally in boldface and/or set in brackets—sprinkled throughout this draft, indicating the parts of the specification that need more work for the final version. These notes are your cue to be on the lookout for changes.

Look for new drafts at the following Web site:

```
http://webspace.sgi.com/moving-worlds/spec/spec.main.html
```

Chapter 5

Creating and Using JavaScript Objects

The previous chapter introduced terminology and concepts associated with object-oriented languages. The object is JavaScript's basic building block. It allows what appears to be a single variable to remember its own private set of variables, called *properties*, and functions, called *methods*. It can even remember other objects.

Before you can explore how to use objects, you must first be able to create them. This chapter explains how to create objects and explores making use of special features such as *arrays* within JavaScript.

Creating JavaScript Objects

The first step in creating an object in JavaScript is to create a *function*. A JavaScript function is different in use than a standalone function or a function to be used as a method. Those functions are concerned with operational actions. Here, a function is used to initialize a structure for a JavaScript object.

Here is an example of a function creation in JavaScript:

```
function house(pcolor, ht, bldr, res) {
  this.paintcolor = pcolor;
  this.height. = ht;
  this.builder = bldr;
  this.residents = res;
}
```

The object `this` is a special keyword used in JavaScript to refer to the current object. In this case, the current object is to be created by the *new* operator and passed to the original function. This will make sense in a minute.

The next step in creating an object is to take the object function `house` and use it as a skeleton to create an instance of `house`. Think of an *instance* as a real set of data with a certain, specified structure defined in the associated function. An instance is related to all other sets of data with the same structure of object form; an instance just has different values.

The actual creation of the object looks like this:

```
myHouse = new house();
myHouse.paintcolor = "grey";
myHouse.height = 23.45;
myHouse.builder = "Abel Baker";
myHouse.residents = 5;
```

Instances of objects are created with the keyword `new`, which creates an entity based on the structure of an original object. In this case, the original object structure is found in the function `house()`. Assignments are made to the properties found in `house` and assigned to the instance name of `myHouse`.

Another way to initialize an object and assign it values is shown in the following example, which assigns the same values as the previous example, but in a less verbose format:

```
myHouse = new house("grey", 23.45, "Abel Baker", 5);
```

Either way, the specific properties are accessed identically. myHouse.paintColor is still grey.

Creating JavaScript Objects from HTML Objects

The examples in the previous section showed an object created by using a constructor function in JavaScript. Another way to create a JavaScript object is to use HTML. HTML implicitly creates JavaScript objects corresponding to links, forms, form elements, and browser objects.

Using the *this* Argument to Pass Information.　　Information created by HTML code can be passed and used within a JavaScript function, as shown in the following example. The argument this represents the current information to be passed.

```
<FORM NAME="chloroform" METHOD="GET" ACTION=" ">
<INPUT TYPE="TEXT" NAME="chlorotype" onChange="register(this);">
</FORM>
```

This example demonstrates the extension of HTML to add the capability to specify an event handler, onChange. The JavaScript function register() is called when the contents of the text input box are changed. The call to register includes the argument this, which refers to the text input box named chlorotype, the current object. The text typed into the input box is available via the this object. The input text may now be manipulated by the JavaScript code in the function register().

Please note that this can be used only in functions used as methods and in event handlers.

Creating Multiple Instances of JavaScript Objects.

This section demonstrates an example of *multiple instances* of JavaScript objects; in other words, several objects with the same structure but different values. This example creates the instances and assigns them values. This is as close as JavaScript gets to the Java/C++ class concept, which is multiple objects that happen to have the same structure.

Consider this example. In keeping with a company health awareness program, employees will have their doughnut intake monitored. (We know, we know—sounds like Big Brother. Just go with it for the sake of the example.) This example uses a JavaScript program fragment that builds a small database of people and their doughnut intake.

The company has four people: Susan, Jeff, Ann, and Larry. As previously mentioned, the first step in creating objects is to create a function. A constructor function facilitates the creation of new person objects and initializes their properties, then values may be assigned.

```
//Constructor for object "person"
function person(fullName, idNum, sal, numDoughnuts, title) {
  this.name = fullName;
  this.id = idNum;
  this.salary = sal;
  this.doughnuts = numDoughnuts;
  this.title = title;
}
//Assign the values
susan = new person("Susan", 23, 3000, 5, "President");
jeff = new person("Jeff", 89, 2600, 3, "Vice President");
ann = new person("Ann", 123, 2200, 4, "Manager");
larry = new person("Larry", 143, 2000, 9, "Engineer");
```

Now that the database is established, let's indicate that Ann ate another doughnut by executing the following statement:

```
ann.numDoughnuts = ann.numDoughnuts + 1;
```

Another way to increment Ann's doughnut intake is with this statement:

```
ann.numDoughnuts++;
```

Each *person* is a separate instance of the object person, and each has data that can be manipulated separately. These multiple instances of an object reside in a database.

Using Methods with JavaScript Objects.   Remember that
a *method* is a function that is associated with an object. A method
allows a program to call a function as if it were a property of the
object. In other words, it "integrates" the function into the object
hierarchy notation. This idea of a method and its notation in the
language is borrowed from C++ and Java.

The syntax for methods is

```
this.methodName = functionName;
```

Before a method may be called, the function behind it must be
defined. Notice the absence of parentheses after the function name in
the preceding code. Putting the parentheses after the function name
causes the function to be called and its return value to be put into
the object. Without the parentheses, the object remembers the function. The object can then call the function in the future.

The example of the health-conscious company continues. It has
been decided to notify an employee if he or she has gone over the
limit of 10 doughnuts. A function, someoneAteDoughnut(), is
defined, which implicitly assumes that one doughnut was eaten.
The someoneAteDoughnut() function will become the method
of the object person. The function is defined here:

```
function someoneAteDoughnut(){
   this.numDoughnuts++;
   if (this.numDoughnuts>10 {
    alert("Doughnut Limit Reached!");
   }
}
```

Now an improved version of the person function is defined, including the AteDoughnut method:

```
//Constructor for object "person"
function person(fullName, idNum, sal, numDoughnuts, title{
   this.name = fullName;
   this.id = idNum;
   this.salary = sal;
   this.doughnuts = numDoughnuts;
   this.title = title;
```

```
  this.ateDoughnut = someoneAteDoughnut;   //define method
}
//Assign the values
susan = new person("Susan", 23, 3000, 5, "President");
jeff = new person("Jeff", 89, 2600, 3, "Vice President");
ann = new person("Ann", 123, 2200, 4, "Manager");
larry = new person("Larry", 143, 2000, 9, "Engineer");
ann.AteDoughnut();   //calls method and does calculation
```

The last line calls the `AteDoughnut` method, which is really a call to the `someoneAteDoughnut()` function. The `this` operator returns the person object `ann`, increases her doughnut number property, and warns her with a pop-up alert window if she has gone over 10.

Other methods could be added to monitor cholesterol and heart rate just as the method to keep track of the number of doughnuts. This may be a contrived example, but the general concept is that the programmer may put as many methods as desired in an object. This supports the object-oriented concept called *encapsulation*, which is the unification of data and functions related to an object.

The same way functions assigned as properties of an object function as methods, other objects can be assigned as properties of an object. The interpretation of this is that one object is a "sub-object" of another.

The assignment is one of a reference to the "sub-object" in question; a copy is not made of the "sub-object." For example, the preceding example above might be improved by the addition of the properties `subordinate` and `boss`:

```
// Designate subordinates
susan.subordinate = jeff;
jeff.subordinate = ann;
ann.subordinate  = larry;
larry.subordinate = null; //sorry Larry

// Designate bosses
susan.boss = null;
jeff.boss  = susan;
ann.boss   = jeff;
larry.boss = ann;
```

This enables us to assign values such as:

```
jeff.subordinate.salary -= 100;
```

If you had declared further methods such as askBossForRaise and giveRaise, and expanded the constructor function to the following:

```
function askBossForRaise(dollars) {
  if (this.boss != null) {
    this.boss.raisePolicy(dollars);
  }
}


function giveRaise(dollars) {
  this.subordinate.salary += dollars / 2;
}


// Constructor for object "person"
function person(fullname, id_no, sal, no_dohnuts, title) {
  this.name    = fullname;
  this.id      = id_no;
  this.salary  = sal;
  this.doughnuts  = no_dohnuts;
  this.AteDoughnut = SomeoneAteDoughnut;    // Define Method
  this.askRaise = askBossForRaise;
  this.raisePolicy = giveRaise;
}
```

then you could use

```
larry.askRaise(200);
```

which would call askBossForRaise. This in turn would call giveRaise, adding 100 to larry.salary.

The special value null is a JavaScript keyword denoting a null value, or no value at all.

Arrays and JavaScript

Most higher level languages, including C++ and Java, have an array datatype, and JavaScript is no exception. The internal implementation of arrays is much different in JavaScript than C++ and Java. The concept of arrays was covered in Chapter 2, "Getting Started: JavaScript Basics." This section goes into detail about array creation and usage as objects.

Arrays as JavaScript Objects

JavaScript arrays are actually implemented as objects, and JavaScript objects and arrays are interchangeable. This means that arrays must be created in the same way as objects with the new operator.

The first step in creating an array is to define a constructor function. Once the function is created, it can be used to create a new object, which is initialized as an array. The following shows the sequence of events to define, create, and initialize an array:

```
function preInitArray(size) {
  for (var i=0; i<size; i++) {
    this[i]=0;
  }
  this.length = size;
}


myArray = new preInitArray(20);
```

A new array named myArray is created with 20 pre-initialized elements, indexed 0 through 19. Setting the property length to the number of elements in the array is a conventional practice. Users can check the property length to find out the number of elements in the array, as in the following:

```
for (var i=0; i < myarr.length; i++) {
  document.writeln("Element " + i + " has value " + myarr[i] +
➥"<BR>");
}
```

It should be pointed out that the programmer may add new elements to the array at any time.

Many people choose to have their array elements start with the element with subscript 0. This practice is mainly due to C++ and Java arrays *only* starting at element 0. Please note that this is simply convention. The programmer could choose to start the array with element 1 or 1000 just as easily.

JavaScript Array Notation. JavaScript array elements may be accessed through the same dot notation as properties. Array elements may also be accessed by element number or integer subscript. A third way to refer to a specific value is by using the string element name as the subscript. Keep in mind that *object* properties may be accessed using array notation.

The following three statements point to the same value:

```
larry.numDoughnuts
larry["numDoughnuts"]
larry[3]
```

The integer subscript corresponds to the order in which the property was defined in the constructor function. In the example, numDoughnuts was fourth after fullName, idNum, and sal. The subscript integer is 3 because subscripts by default start with the index value 0.

This mechanism implements what is known as an *associative array*, or a string addressable array. PERL and AWK also have this built-in capability, but Java does not.

Using the *for..in* Statement in JavaScript

JavaScript provides the for..in loop structure to make it possible for a program to execute a loop once for each property of an object. This was discussed in Chapter 2, but here we cover usage of this structure.

The for..in example uses the object structure assigned in the constructor function person:

```
//Constructor for object "person"
function person(fullName, idNum, sal, numDoughnuts, title){
   this.name = fullName;
   this.id = idNum;
   this.salary = sal;
   this.doughnuts = numDoughnuts;
   this.title = title;
   this.ateDoughnut = someoneAteDoughnut   //define method
}
//Assign the values
susan = new person("Susan", 23, 3000, 5, "President");
```

```
for (myVar in susan) {
  document.write("The var susan." + myVar);
  document.writeln(" = " + susan[myvarO]);
}
```

The preceding loop executes once for each property of the object susan. The following is the output to the browser:

```
The var susan.ateDoughnut =
function someoneAteDoughnut() {
  this.doughnuts++;
  if (this.doughnuts>10) {
   alert("Doughnut Limit Reached!");
  }
}
The var susan.doughnuts = 5
The var susan.salary = 3000
The var susan.id = 23
The var susan.name = Susan
```

Yes, this is the actual output from the code. for..in makes no promises about the order in which it will execute, only that it will execute once for each property. In this case, the properties have printed in reverse order.

A very interesting item in this output is the ateDoughnut method, which was printed in source form. In fact, this method is defined as a property of person. When JavaScript was asked to print all of the properties, the method was translated into its source code and printed out as the representation of property susan.ateDoughnut. This is one example that you will probably want to try for yourself.

Using the *with* Statement in JavaScript

The with statement is provided by JavaScript in an attempt to reduce typing and increase understanding of code. If there are several operations to be performed on properties of an object, the with statement can establish that object as the default object to use.

The following two sets of statements are equivalent:

```
with (myHouse) {  //using the with statement
  paintColor = "grey";
```

```
    height = 23.45;
    builder = "Abel Baker";
    residents = 5;
}

myHouse.paintColor = "grey";  // using properties and notation
➥explicitly
myHouse.height = 23.45;
myHouse.builder = "Abel Baker";
myHouse.residents = 5;
```

Summary

This chapter covered the creation of JavaScript objects. You learned that objects may be created either through function creation in JavaScript or by using HTML objects. Objects passed in through HTML may be referenced by using the `this` keyword.

This chapter also covered methods, which allow objects to use a function as if it were a property of the object. In other words, a function may be called just by using JavaScript notation. This saves a lot of coding. It also allows JavaScript to be more object-like.

You also learned that arrays are JavaScript objects. One of the basic concepts of JavaScript is that it allows HTML objects to be accessed as a series of elements in an array. Arrays are formatted through functions and created by using the `new` command. The `for..in` and `with` control flow structures allow loop access to arrays.

The next chapter, "JavaScript Events," concludes the discussion of the structural elements in JavaScript programs and applications.

Chapter 6

JavaScript Events

This chapter introduces the JavaScript concept of *events*. Events are things that occur that can be used to trigger other activities. Events are associated with objects. Event recognition and actions allow JavaScript to be a non-procedural language.

Definition of JavaScript Events

Three things are defined when an object is created: the object's data, methods, and event handlers. Each object has all the information it needs to be a competent actor in the play, which is the program. Unification of these three things allows an object to exist independently from other objects. This supports the fundamental object-oriented concepts of encapsulation and abstraction, and aids code re-use.

The object's *data* tells the object its current state, and perhaps its past state. *Methods* give the "actor," the object, a repertoire, or its instructions for executing its actions of which it is capable. The *event handlers* define how the object should behave in response to certain events. An *event* is input received from the environment or from other objects. For example, an actor waits for the curtain to rise to begin speaking. The rising curtain is an event that triggers action on the part of the actor. It's a cue to the actor.

Events may be *asynchronous*, meaning they may be received at any time, possibly unpredictably. Think of a teacher lecturing a class. The teacher has a precise procedure to follow in the event of a fire. However, a teacher does not constantly monitor the smoke alarm while teaching. Suppose that one day the teacher is lecturing on fractions when the fire alarm rings. The alarm is a signal that is noticed when it rings. The alarm interrupts the current actions of the teacher and causes invocation of the fire procedures. Usually, the teacher doesn't have to go about shouting "HELP! FIRE!" She has an orderly procedure to follow. Nor does the teacher ignore the event, even if it is the third time in the day that the alarm has been triggered. In this way, the JavaScript program recognizes an event, handles it nicely in a preset fashion, and smoothly goes about its business.

Non-object-oriented programming languages need to constantly check for events or simulate object orientation with state-machines and event loops. There is very little structure for handling events other than errors. Having objects respond to events with event handlers allows the programmer to isolate the code relating to an object. This leads to a greater probability that the code for each object will be reusable.

Following is pseudocode representing the sequence of events from the example of the teacher and the smoke alarm. This is from a procedural, non-object-oriented programming language:

```
Lecture-loop:
  Teacher lectures
  Teacher checks the smoke alarm
  If the smoke alarm goes off,
   do something
  else
   continue
  go to Lecture-loop
```

Instead, an object-oriented approach to this scenario would be

```
Teacher, in event of alarm perform Alarm-procedure
  Lectures


Alarm-procedure, in event of all-clear perform Return-to-Class:
  Close windows
  Get class out immediately
  Go to pre-assigned spot
  Count students
...
```

The object "knows" what to do when something happens. There is no need to constantly check the status of something. The program is automatically interrupted at its current point. The predefined event-triggered action is then performed.

JavaScript Events

JavaScript has defined several types of events, as shown in Table 6.1. Each object responds to its own set of events.

It's important to distinguish between events and errors. Errors are also interruptions in processing; however, these interruptions may terminate the program with no recovery available at this stage in the development of JavaScript.

Events are very different from errors. True, they interrupt the current processing, but they also allow for a change in direction in further processing. However, these events could be ignored if the program chose not to recognize them.

Table 6.1.
Events for
JavaScript Objects.

Event	JavaScript Object
Focus	TEXT (Input), PASSWORD (Input), TEXTAREA, SELECT
Blur	TEXT (Input), PASSWORD (Input), TEXTAREA, SELECT
Change	TEXT (Input), PASSWORD (Input), TEXTAREA, SELECT
Select	TEXT (Input), PASSWORD (Input), TEXTAREA
Click	BUTTON, RADIO (Button), CHECKBOX, RESET (Button), SUBMIT (Button), LINK
MouseOver	LINK
Submit	FORM
Load	WINDOW
Unload	WINDOW
Timeouts	WINDOW

Clicking on a button is an event. The button object could choose to ignore the click and go on processing its merry way. Users would probably get a little testy about a click being ignored, but it's not necessary to do anything with an event.

JavaScript event handlers allow for a wide range of event recognition and are easy to insert into code. Applications are a lot more user friendly and have more of the look-and-feel of windows applications if events are used wisely. The following sections cover the recognized JavaScript events.

Focus and *Blur* Events

The Focus event occurs when the user directs the keyboard focus at an object. An example of such an object is the text input box of a form. The user can do this by clicking the mouse in the text box. Another way is by pressing the Tab key to move focus from another input object. The Blur event occurs when an object that has keyboard focus loses it. Think of blur as loss of focus.

The Focus and Blur events can be accepted by the three form text input mechanisms, TEXT, PASSWORD, and TEXTAREA, as well as by the form pulldown selector, SELECT. One idea of the use of these events is to pop up dialog boxes advising the user of the proper way of filling in the relevant fields. This could happen either before the fact when focus is obtained or after the fact when focus is lost, or if a problem was detected.

Change Event

The Change event is a higher-level event than Blur and Focus. Change occurs when the user changes the contents or state of an object, such as a text area. The user must give focus to the text area, modify the contents of the text area, and then remove keyboard focus to constitute a Change event.

The Change event can be accepted by the three form text input mechanisms, TEXT, PASSWORD, and TEXTAREA, and by the form pulldown selector, SELECT. Just like Focus and Blur, Change might be used to analyze the modification done to an object and then pop up an advice dialog. Change might then run a routine to process the new data.

Select Event

The Select event occurs when the user highlights text within a text input object. This can be done by clicking and dragging on the text to highlight the entire object. Selection of text in this way is a standard supported in the window system for purposes of cutting and pasting text between windows. This selection can now be used to generate an event that could initiate execution of JavaScript code.

The Select event can be accepted by the three form text input mechanisms, TEXT, PASSWORD, and TEXTAREA. The Select event could be used to allow the user to choose from an arbitrary set of strings from within a text area. Imagine an instructional program for grammar in which the user is asked to select the verb from a sentence. Select could be used to indicate the selected text.

Click Event

The Click event occurs whenever a button or hyperlink object is clicked on with the mouse. Click works for all button type objects, including form BUTTONs, RESETs, CHECKBOXes, RADIO buttons, and SUBMIT buttons. Click also works for links.

The basic BUTTON, which does not exist in the CGI forms, is often used as a control button. Its Click event handler runs code to accomplish its function. It is the same as a SUBMIT or RESET button object except that it doesn't have any side effects.

The Click event handler may also be specified as a supplement to the other objects' functions. RADIO buttons and CHECKBOXes may have their states checked to see if they make sense. These states may be modified to obey program constraints.

An example of this use of event handling is a pizza selection program. CHECKBOXes may be used to select toppings for pizza. In this program, up to 5 of the 12 possible toppings can be checked for inclusion on the pizza. A check routine could be run every time a CHECKBOX is clicked. The routine could pop up an alert to inform the user of the exceeded limit and then un-select the CHECKBOX just checked.

The Click event handler will also work with the RESUBMIT and SUBMIT button objects. The onClick event handler cannot be used to prevent form reset or submission, however. The FORM object's submit event handler should be used instead to prevent form submittal.

The Click event handler can be used with a link to dynamically change the link's HREF. This allows the programmer to choose the destination of the link according to program conditions, including doing load balancing. There are a lot of possibilities of usage with the Click event handler.

MouseOver Event

The MouseOver event occurs when the mouse is moved over a link object. A *link object* is a piece of text or an image that has been identified as a hypertext link.

MouseOver is an event that happens only to link objects. The event handler can do anything that the programmer desires, but it is more commonly used to set the text in the browser status bar (where the URL for the HREF is normally displayed). The programmer might also like to have a pop-up alert appear the first time the user moves the mouse over the link.

Submit Event

The Submit event occurs when a form is submitted. This happens when the form's Submit button is pressed or the form's Submit method is called. Only the FORM object can specify a Submit event handler.

The Submit event handler can be used to approve and clean up form data. If the Submit event handler returns the value false, the submit will be aborted. If the event handler returns anything else or doesn't return anything, the submit will proceed.

Load Event

The Load event occurs after the browser has finished loading and rendering a document or all the frames of a frameset into a window. The Load event occurs every time the window is rendered, not just the first time. The load event is generated when a page has completed loading. The onLoad event handler enables the programmer to script JavaScript program code to execute. For instance, the onLoad event enables the programmer to be sure a page including associated graphics has loaded completely before executing the event handler.

The programmer specifies the Load event handler in either the <FRAMESET> tag or the <BODY> tag with the onLoad attribute, but the Load event handler is actually an event handler of the window object. There can be only one Load event handler for each window object. The Load event can be used to perform initialization, which should occur only after the page has been fully loaded.

Unload Event

The Unload event occurs upon departure from the current page. The programmer specifies the Unload event handler in either the <FRAMESET> tag or the <BODY> tag with the onUnload attribute. However, the Unload event handler, like the Load event handler, is actually an event handler of the window object.

There can be only one Unload event handler for each window object. The Unload event can be used to perform actions to take when the user leaves the current page. This might be to pop up a farewell message or to store state information in a cookie to remember what the user did while in that page. (Cookies provide a method to store information at the client side and have the browser provide that information to the server along with a page request.) This allows for things such as forms with persistent data.

Timer Events

Timer events allow the programmer to schedule any code to execute after a given delay period. Timer events are not events associated with particular objects. Other events are associated with something a user does, such as move the mouse or click on something. Instead, Timer events are events triggered by elapsed time.

Timer events are general events that may be delivered to any object, including JavaScript built-in objects. Timer events are scheduled with the setTimeout method. Scheduled Timer events may be canceled using the clearTimeout method. As with other JavaScript timekeeping functions, Timer resolution is down to the millisecond.

Timer events have a myriad of applications. These applications include setting time limits, sequencing a series of events, animating a message, implementing a timed academic examination form, helping users navigate a site by guiding them back to a help page if they haven't done anything for a long period, and so on. Basically, any timed event is schedulable for execution asynchronous to other running code.

 Using JavaScript Events

All events, excluding `Timer` events, are specified in the HTML tag for the relevant object. The event handler code is identified by one of the HTML attributes: `onBlur`, `onChange`, `onClick`, `onFocus`, `onLoad`, `onMouseOver`, `onSelect`, `onSubmit`, or `onUnload`. Each of these attributes is identified as a string value to the JavaScript code to be executed when the given event happens to the object. Remember that each object has its own limited set of events it's capable of responding to.

All of the text input form elements, including the TEXT input box, the PASSWORD input box, the TEXTAREA, and the SELECT pulldown, are capable of receiving the `Focus` and `Blur` events.

One idea of the use of the `Focus` event is to remind the user of input constraints. For example, consider this form that pops up an alert when the user first selects the text input box:

```
<HTML>
<BODY>
<FORM NAME="stateform" ACTION="/cgi-bin/stform.pl" METHOD="GET">
Please type the state name:
<INPUT TYPE="TEXT" NAME="state"
    onFocus="document.stateform.message.value='Capital letters
➡only';">
<BR> Message: <INPUT TYPE="TEXT" NAME="message">
<INPUT TYPE="SUBMIT" NAME="sub1" VALUE="Send Form In">
</FORM>
</BODY>
</HTML>
```

If we had wanted to warn users only when they explicitly selected or highlighted text with the mouse, we could have changed our `onFocus` event handler to be an `onSelect` event handler. The example may be improved by adding an event handler that validates the user's data when the user "blurs" the keyboard focus by selecting something else:

```
<HTML>
<BODY>
<FORM NAME="stateform" ACTION="/cgi-bin/stform.pl" METHOD="GET">
```

```
Please type the state name:
<INPUT TYPE="TEXT" NAME="state"
onBlur="if (this.value != this.value.toUpperCase()) alert('I said
➥CAPITALS!');">
onFocus="document.stateform.message.value='Capital letters
➥only';">
<BR> Message: <INPUT TYPE="TEXT" NAME="message">
<INPUT TYPE="SUBMIT" NAME="sub1" VALUE="Send Form In">
</FORM>
</BODY>
</HTML>
```

Note that the keyword this is used to access the current object, the
text input box. this.value is much simpler and more general than
document.stateform.state.value. It could be used the same way
with a series of objects without having to come up with the precise
hierarchical name of each one.

The onChange event is a composite event that occurs when an object
gets keyboard focus, is modified, then looses keyboard focus. To
improve the preceding example, we could avoid unnecessary harass-
ment of the user by popping up the I said CAPITALS alert when the
user actually modifies the contents of the text input box. The onLoad
and onUnload event handlers have also been added to the <BODY> tag
to print a friendly greeting and farewell messages:

```
<HTML>
<BODY onLoad="alert('Welcome to Choose-A-State!');"
➥onUnload="alert('Bye Now!');">
<FORM NAME="stateform" ACTION="/cgi-bin/stform.pl" METHOD="GET">
Please type the state name:
<INPUT TYPE="TEXT" NAME="state"
onChange="if (this.value != this.value.toUpperCase()) alert('I
➥said CAPITALS!');">
onFocus="document.stateform.message.value='Capital letters
➥only';">
<BR> Message: <INPUT TYPE="TEXT" NAME="message">
<INPUT TYPE="SUBMIT" NAME="sub1" VALUE="Send Form In">
</FORM>
</BODY>
</HTML>
```

Further improving the example, we simply convert the state name to uppercase, then check the string's value:

```
<HTML>
<HEAD>
<SCRIPT LANGUAGE="JavaScript">
<!--

function makeStates() {
  this[0] = "ALABAMA";
  this[1] = "ALASKA";
  this[2] = "ARIZONA";
  this[3] = "ARKANSAS";
...
  this[48] = "WISCONSIN";
  this[49] = "WYOMING";

  this.length = 50;
}


function checkState(textinput) {
  // Translate the value string to uppercase
  textinput.value = textinput.value.toUpperCase();

  // Check for valid state name
  var found = false;
  for (var i=0; i < states.length; i++) {
   if (textinput.value == states[i]) {
     found = true;
     break;
   }
  }

  if ( ! found ) {
   alert("Sorry, unrecognized state name\nPlease try again");
  }
}
```

```
states = new makeStates();


// ->
</SCRIPT>
<BODY onLoad="alert('Welcome to Choose-A-State!');" onUnload=
➥"alert('Bye Now!');">
<FORM NAME="stateform" ACTION="/cgi-bin/stform.pl" METHOD="GET">
Please type the state name:
<INPUT TYPE="TEXT" NAME="state" onChange="checkState(this);">
<INPUT TYPE="SUBMIT" NAME="sub1" VALUE="Send Form In">
</FORM>
</BODY>
</HTML>
```

Taking our example to the next stage, we could add a Submit event
handler, which should prevent submissions if the state data is invalid:

```
<HTML>
<HEAD>
<SCRIPT LANGUAGE="JavaScript">
<!-

function makeStates() {
   this[0] = "ALABAMA";
   this[1] = "ALASKA";
   this[2] = "ARIZONA";
   this[3] = "ARKANSAS";
...
   this[48] = "WISCONSIN";
   this[49] = "WYOMING";

   this.length = 50;
}


function checkState(textinput) {
   // Translate the value string to uppercase
   textinput.value = textinput.value.toUpperCase();

   // Check for valid state name
```

```
var found = false;
for (var i=0; i < states.length; i++) {
 if (textinput.value == states[i]) {
   found = true;
   break;
 }
}

if ( ! found ) {
 alert("Sorry, unrecognized state name\nPlease try again");
 // Prevent submission when called by onSubmit
 return false;
}

// Allow submission when called by onSubmit
return true;
}

states = new makeStates();

// ->
</SCRIPT>
<BODY onLoad="alert('Welcome to Choose-A-State!');" onUnload=
➡"alert('Bye Now!');">
<FORM NAME="stateform" ACTION="/cgi-bin/stform.pl" METHOD="GET"
onSubmit="return checkState(this.state);">
Please type the state name:
<INPUT TYPE="TEXT" NAME="state"
onChange="checkState(this);">
<INPUT TYPE="SUBMIT" NAME="sub1" VALUE="Send Form In">
</FORM>
</BODY>
</HTML>
```

Note that the onSubmit attribute in the <FORM> tag needs to have the
return statement. The form submission cannot be inhibited without
the return statement. Of course, the corresponding return statements
in the checkState function also had to be added. Returning false

prevents the form from being submitted, while returning `true` validates and permits the submission.

One last enhancement can be made to illustrate the use of `Timer` events: a timer that displays a pop-up alert window if the user has not tried to type anything for 10 seconds:

```html
<HTML>
<HEAD>
<SCRIPT LANGUAGE="JavaScript">
<!-

function makeStates() {
   this[0] = "ALABAMA";
   this[1] = "ALASKA";
   this[2] = "ARIZONA";
   this[3] = "ARKANSAS";
...
   this[48] = "WISCONSIN";
   this[49] = "WYOMING";

   this.length = 50;
}


function checkState(textinput) {
   // Translate the value string to uppercase
   textinput.value = textinput.value.toUpperCase();

   // Check for valid state name
   var found = false;
   for (var i=0; i < states.length; i++) {
    if (textinput.value == states[i]) {
       found = true;
       break;
     }
   }

   if ( ! found ) {
    alert("Sorry, unrecognized state name\nPlease try again");
```

```
    // Prevent submission when called by onSubmit
    return false;
  }

    // Allow submission when called by onSubmit
    return true;
}

states = new makeStates();
// If 10 seconds (10000 milliseconds) go by without user
➥action...
// The ID 'myID' allows us to disable the timeout action.
myID = setTimeout("alert('Hello? Are you awake?');", 10000)

// ->
</SCRIPT>
<BODY onLoad="alert('Welcome to Choose-A-State!');" onUnload=
➥"alert('Bye Now!');">
<FORM NAME="stateform" ACTION="/cgi-bin/stform.pl" METHOD="GET"
onSubmit="return checkState(this.state);">
Please type the state name:
<INPUT TYPE="TEXT" NAME="state" onFocus="clearTimeout(myID);"
onChange="checkState(this);">
<INPUT TYPE="SUBMIT" NAME="sub1" VALUE="Send Form In">
</FORM>
</BODY>
</HTML>
```

The timer that is set by setTimeout at the end of the <SCRIPT> section is disabled by clearTimeout in the onFocus event handler. If the Focus event doesn't happen before the timeout expires, the alert window will appear.

To illustrate the onClick event, the following example implements a stopwatch program:

```
<HTML>
<HEAD>
<TITLE>JavaScript StopWatch</TITLE>
<SCRIPT LANGUAGE="JavaScript">
```

```
<!- JavaScript StopWatch

var ms = 0;   // Stopwatch Elapsed Time in milliseconds
var state = 0;   // Stopwatch State: 0=stopped, 1=running

// StopWatch Start/Stop
function startstop() {
  if (state == 0) {          // If currently stopped
   state = 1;        // "Start";
   then = new Date(); // What time is it now?
   then.setTime(then.getTime() - ms); // Adjust back
  } else {                // If currently running
   state = 0;        // "Stop";
   now  = new Date(); // What time is it now?
   ms  = now.getTime() - then.getTime(); // Compute
   document.stpw.time.value = ms;        // Display
  }
}


// StopWatch Reset
function swreset() {
  state = 0;            // "Stop"
  ms  = 0;              // Reset elapsed time to 0
  document.stpw.time.value = ms; // Display
}

// Display the current time every 50 milliseconds
function display() {
  setTimeout("display();", 50);

  // Display new time only if StopWatch is running
  if (state == 1) {
  now  = new Date();
  ms  = now.getTime() - then.getTime();
  document.stpw.time.value = ms;
  }
```

```
     }

     // ->
     </SCRIPT>
     </HEAD>
     <BODY onLoad="display();">

     <FORM NAME="stpw">
     Time:
     <INPUT TYPE="TEXT" NAME="time">
     <INPUT TYPE="BUTTON" NAME="ssbutton" VALUE="Start/Stop" onClick=
     ➡"startstop();">
     <INPUT TYPE="BUTTON" NAME="reset" VALUE="Reset" onClick=
     ➡"swreset();">
     </FORM>
     </BODY>
     </HTML>
```

Two buttons labeled Start/Stop and Reset are created in a form .
The onClick event handler for each button executes a corresponding
function. The startstop function keeps track of the state of the
stopwatch, running or stopped, with the state variable state. If the
stopwatch is not running, the function starts it by making a note of
the start time and changing the state variable to 1, or running. If the
stopwatch is running, the function stops the stopwatch by changing
the state variable to 0, or stopped. It also makes a note of the stop
time. The Date object method getTime() is used to convert the start
and stop times to milliseconds. The millisecond times are then sub-
tracted to get the difference between the two times, which is displayed in the text input box.

The onLoad event handler schedules a call to the display() function.
The display() function in turn schedules a call to itself, which causes it to be executed every 50 milliseconds. The display routine repeatedly updates the time in the output text box to give the user a sense
of the progression of time.

The last type of event is the MouseOver event type, which is only recognized by the link object. Normally, when the mouse is moved over a
link, the HREF attribute's information is displayed in the status bar
at the bottom of the browser window. The onMouseOver event handler
allows specification of any additional action to occur. Among the
things onMouseOver can do is display alternate text in the status bar.

If the onMouseOver event handler returns true, the value of property window.status is used for the status bar. If the event returns false, the normal HREF of that link is displayed.

The following example also uses a timeout event to change the default status bar message, which is displayed whenever other status messages are not:

```
<HTML>
<HEAD>
<TITLE>Link Message Demo</TITLE>
<SCRIPT LANGUAGE="JavaScript">
<!- Link message changer

messageNum = 0;
// Schedule the initial message to be displayed in 3 seconds
setTimeout("messageChanger();", 3000);


// Display alternating default status messages every 3 seconds
function messageChanger() {
  if (messageNum == 0) {
    defaultStatus = "Qvid me anxivs svm?";
    messageNum = 1;
  } else {
    defaultStatus = "- Alfredus E. Neumanus";
    messageNum = 0;
  }

  // Schedule the next message
  setTimeout("messageChanger();", 3000);
}


// ->
</SCRIPT>
</HEAD>
<BODY>
<BR>
All done.
<p>
```

```
This is <a HREF="other.html" onClick="alert('You clicked on the
➥link');"
onMouseOver="status='Yep, thats a link'; return true;">a link</a>
with status.
</BODY>
</HTML>
```

When the user moves the mouse over the link text, Yep, thats a link
appears in the status bar and disappears when the mouse moves off.

The onClick event handler in the preceding code occurs before the
HREF is followed. Thus, it is possible to dynamically modify the
HREF. The programmer might custom tailor a destination based on
the values the user has entered in other form input elements.

Summary

In this chapter, you have made a big step towards being able to write
the type of interactive Web pages and scripts that JavaScript is widely
used for today.

You learned about events and event handlers. Events allow JavaScript
to interrupt the current processing of a program and go off to do
something else. The events are set up to mirror typical windows-type
environment activity. Specific user initiated events are recognized by
JavaScript. These events are focus, blur, change, select, click,
mouseOver, submit, load and unload. There are also timeout events
that may be scheduled.

Events are easy to use. There is no specific programming necessary
for the programmer to do to test for an event. The
JavaScript/Browser environment is designed to recognize an event
and look to see if anything needs to be done when one occurs.

Object definition statements notify the interpreter which events to
recognize. Likewise, the programmer may choose to ignore an event.
Good usage of events make a JavaScript application a whole lot more
fun to program and use.

The next chapter discusses in detail JavaScript objects, their syntax,
and how to use them.

Chapter 7

JavaScript Objects

JavaScript is designed to be easy to learn and easy to use. Because the designers of JavaScript have had this mind, they have provided you, the programmer, with many built-in objects that you are likely to use often. These built-in objects are available through JavaScript (inside the Netscape Navigator on your desktop).

Objects make programming with JavaScript easy. Objects such as buttons, checkboxes, and radio objects are used to interact with and alert users. There are many types of JavaScript objects: math objects manipulate data; date objects manipulate and display time and dates; the document, form, and form elements objects bring order and structure to HTML documents. This chapter includes a full list of currently available JavaScript objects and ideas for their use.

There are only a few things you need to know to effectively use these objects. You need to know how JavaScript objects and HTML code interact. Each object has methods associated with it that perform certain actions. Most objects have properties that are associated with HTML attributes and set various characteristics of the object. Also, most objects recognize certain events.

This chapter lists the JavaScript objects in alphabetical order. The properties, methods, and events for each object are also listed. This chapter also provides examples for each object. Try out some of the examples for yourself to get a feel for using these objects.

Anchor Object

The `Anchor` object is a JavaScript array. Every HTML anchor in the document containing an a `NAME` attribute will result in the creation of an element in the `Anchor` array. At the present stage in the development of JavaScript, the value of all `Anchors` array elements is `null`. Therefore, the `Anchor` object is not useful beyond being able to tell the number of `anchors` on the current page. Use the `Links` array for more useful information on HTML anchors with HREF attributes.

Like other JavaScript arrays, the number of elements in the array is stored in `anchors.length`. Elements of anchors start at element number 0.

Syntax:

```
<A NAME="AnchorName" HREF="URL" TARGET="WinOrFrameName"> Anchor
➥Text </A>
```

Required Attributes:

⊙ NAME: The name of the anchor, also known as the "hash" name.

The anchor may be linked to from elsewhere by using a URL that appends a # and the NAME of the anchor. Such a URL specifies not only the document, but also the position within the document.

Optional Attributes:

⊙ HREF: A destination URL.

⊙ TARGET: The name of the window or frame in which to display the resulting page.

Usage Example:

```
<A NAME="myAnchor" HREF="http://foo.com/bar" TARGET=
➥"Otherwin">Move to foo</A>
```

Parent Object:

```
document
```

Properties:

❺ `length`: The number of elements in the `anchors` array.

Methods:

None.

Event Handlers:

None.

Example:

This example prints the number of HTML anchors found in the page at the bottom of the page:

```
<HTML>
<BODY>
<A NAME="TOP"></A>
This is the first line.<BR>
...other lines...
<A NAME="MIDDLE"></A>
This is line 100.<BR>
...other lines...
<A NAME="BOTTOM"></A>
This is line 200.<BR>
<SCRIPT LANGUAGE="JavaScript">
 document.writeln("Anchor count on this page is: " + document.
➥anchors.length);
</SCRIPT>
</BODY>
</HTML>
```

See Also:

The Links array object, Anchor method, and Link method.

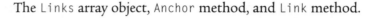

Button Object

The Button object creates a pushbutton widget with a given label in an HTML form. The Button object can exist only within an HTML form. If the programmer specifies event handler code by using the onClick attribute, the code will be executed when the button is pressed.

As with all form elements, the button is accessible both via its name and the form's elements array.

Please note that changing the value property of the button after it has been rendered by the browser *will not* modify its appearance on the screen but *will* change the property's value.

Syntax:

```
<INPUT
  TYPE="BUTTON"
  NAME="ButtonName"
  VALUE="ButtonLabel"
  [onClick="HandlerCode"]>
```

Required Attributes:

- ⊕   TYPE: Must be set to the string "BUTTON".

- ⊕   NAME: The name by which the Button object will be known. NAME should be a valid JavaScript identifier and unique among form elements.

- ⊕   VALUE: The label text to be printed on the face of the button.

Optional Attributes:

- ⊕   onClick: JavaScript event handler code to be executed when the mouse is clicked on the button.

Usage Example:

```
<INPUT TYPE="BUTTON" NAME="btn1" VALUE="Explode" onClick=
➥"firecracker.pop();">
```

Parent Object:

form

Properties:

- name: Corresponds to the HTML attribute NAME.

- value: Corresponds to the HTML attribute VALUE.

Methods:

- click: Simulates clicking the button.

Event Handlers:

- onClick: Executes the indicated JavaScript code when the button is clicked.

Example:

When the "Ate one" button is pushed, the person whose name appears in the text input box will have his or her doughnut count increased by 1:

```
<HTML>
<HEAD>
<SCRIPT LANGUAGE="JavaScript">
function DoughnutDB()
{
    this.andy   = 0;
    this.emily  = 0;
    this.ali    = 0;
    this.liz    = 0;
    this.mark   = 0;
    this.laszlo = 0;
}
NumDoughnuts = new DoughnutDB();
</SCRIPT>
</HEAD>
<BODY>
<FORM NAME="doughnutOmatic">
<INPUT TYPE="TEXT" NAME="username" SIZE="25"> Name
<BR>
<INPUT TYPE="BUTTON" NAME="doughnutPlus" VALUE="Ate One"
    onClick="NumDoughnuts[this.form.username.value]++;
                        alert('Count_incremented!');">
<INPUT TYPE="BUTTON" NAME="showNum" VALUE="Show Number"
    onClick="alert(NumDoughnuts[this.form.username.value]);">
</FORM>
</BODY>
</HTML>
```

See Also:

The other button form elements: reset and submit.

The other form elements: Checkbox, Hidden, Password, Radio, Select, Text, and Textarea.

Checkbox **Object**

The Checkbox object creates a click-on, click-off widget in an HTML form. The Checkbox object can exist only within an HTML form.

The checkbox is examined at the time the form is submitted. If the checkbox is checked, the checkbox name will have the value specified in the value property submitted. If the checkbox is not checked, the value will be an empty string.

If the programmer specifies event handler code by using the onClick attribute, the code will be executed when the checkbox is clicked. As with all form elements, the checkbox object is accessible via its name and the form's elements array.

Syntax:

```
<INPUT TYPE="CHECKBOX" NAME="CheckBoxName" VALUE="ValueIfChecked"
➥CHECKED onClick="HandlerCode">
```

Required Attributes:

- ◑ TYPE: Must be set to the string CHECKBOX.

- ◑ NAME: The name by which the checkbox object will be known. It should be a valid JavaScript identifier and unique among form elements.

- ◑ VALUE: If the checkbox is checked, this value is returned with the checkbox name when the form is submitted.

Optional Attributes:

- ◑ CHECKED: Indicates that the checkbox is to appear checked by default.

- ◑ onClick: JavaScript event handler code to be executed when the mouse is clicked on the checkbox.

Usage Example:

```
<INPUT TYPE="CHECKBOX" NAME="smoking" VALUE="Y" CHECKED onClick=
➥"cough();">
```

Parent Object:

```
form
```

Properties:

- **name:** Corresponds to the HTML attribute NAME.

- **value:** Corresponds to the HTML attribute VALUE.

- **checked:** The Boolean state of the checkbox. Assign true to have this property checked or false to un-check a box.

- **defaultChecked:** The Boolean default (reset) state of the checkbox. This corresponds to the HTML CHECKED attribute.

Methods:

- **click:** Simulates clicking the button.

Event Handlers:

- **onClick:** Executes when the checkbox is clicked.

Example:

When the following form for ordering at Burger Czar is submitted, the order is printed out in a pop-up alert window. Note that the form elements may be accessed via the document object or via the form object passed from the onSubmit event handler using the this keyword. This is shown in the cheese and pickles checkbox objects:

```
<HTML>
<HEAD>
<SCRIPT LANGUAGE="JavaScript">
function processform(theform) {
    var  result = "You have ordered two tofu patties, ";
    if (document.burger.sauce.checked)
        result += "special sauce, ";
    if (document.burger.lettuce.checked)
```

```
            result += "lettuce, ";
    if (theform.cheese.checked)
            result += "cheese, ";
    if (theform.pickles.checked)
            result += "pickles, ";
    if (document.burger.onions.checked)
            result += "onions, ";
    result += "on a sesame seed bun.";
    alert(result);
    return true;
}
</SCRIPT>
</HEAD>
<BODY>
<FORM NAME="burger" ACTION="/cgi-bin/kitchen.pl" METHOD="POST"
    onSubmit="return processform(this);">
What would you like on your Burger Czar Tofu Burger:
<BR>
<INPUT TYPE="CHECKBOX" NAME="sauce"   VALUE="Y"> Special Sauce?
<INPUT TYPE="CHECKBOX" NAME="lettuce" VALUE="Y"> Lettuce?
<INPUT TYPE="CHECKBOX" NAME="cheese"  VALUE="Y"> Cheese?
<INPUT TYPE="CHECKBOX" NAME="pickles" VALUE="Y"> Pickles?
<INPUT TYPE="CHECKBOX" NAME="onions"  VALUE="Y"> Onions?
<BR>
<INPUT TYPE="SUBMIT" NAME="sbm" VALUE="Process Form">
</FORM>
</BODY>
</HTML>
```

See Also:

The other form elements: Button, Hidden, Password, Radio, Reset, Select, Submit, Text, and Textarea.

Date Object

A Date object is JavaScript's internal way of storing and handling date and time information. Date has a wide range of methods, which retrieve, set, convert, and compute times and dates.

Date is a JavaScript only object and is not related to HTML at all. In order to deal with dates, an instance of a Date object must be created with the new operator.

Please note that an unusual feature of Date's numeric representation for the year, month, and date numbers. Months are numbered from 0: January is 0, February is 1, and so on, through December, which is 11. The year number is the year minus 1900. The date within the month is the same as conventional time. Hours are represented in military time (Military times use a 24-hour format and can be worked out by adding 12 to the hour time.) Hour 0 is midnight, hour 17 is 5 p.m.. Minutes and seconds are the same as conventional time.

There are three internal forms used for storing time information in JavaScript. The first form is a single integer that is the number of milliseconds since midnight, January 1, 1970 GMT, called "the epoch." The second form is as a series of integers representing year, month, date, hour, minute, and second. The third form is in the IETF string standard date format, which is used by HTTP and produces a string such as "Sat Oct 09, 14:08:52 GMT 1982".

Syntax:

```
dateObjectInstance.dateMethodInstance([Parameters])
Date.staticDateMethod(Parameters)
```

Usage Example:

```
now  = new Date();
then = new Date("January 20, 1979 09:40:00");
then2 = new Date(79, 0, 20, 9, 40, 0);
then3 = new Date(79, 0, 20);
```

Parent Object:

None.

Properties:

None that are user accessible.

Methods:

- getDate: Extract the day of the month from a Date object.

- ❂ `getDay`: Extract the day of the week from a `Date` object.

- ❂ `getHours`: Extract the hour of the day from a `Date` object.

- ❂ `getMinutes`: Extract the minute of the hour from a `Date` object. ·

- ❂ `getMonth`: Extract the month of the year from a `Date` object.

- ❂ `getSeconds`: Extract the second of the minute from a `Date` object.

- ❂ `getTime`: Compute the number of milliseconds since the epoch from a `Date` object.

- ❂ `getTimezoneOffset`: Get the number of minutes GMT and local time differ by.

- ❂ `getYear`: Extract the year from a `Date` object.

- ❂ `parse`: Compute milliseconds in the epoch, from IETF format local time (`Static` method).

- ❂ `setDate`: Modify the day of the month in a `Date` object.

- ❂ `setHours`: Modify the hour of the day in a `Date` object.

- ❂ `setMinutes`: Modify the minute of the hour in a `Date` object.

- ❂ `setMonth`: Modify the month of the year in a `Date` object.

- ❂ `setSeconds`: Modify the second of the minute in a `Date` object.

- ❂ `setTime`: Set a `Date` object to represent the time given in milliseconds since the epoch.

- ❂ `setYear`: Modify the year from a `Date` object.

- ❂ `toGMTString`: Extract the IETF string format from a `Date` object, GMT time.

- ❂ `toLocaleString`: Extract local customary string format from a `Date` object, local time.

- ❂ `UTC`: Return the number of milliseconds in the epoch given a list of integers (`Static` method).

Event Handlers:

None.

Example:

Compute and print the older of two people. Note: This will work only for people born January 1, 1970 and after, or the beginning of the epoch.

```
<HTML>
<HEAD>
<SCRIPT LANGUAGE="JavaScript">

function whoisolder(theform) {
    bd1 = new Date(theform.bday1.value);
    bd2 = new Date(theform.bday2.value);

    if (bd1.getTime() < bd2.getTime()) {
        // Compute age difference in days (1 day = 86400000ms)
        agediff = (bd2.getTime() - bd1.getTime()) / (86400000);
        alert(theform.name1.value+" is older than "+theform.name2.value +
            " by " + agediff + " days."
            + "\n" + theform.name1.value + " born on " +
bd1.toLocaleString()
            + "\n" + theform.name2.value + " born on " +
bd2.toLocaleString() );
    } else {
        // Compute age difference in days
        agediff = (bd1.getTime() - bd2.getTime()) / (86400000);
        alert(theform.name2.value+" is older than "+theform.name1.value +
            " by " + agediff + " days."
            + "\n" + theform.name1.value + " born on " +
bd1.toLocaleString()
            + "\n" + theform.name2.value + " born on " +
bd2.toLocaleString() );
    }
}
</SCRIPT>
</HEAD>
<BODY>
<FORM NAME="seniority">
Care to compare ages?
<BR>
```

```
<INPUT TYPE="TEXT" NAME="name1"> Person 1 Name <BR>
<INPUT TYPE="TEXT" NAME="bday1"> Person 1 Birthdate <BR>
<INPUT TYPE="TEXT" NAME="name2"> Person 2 Name <BR>
<INPUT TYPE="TEXT" NAME="bday2"> Person 2 Birthdate <BR>
<BR>
<INPUT TYPE="BUTTON" NAME="doit" VALUE="Compute" onClick=
➥"whoisolder(this.form);">
</FORM>
</BODY>
</HTML>
```

See Also:

`setTimeout()`and `clearTimeout()`

Document **Object**

The `Document` object is used to access, set, and use items relating to the document loaded into the current window or frame. The `Document` object corresponds directly to an HTML input file or stream. The `Document` object is the parent object of all objects that reside within it, including `Anchor`, `Form`, `History`, and `Link` objects.

Usage Example:

```
<BODY BACKGROUND="matterhorn.gif" TEXT="darkgreen" LINK="#0080FF"
➥ALINK="#FFA800" VLINK="#0080FF" onLoad="alert('Page loaded');">
```

Syntax:

```
<BODY
   [BACKGROUND="BackgroundImage"]
   [BGCOLOR="BackgroundColor"]
   [TEXT="ForegroundColor"]
   [LINK="LinkColor"]
   [ALINK="ActiveLinkColor"]
   [VLINK="VisitedLinkColor"]
   [onLoad="HandlerCode"]
   [onUnload="HandlerCode"]>
</BODY>
```

Required Attributes:

None.

Optional Attributes:

- BACKGROUND: Specifies an image to be tiled on the document background; usually a pattern.

- BGCOLOR: In lieu of a BACKGROUND image, make the background this color instead of gray.

- TEXT: Make the text this color instead of black.

- LINK: Make links this color instead of light blue.

- ALINK: Make activated links this color instead of red.

- VLINK: Make previously visited links this color instead of dark blue.

- onLoad: JavaScript event handler code to be executed after the current document has been loaded in its entirety.

- onUnload: JavaScript event handler code to be executed when the user departs from current document.

Parent Object:

window

Properties:

- alinkColor: Corresponds to the HTML ALINK attribute

- anchors: An array containing elements corresponding to anchors containing NAME attributes. See *anchors*.

- bgColor: Corresponds to the HTML BGCOLOR attribute.

- fgColor: Corresponds to the HTML TEXT attribute.

- forms: An array containing elements corresponding to each form in the document.

- lastModified: The string time and date of last modification of the document HTML file.

- **linkColor:** Corresponds to the LINK HTML attribute

- **links:** An array containing elements corresponding to anchors containing HREF attributes. See *links*.

- **location:** A location object containing the location of this document.

- **referrer:** The string URL of the document whose anchor led to this document.

- **title:** The title of the document, which appears in the window title bar.

- **vlinkColor:** Corresponds to the HTML VLINK attribute.

- **history:** An object allowing movement forward or backward in the browser history.

Methods:

- **clear:** Clear the document to a blank page.

- **close:** Terminate sending output to the document from JavaScript.

- **open:** Initiate sending a new page of output to the document from JavaScript.

- **write:** Send output to the document.

- **writeln:** Send output to the document, with a newline added on to the end.

Event Handlers:

- **onLoad:** After the entire document and all its component parts have been loaded by the browser, execute this JavaScript code.

- **onLoad:** After the user departs this document, execute this JavaScript code.

Example:

Every five seconds, update the document in a new window to show a different quotation:

```
<HTML>
<HEAD>
<SCRIPT LANGUAGE="JavaScript">

/*
** State Variables
*/
var quoteNum=0;

/*
** makeQuotes() — Constructor function for the quotes array.
*/
function makeQuotes() {
   this[0] = "The sun was shining on the sea\nShining with all
➥its might";
   this[1] = "He did his very best to make\nThe billows smooth
➥and bright";
   this[2] = "And this was odd because it was\nthe middle of the
➥night.";
   this[3] = "The moon was shining sulkily\nbecause she thought
➥the sun";
   this[4] = "Had got no business to be there\n after the day was
➥done";
   this[5] = "He's got no right, she said,\nto come and spoil the
➥fun.";
   this.length = 6;
}

/*
**   showNextQuote()  — Display quotation, and schedule the next
➥quotation.
*/
function showNextQuote() {
   w.document.clear();                    // Clear the document frame
   w.document.open("text/plain");   // Begin display of document
   w.document.writeln(quotes[quoteNum]); // Display quote
   w.document.close();               // End, flush output and display
   quoteNum++;
```

```
    // If there are more quotes to display, schedule another in 5
➥sec.
    if (quoteNum < quotes.length)
        setTimeout("showNextQuote();", 5000);
}


// Initialize quotes array
quotes = new makeQuotes();


// Create output window
w = window.open("", "outputWin7_5", "width=300,height=100");


// Show first quote:
showNextQuote();


</SCRIPT>
</HEAD>
</HTML>
```

See Also:

The Window object.

Elements Array

The Elements array is an alternate method of accessing elements of
an HTML form. Normally, forms elements are accessed in JavaScript
by using their name, which is set by the HTML NAME attribute. The
elements within the Elements array are numbered starting from zero,
according to their order of definition in the HTML source.

Syntax:

```
document.FormName.elements[n]
document.FormName.elements.length
```

Parent Object:

```
form
```

Properties:

```
length
```

Example:

Given this HTML form:

```
<FORM NAME="chooser" ACTION="javascript:processform()"
➥METHOD="POST">
<INPUT TYPE="TEXT" NAME="city" SIZE="30" MAXLENGTH="30"> City
➥name
<BR>
<INPUT TYPE="RADIO" NAME="emmm" VALUE="eenie"> Eenie
<INPUT TYPE="RADIO" NAME="emmm" VALUE="meenie"> Meenie
<INPUT TYPE="RADIO" NAME="emmm" VALUE="mienie"> Mienie
<INPUT TYPE="RADIO" NAME="emmm" VALUE="moe"> Moe
<BR>
<INPUT TYPE="CHECKBOX" NAME="vegie" VALUE="Y"> Vegetarian?
<BR>
<INPUT TYPE="SUBMIT" NAME="sbm" VALUE="Process Form">
</FORM>
```

JavaScript automatically builds the Elements array in source order. The text input box is element 0, the radio buttons are elements 1 through 4, and the checkbox and submit are elements 5 and 6. The following code:

```
cityname = document.chooser.city.value;
document.chooser.emmm[2].checked = true;
if (document.chooser.vegie.value == "Y") {
  document.writeln("Tofu");
} else {
  document.writeln("Steak");
}
```

is identical in function to this code

```
cityname = document.chooser.elements[0].value;
document.chooser.elements[3].checked = true;
if (document.chooser.elements[5].value == "Y") {
  document.writeln("Tofu");
} else {
  document.writeln("Steak");
}
```

See Also:

The other form objects: Button, Checkbox, Hidden, Password, Radio, Reset, Select, Submit, Text.

The other alternate access arrays: Anchors, Forms, Frames, Links, Options.

Form and *Forms* Array Object

The form is the Web builder's primary method of interactively exchanging data with the user. The Form object is created by using HTML and encloses form elements. The form elements may include objects such as Button, Checkbox, Hidden, Password, Radio, Reset, Select, Submit, Text, and Textarea. These elements allow user interaction for various types of data input, as well as display.

Forms are accessible via their name, or alternately, through an automatically created Forms array. The Forms array numbers forms sequentially from 0 in HTML source order. The first form will be form 0, the second will be 1, and so on.

Every element in the form also becomes a property of the form, named according to the NAME attribute of the respective element. For example, if a form contains a text input box named "zoom," then zoom becomes a property of the form, allowing access to the text input box.

Syntax:

```
<FORM
    [NAME="FormName"]
    [TARGET="WindowOrFrameName"]
    [ACTION="ServerURL"]
    [METHOD="GET" | "POST"]
    [ENCTYPE="MIMEencodingType"
    [onSubmit="HandlerCode"]>
</FORM>
```

Required Attributes:

None.

Optional Attributes:

🌑 NAME: Names the Form object so it can be accessed from the Document object. If the NAME attribute is not used, the Forms *array* may still be used to access the component elements of the form.

🌑 TARGET: The window or frame name that any output resultant from submitting the form should be loaded into.

🌑 ACTION: The server URL the form should request when submitting the form data according to METHOD.

🌑 METHOD: The HTTP method to use when submitting the form, either GET or POST. If the form is to be submitted to a URL with the protocol javascript:, use the POST method. If the form is to be submitted to a URL with the http: protocol and the form will be processed by a JavaScript program, use the GET method. If the URL has protocol http: and the form data is to be processed by a standard CGI script on the server, use either method. It's important not to confuse the HTTP method with JavaScript methods.

🌑 ENCTYPE: The MIME encoding type to be sent to the server in an HTTP

🌑 POST request method: The standard value for normal CGI forms submission is application/x-www-form-urlencoded. If the new Netscape form element <INPUT TYPE="FILE"> is used to transport a file from the browser machine to the server, the MIME encoding type should be set to multipart/form-data, as detailed in RFC 1867. Don't waste your time with this unless you need to transmit files from the browser machine to the server.

🌑 onSubmit: The JavaScript event handler code to be executed when the form is submitted. This code can abort the submission if it returns the Boolean value false.

Parent Object:

document

Properties:

🌑 action: Corresponds to the HTML ACTION attribute

🌑 elements: An array object, this is an alternate mechanism to access form elements. See Elements, earlier.

- **encoding:** Corresponds to the HTML ENCTYPE attribute

- **length:** The number of elements in the Elements array. This is identical to the Length property of the Elements array.

- **method:** Corresponds to the HTML METHOD attribute

- **target:** Corresponds to the HTML TARGET attribute.

Methods:

- **submit:** Causes the form to be submitted. This bypasses the normal onSubmit code.

Event Handlers:

- **onSubmit:** This JavaScript code is executed when the Submit button is pressed but before the form data is transmitted to the URL indicated in the ACTION attribute. If it returns a Boolean false, the submit action is aborted; otherwise, the submit occurs.

Example:

Given these HTML forms

```
<FORM NAME="chooser" ACTION="javascript:processchooserform()"
➡METHOD="POST">
<INPUT TYPE="TEXT" NAME="city" SIZE="30" MAXLENGTH="30"> City
➡name
<BR>
<INPUT TYPE="RADIO" NAME="emmm" VALUE="eenie"> Eenie
<INPUT TYPE="RADIO" NAME="emmm" VALUE="meenie"> Meenie
<INPUT TYPE="RADIO" NAME="emmm" VALUE="mienie"> Mienie
<INPUT TYPE="RADIO" NAME="emmm" VALUE="moe"> Moe
<BR>
<INPUT TYPE="CHECKBOX" NAME="vegie" VALUE="Y"> Vegetarian?
<BR>
<INPUT TYPE="SUBMIT" NAME="sbm" VALUE="Process Form">
</FORM>
<P>
<FORM NAME="allergies" ACTION="javascript:processallergiesform()"
➡METHOD="POST">
<INPUT TYPE="RADIO" NAME="plants" VALUE="Pivy"> Poison Oak
```

```
<INPUT TYPE="RADIO" NAME="plants" VALUE="Psumac"> Poison Sumac
<INPUT TYPE="RADIO" NAME="plants" VALUE="ragweed"> Ragweed
<INPUT TYPE="RADIO" NAME="plants" VALUE="poisonivy"> Queen Anne's
➥Lace
<BR>
<INPUT TYPE="RADIO" NAME="foods" VALUE="dairy"> Milk
<INPUT TYPE="RADIO" NAME="foods" VALUE="chocolate"> Chocolate
<INPUT TYPE="RADIO" NAME="foods" VALUE="eggs"> Eggs
<INPUT TYPE="RADIO" NAME="foods" VALUE="peanuts"> Peanuts
<BR>
<INPUT TYPE="SUBMIT" NAME="sbm" VALUE="Process Allergies">
</FORM>
```

JavaScript automatically builds the Forms array in source order. The chooser form is form 0, and the allergies form is form 1:

```
cityname = document.chooser.city.value;
document.chooser.emmm[2].checked = true;
if (document.chooser.elements[5].value == "Y") {
  document.writeln("Tofu");
} else {
  document.writeln("Steak");
}
alerRagw = document.allergies.plants[2].checked;
document.write.("Would you like some ");
if ( ! document.allergies.foods[1].checked)) {
  document.write.("ice cream");
} else if ( ! document.allergies.foods[2].checked)) {
  document.write.("chocolate cake");
} else if ( ! document.allergies.foods[3].checked)) {
  document.write.("custard pie");
} else if ( ! document.allergies.foods[4].checked)) {
  document.write.("peanut brittle");
} else {
  document.write.("distilled ice water");
}
document.write.(" for desert?");
```

The preceding code is identical in function to this code:

```
cityname = document.forms[0].city.value;
document.forms[0].emmm[2].checked = true;
if (document.forms[0].elements[5].value == "Y") {
  document.writeln("Tofu");
} else {
  document.writeln("Steak");
}
alerRagw = document.form[1].plants[2].checked;
document.write.("Would you like some ");
if ( ! document.form[1].foods[1].checked)) {
  document.write.("ice cream");
} else if ( ! document.form[1].foods[2].checked)) {
  document.write.("chocolate cake");
} else if ( ! document.form[1].foods[3].checked)) {
  document.write.("custard pie");
} else if ( ! document.form[1].foods[4].checked)) {
  document.write.("peanut brittle");
} else {
  document.write.("distilled ice water");
}
document.write.(" for desert?");
```

See Also:

The other form element objects: Button, Checkbox, Hidden, Password, Radio, Reset, Select, Submit, and Text.

The other alternate access arrays: Anchors, Forms, Frames, Links, and Options.

Frames Object

Every browser window may be subdivided into sub-windows called *frames*. Each frame is capable of displaying anything a full browser window can, even when the loaded HTML file is further subdivided into frames! For most purposes, frames are the functional equivalents of windows.

The subdivision of a window into frames may be into multiple vertical windows side by side, called *columns*, or into multiple horizontal windows one above the other, called *rows*. The subdivisions are specified in framesets using the `<FRAMESET>` HTML tag pair. These tags define the geometry of the enclosed frames. Framesets may contain frames specified with the `<FRAME>` HTML tag, or further framesets.

Note that the number of source files is actually one greater than the number of frames. One HTML file defines the frameset, which specifies the geometry of the frames and which source files to load into each, one file per frame.

Every window has a `Frames` array. The window's `Frames` array automatically keeps track of all frames subdividing it. These frames were created by a frameset declaration in its main HTML file. If documents loaded into frames specify framesets themselves, elements of the `Frames` array will themselves be subdivided and have another `Frames` array within them as a property. The `Frames` array is created starting from the index 0, in the order that frames were defined in the HTML source. Like other JavaScript arrays, `frames.length` indicates the number of elements in the `Frames` array.

If you specify both rows and columns in your `<FRAMESET>` tag, frames will be ordered in row-major order, just as with HTML tables. `ROWS` and `COLS` slice the frame into horizontal and vertical strips. The width of each of these strips is specified in a string. See Chapter 3, "An HTML Overview and Primer," for the specification of this string.

Syntax:

```
<FRAMESET
   ROWS="RowSpecList"
   COLS="ColumnSpecList"
   [onLoad="HandlerCode"]
   [onUnload="HandlerCode"]>
   <FRAME SRC="URL" NAME="FrameName">
   <FRAMESET ...>
   [<FRAME ...> ...]
   [<FRAMESET ...> ...]
</FRAMESET>

FrameOrWindowName.property
frames[n].property
```

Required Attributes:

- ROWS and COLS: One or both ROWS and COLS should be included.

- <FRAME>: The <FRAME> tag indicates the URL to load into the frame with its SRC attribute and identifies its name with the NAME attribute.

- NAME: The name of the frame. This name can be used as the *target* of a link by using the TARGET attribute of the <A>, <BASE>, and <FORM> tags, as well as in client-side image map <AREA> tags.

- <FRAMESET>: Further nested framesets may be included in framesets.

Optional Attributes:

- onLoad: Specifies the Load event handler.

- onUnload: Specifies the Unload event handler.

Parent Object:

Window and Frames (for nested framesets).

Properties:

- frames: An array referencing sub-windows within the document. Elements are numbered from 0, in source order.

- length: Shorthand for frames.length, the number of elements in frames.

- name: The name of the frame or window. frame[2].name will be the name of frame number 2. window.name is the name of the window.

- parent: The parent window or Frame object. This is the window that specified the current document in a <FRAME> HTML tag.

- self: Alias for the current frame.

- window: Alias for the current frame.

Methods:

- clearTimeout: Cancel a pending timer event.

- setTimeout: Schedule a timer event.

Event Handlers:

- `onLoad`: After the entire document including all its component parts has been loaded by the browser, execute this JavaScript code.

- `onUnload`: After the user departs this document, execute this JavaScript code.

Example:

This example shows loading multiple frames. Your browser window is to be subdivided into three windows. At the left will be a tall narrow window; the remaining right side of the window will be divided into a top half and a bottom half.

Consider this HTML file to be loaded into your browser main window:

```
<HTML>
<HEAD>
<SCRIPT LANGUAGE="JavaScript">
</SCRIPT>
</HEAD>

<FRAMESET COLS="30%,70%">
  <FRAME SRC="dir.html" NAME="left">
  <FRAMESET ROWS="50%,50%">
   <FRAME SRC="main.html" NAME="top">
   <FRAME SRC="ref.html" NAME="bottom">
  </FRAMESET>
</FRAMESET>
```

Observe that `frames[0]` will contain `dir.html`, `frames[1]` will contain `main.html`, and `frames[2]` will contain `ref.html`. This is what `dir.html` looks like:

```
<HTML>
<HEAD>
<SCRIPT LANGUAGE="JavaScript">
</SCRIPT>
</HEAD>
<BODY>
```

```
Click <A HREF="rules.html" TARGET="top"> here </A> to see the
➥rules.<BR>
Click <A HREF="regs.html" TARGET="bottom"> here </A> to see the
➥regulations.<BR>
<FORM>
And press this button to see both:
<INPUT TYPE="BUTTON" NAME="rNr" VALUE="rules and regulations"
  onClick="frames[1].location='rules.html'; frames[2].location=
➥'regs.html';">
</FORM>
</BODY>
</HTML>
```

To be more explicit, `window.frames[1].location` could have been used in lieu of `frames[1].location`.

To enable the `regs.html` file to pull up the related file, `procedure.html`, the following code can be inserted into `regs.html`:

```
<FORM>
<INPUT TYPE="BUTTON" NAME="b1" VALUE="Show Procedures" onClick=
➥"parent.frames[1]='procedure.html';">
</FORM>
```

See Also:

`window`

Hidden Object

The `Hidden` object is a form input element. It doesn't have a rendering in the browser window. Rather, `Hidden` is intended to be used to communicate additional data back to the form handler with the other form data when the form is submitted. The `Hidden` element can exist only within a form.

Think of a Web site with multiple forms with which it would be desirable to have a single common CGI script handle. The `Hidden` element could be used to communicate which Web form is the origin of the page. `Hidden` can also include other information involving the previous state or prior events to be passed on to the CGI or JavaScript form handler.

Syntax:

```
<INPUT
  TYPE="HIDDEN"
  NAME="HiddenName"
  [VALUE="HiddenValue"]>
```

Required Attributes:

- TYPE: Must be the string "HIDDEN".

- NAME: The name by which the hidden object will be known. It should be a valid JavaScript identifier and unique among the form's elements.

Optional Attribute:

- VALUE: The value of the hidden object, which may be overwritten.

Parent Object:

form

Properties:

- name: Corresponds to the HTML attribute NAME.

- value: Corresponds to the HTML attribute VALUE.

Methods:

None.

Event Handlers:

None.

Example:

The following displays two forms, both to be submitted to the same CGI form handler script. The script can know which form was used to send in the data by checking the value of the stat CGI variable. The script might then compute an insurance quotation giving the auto club member a discount.

```
<HTML>
<BODY>
If you are an Auto Club member fill this form in:
Select your Insurance coverage:
<FORM ACTION="/cgi-bin/order.pl" METHOD="POST">
<INPUT TYPE="CHECKBOX" NAME="liab" "VALUE="Y"> Liability<BR>
<INPUT TYPE="CHECKBOX" NAME="coll" "VALUE="Y"> Collision<BR>
<INPUT TYPE="CHECKBOX" NAME="comp" "VALUE="Y"> Comprehensive<BR>
<INPUT TYPE="TEXT"    NAME="ID"> Your Club ID number<BR>
<INPUT TYPE="HIDDEN"  NAME="stat" "VALUE="AutoClubMember">
<INPUT TYPE="SUBMIT"  NAME="sub1" "VALUE="Send In">
</FORM>

If you are NOT an Auto Club member fill this form in:
Select your Insurance coverage:
<FORM ACTION="/cgi-bin/order.pl" METHOD="POST">
<INPUT TYPE="CHECKBOX" NAME="liab" "VALUE="Y"> Liability<BR>
<INPUT TYPE="CHECKBOX" NAME="coll" "VALUE="Y"> Collision<BR>
<INPUT TYPE="CHECKBOX" NAME="comp" "VALUE="Y"> Comprehensive<BR>
<INPUT TYPE="HIDDEN"  NAME="stat" "VALUE="SomeSchmo">
<INPUT TYPE="SUBMIT"  NAME="sub1" "VALUE="Send In">
</FORM>
</BODY>
</HTML>
```

See Also:

The other form elements: Button, Checkbox, Password, Radio, Reset, Select, Submit, Text, and Textarea.

History **Object**

The History object is JavaScript's way of allowing the programmer to command it based on its recollection of the pages that have been visited. The History object is a list that contains the location of all the URLs that have been visited. You can move backward and forward through the history list. For security and privacy reasons, the actual content of the list is not reflected into JavaScript.

The History object may be used only to tell the browser to go to a certain location in its history, simply an interface to the browser's

Forward and Back toolbar buttons, and to the Go pulldown menu. The History object may be used within any document, including within frames.

The History object has a couple of current shortcomings. First, the referenced URLs are not available. Second, although the length property indicates the number of elements in the history memory, the current position within the list is unavailable.

Syntax:

```
history.length
history.back()
history.forward()
history.go(params)
```

Parent Object:

```
document
```

Properties:

- ○ length: The number of entries in the History object's list.

Methods:

- ○ back: Go back one in the history list.

- ○ forward: Go forward one in the history list.

- ○ go: Go to the indicated element in the history.

Event Handlers:

None.

Examples:

Example 1: Reload the page every 60 seconds:

```
<HTML>
<HEAD>
<TITLE>Up-to-the-minute Stock Report</TITLE>
<SCRIPT LANGUAGE="JavaScript">
setTimeout("history.go(0);", 60000);
```

```
</SCRIPT>
</HEAD>
<BODY>
Here are the latest stock figures:
...
</BODY>
</HTML>
```

Example 2: Return to the page arrived from after 20 seconds:

```
<HTML>
<HEAD>
<TITLE>Product Information Screen</TITLE>
<SCRIPT LANGUAGE="JavaScript">
setTimeout("history.back();", 20000);
</SCRIPT>
</HEAD>
<BODY>
This data display system was implemented by Seymour Graf.
Thanks for visiting!
</BODY>
</HTML>
```

See Also:

The go method.

Links Object

The Links object is a JavaScript array. Every HTML anchor in the document containing an HREF attribute will have an entry in the Links array. This allows access to the HREF information.

Like other JavaScript arrays, the number of elements in the array is stored in links.length. Elements of links start at element number 0.

The Links array doesn't facilitate write access to the link text, which is the text between the <A> and </A> HTML tags. The Links array is read-only at this stage in the development of JavaScript. The destination URL of the link can be known but not modified. To have a dynamically generated link, use the onClick event handler to call a routine that modifies document.location to jump to a new page.

Syntax:

```
<A
  HREF="URL"
  [NAME="AnchorName"]
  [TARGET="WinOrFrameName"]
  [onClick="HandlerCode"]
  [onMouseOver="HandlerCode"]>
  Link Text
</A>
```

Required Attributes:

- HREF: The destination URL that should be loaded when the link is clicked.

Optional Attributes:

- NAME: Name of the anchor within the current document, the "hash" location.

- TARGET: Name of the window or frame to load the given HREF URL into.

- onClick: The JavaScript event handler code for the Click event.

- onMouseOver: The JavaScript event handler code for the MouseOver event.

Parent Object:

```
document
```

Properties:

The Links object itself has the following property:

- length: The number of elements in the Links array; the number of links in the document.

Every object in the Links array has the following properties:

- hash: Extracts the anchor name, the part after a # and before a ? in the URL.

- host: Extracts the full hostname and port specification portion from the URL, the part after the protocol:// and before the next /.

- hostname: Extracts the hostname, not including the port, from the URL.

- href: Returns the entire URL.

- pathname: Extracts the local path, everything after the host and before a ?, from the URL.

- port: Extracts the TCP/IP port number from the host property, discussed earlier.

- protocol: Extracts the protocol from the URL, including the colon. This may be one of the strings javascript:, about:, http:, file:, ftp:, mailto:, news:, gopher:, or wais:.

- search: Extracts the QUERY_STRING, the part after the ?. This is normally used to communicate form data via the HTTP GET method.

- target: Corresponds to the TARGET HTML attribute.

Methods:

None.

Event Handlers:

- onClick: Executes the indicated JavaScript code when the link is clicked.

- onMouseOver: Executes the indicated JavaScript code when the mouse is moved over the link. Note that the onMouseOver event handler code must return Boolean true to cause the modification of window.status to actually modify the window's status bar.

Example:

In order to pacify easily startled users, the event handler onMouseOver is used to edit the link's URL to show only the hostname and the filename, rather than the full URL:

```
<HTML>
<HEAD>
<TITLE>Link Message Cleaner-upper</TITLE>
```

```
<SCRIPT LANGUAGE="JavaScript">
<!-- Link message cleaner

/*
** clean(lnk) -- Given a link object, return a string of the
➥form:
**      "Host: hostname.foo.com Doc: blah.html"
*/
function clean(lnk) {
  // Get link pathname
  fname    = lnk.pathname;
  // Find position of last '/'
  lastSlash = fname.lastIndexOf("/", fname.length);
  // Extract filename (after last '/')
  fname    = fname.substring(lastSlash+1, fname.length);
  // Build return string
  return("Host: " + lnk.hostname + " Doc: " + fname);
}


// -->
</SCRIPT>
</HEAD>
<BODY>
<BR>
All done.
<p>
This is <a HREF="http://www.cs.colorado.edu/95-96/courses/
➥courses.html?res"=N
  onMouseOver="window.status=clean(this); return true;">a
➥link</a>
with status.
</BODY>
</HTML>
```

See Also:

The Anchor object.

The Link method.

 *Location* **Object**

The Location object holds the browser's notion of the currently displayed URL. Modifying the Location object causes the browser to display a new URL.

The Location object is different from the Document object's location property, which is read-only. The Location object has properties that allow easy disassembly and extraction of URL components. This can be particularly useful when extracting HTTP GET method form data, enabling a JavaScript program to process form data. This can also be invaluable when writing a CGI form handler is impractical.

Syntax:

WindowOrFrame.location

WindowOrFrame.location.property

Parent Object:

Window

Properties:

- ⊙ hash: Extracts the anchor name, which is the part after a # and before a ? in the URL.

- ⊙ host: Extracts the full hostname and port specification portion from the URL. This is the part after the protocol:// and before the next /.

- ⊙ hostname: Extracts the hostname, not including the port, from the URL.

- ⊙ href: Returns the entire URL. Using the Location object with no property, as in window.location, is a shorthand for window.location.href.

- ⊙ pathname: Extracts the local path, which is everything after the host and before a ?, from the URL.

- ⊙ port: Extracts the TCP/IP port number from the host property, listed earlier.

- **protocol:** Extracts the protocol from the URL, including the colon. This may be one of the strings javascript:, about:, http:, file:, ftp:, mailto:, news:, gopher:, or wais:.

- **search:** Extracts the QUERY_STRING, which is the part after the ?. This is normally used to communicate form data via the HTTP GET method.

- **target:** Corresponds to the TARGET HTML attribute.

Methods:

None.

Event Handlers:

None.

Examples:

Example 1: Display a slide-show of URLs in the browser's lower frame. Here is the file slideshow.html:

```
<HTML>
<HEAD>
<SCRIPT LANGUAGE="JavaScript">
<!-- location object demo

/*
** State Variable
*/
var Num=0;   // current document number

/*
** makeURLs() -- Constructor function for the url array.
*/
function makeURLs() {
    this[0] = "http://www.foo.com/mumbo/jumbo1.html";
    this[1] = "http://www.foo.com/mumbo/jumbo2.html";
    this[2] = "http://www.foo.com/mumbo/jumbo3.html";
    this[3] = "http://www.foo.com/mumbo/jumbo4.html";
    this[4] = "http://www.foo.com/mumbo/jumbo5.html";
```

```
      this.length = 5;
  }


  /*
  ** showNextDoc() -- Display next document, and schedule the next
  ➥timeout.
  */
  function showNextDoc() {
    top.frames[1].location.href = url[Num];
    Num++;


    // If there are more docs to display, schedule another in 5
  ➥sec.
    if (Num < url.length)
      setTimeout("showNextDoc()", 5000);
  }


  // Initialize URL array
  url = new makeURLs();


  // The reason we can't put showNextDoc() here is that the
  ➥frameset
  // doesn't exist yet. Show first document after frameset is
  ➥loaded.


  // -->
  </SCRIPT>
  </HEAD>


  <FRAMESET ROWS="50,*" NAME="f1" onLoad='showNextDoc();'>
    <FRAME NAME="hi" SRC="http://www.foo.com/mumbo/top.html">
    <FRAME NAME="low" SRC="http://www.foo.com/mumbo/welcome.html">
  </FRAMESET>


  </HTML>
```

Example 2: The showNextDoc() function from Example 1 is modified
to loop through the series of documents in an endless slideshow:

```
/*
** showNextDoc() -- Display next document, and schedule the next
➡timeout.
*/
function showNextDoc() {
  top.frames[1].location.href = url[Num];
  Num++;

  // If end of sequence reached, recycle
  if (Num >= url.length)
   Num = 0;

  // Schedule another in 5 sec.
  setTimeout("showNextDoc()", 5000);
}
```

See Also:

Document location **property**

Links **object**

Math **Object**

The Math object is an abstract, built-in object that serves simply to provide access to math related functions in the form of methods, and constants in the form of properties.

Syntax:

Math.property

Math.method(parameters)

Parent Object:

None.

Properties:

- ⊕ E: Euler's number, the base of natural logarithms, about 2.7182818.

- ⊕ LN2: Natural log (base e) of 2, about 0.693147.

- ☉ LN10: Natural log (base e) of 10, about 2.302585.

- ☉ LOG2E: Log base 2 of e, about 1.442695.

- ☉ LOG10E: Log base 10 of e, about 0.434294.

- ☉ PI: The ratio between a circle's circumference to its diameter, about 3.1415927.

- ☉ SQRT1_2: The reciprocal of the square root of 2, about 0.707107.

- ☉ SQRT2: The square root of 2, about 1.4142135.

Methods:

- ☉ abs: Absolute value.

- ☉ acos: Inverse cosine.

- ☉ asin: Inverse sine.

- ☉ atan: Inverse tangent.

- ☉ ceil: Round to nearest higher integer.

- ☉ cos: Cosine.

- ☉ exp: Exponential (raise e to a power).

- ☉ floor: Round to nearest lower integer.

- ☉ log: Natural log.

- ☉ max: Maximum of two numbers.

- ☉ min: Minimum of two numbers.

- ☉ pow: Raise a number to a power.

- ☉ random: Generate a random number.

- ☉ round: Round to nearest integer.

- ☉ sin: Sine.

- sqrt: Square root.

- tan: Tangent.

Event Handlers:

None.

Examples:

Example 1: Display coordinates in rectangular coordinates for a cardioid polar graph with radius 50:

```
for (var theta=0.0; theta < 2*Math.PI; theta += 0.1) {
  r = Math.sin(0.5*theta) * 50.0;
  x = r * Math.cos(theta);
  y = r * Math.sin(theta);
  document.writeln("(" + x + ", " + y + ")");
}
```

Example 2: Use the with statement to rewrite Example 1:

```
with (Math) {
  for (var theta=0.0; theta < 2*PI; theta += 0.1) {
   r = sin(2 * theta) * 50.0;
   x = r * cos(theta);
   y = r * sin(theta);
   document.writeln("(" + x + ", " + y + ")");
  }
}
```

Navigator **Object**

The Navigator object allows the programmer to query the Netscape navigator browser for version, code name, operating system, and platform information.

Syntax:

navigator.*property*

Parent Object:

None.

Properties:

- ⊕ `appCodeName`: Name of the code base.

- ⊕ `appName`: Name of the application program.

- ⊕ `appVersion`: Version, OS, and platform information.

- ⊕ `userAgent`: HTTP MIME user-agent string.

Methods:

None.

Event Handlers:

None.

Example:

Check version number and advise user:

```
// Get version
ver = navigator.appVersion.substring(0,4);

if (ver == "2.00") {
  document.write("Whooooa... better ");
  document.write("download".link("http://home.netscape.com/
➥comprod/mirror/client_download.html"));
  document.write(" a newer version of Netscape.");
}
```

The values of the preceding navigator object properties are

```
navigator.appCodeName Mozilla
navigator.appName    Netscape
navigator.appVersion 2.01 (X11; I; SunOS 4.1.4 sun4)
navigator.userAgent  Mozilla/2.01 (X11; I; SunOS 4.1C sun4)
```

Options Object

See `Select` object.

Password Object

The Password object creates a scrollable text input box in an HTML form. Text typed into the box appears as * characters instead of the characters typed. The Password input box object can exist only within an HTML form. Specifying a Password object in HTML creates a new property, named according to its HTML NAME attribute, in the enclosing Form object.

If the programmer specifies event handler code by using the onFocus, onBlur, onChange, or onSelect HTML attributes, that code will be executed, respectively, when focus is obtained, lost, or text is changed or selected by clicking and dragging the mouse.

It's important to note that even though the password text does not print out while the user inputs data, it is transmitted in clear text when the form contents are submitted. Therefore, passwords in this situation should be considered completely insecure.

As with all Form elements, the Password object is accessible as a property of its enclosing Form object via both its name and the form's Elements array.

Syntax:

```
<INPUT
   TYPE="PASSWORD"
   NAME="TextInputName"
   [VALUE="InitialText"]
   [SIZE="number"]
   [MAXLENGTH="number"]
   [onFocus="HandlerCode"]
   [onBlur="HandlerCode"]
   [onChange="HandlerCode"]
   [onSelect="HandlerCode"]>
```

Required Attributes:

- **❂** TYPE: Must be set to the string "PASSWORD".

- **❂** NAME: The name by which the password object will be known. It should be unique within the form.

Optional Attributes:

- ⊙ VALUE: The initial contents of the password input box.

- ⊙ SIZE: The number of characters the width of the password input box should be. SIZE defaults to 20 characters if you do not specify COLS.

- ⊙ MAXLENGTH: The maximum limit for the number of characters that may be typed into the password input box.

- ⊙ onFocus: Specifies the JavaScript event handler for the Focus event.

- ⊙ onBlur: Specifies the JavaScript event handler for the Blur event.

- ⊙ onChange: Specifies the JavaScript event handler for the Change event.

- ⊙ onSelect: Specifies the JavaScript event handler for the Select event.

Usage Example:

```
<INPUT TYPE="PASSWORD" NAME="pass" SIZE="8" MAXLENGTH="8"
➥onFocus="alert('Warning: Not Secure!');">
```

Parent Object:

Form

Properties:

- ⊙ name: Corresponds to the HTML attribute NAME.

- ⊙ value: Corresponds to the HTML attribute VALUE.

- ⊙ defaultValue: The default (reset) state contents of the password input box. This corresponds to the HTML VALUE attribute.

Methods:

- ⊙ focus: Directs keyboard focus to the password input box.

- ⊙ blur: Removes keyboard focus from the password input box.

- ⊙ select: Selects the text contents of the password input box.

Event Handlers:

- onFocus: JavaScript event handler code to be executed when the keyboard focus is directed at the password input box.

- onBlur: JavaScript event handler code to be executed when the keyboard focus is removed from the password input box.

- onChange: JavaScript event handler code to be executed when the contents of the text input box are changed by the user.

- onSelect: JavaScript event handler code to be executed when the contents of the password input box are selected with the mouse.

Example:

```
<FORM ACTION="/cgi-bin/register.pl" METHOD="POST">
<INPUT TYPE="TEXT" NAME="username" VALUE="root" MAXLENGTH="8">
➥Username <BR>
<INPUT TYPE="TEXT" NAME="FullName"> Full Name <BR>
<INPUT TYPE="PASSWORD" NAME="passw" MAXLENGTH="8"> Password <BR>
<INPUT TYPE="TEXT" NAME="favCol" onFocus="alert('Choose
➥wisely');">
   Favorite Color.<BR>

<INPUT TYPE="SUBMIT" NAME="subm" VALUE="Register Now">
</FORM>
```

See Also:

The other form elements: Checkbox, Button, Hidden, Radio, Reset, Select, Submit, Text, and Textarea.

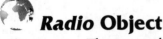

Radio Object

The Radio object creates an exclusive selection button widget in an HTML form. The Radio button object can exist only within an HTML form. If the radio button is checked when the form is submitted, the radio button's name will have the value specified in the Value property submitted.

Radio buttons are created in exclusive selection groups. They all have the same NAME attribute. This indicates that when one radio button of a group is selected, all other buttons of that group should be deselected. This behavior is similar to that of old car radio station selectors, hence the term "radio button." If a radio button is not selected, the value will be the empty string. If the programmer specifies event handler code by using the `onClick` attribute, the code will be executed when the radio button is pressed.

A single array object is created for all objects in a radio button group, with the array name being the same as the radio button's `NAME` attribute.

As with all form elements, the `Radio` object is accessible as a property of its enclosing form object both via its name and the form's `Elements` array. Each radio button is created in its own individual element of the `Elements` array.

Syntax:

```
<INPUT
  TYPE="RADIO"
  NAME="RadioButtonName"
  VALUE="ValueIfSelected"
  [CHECKED]
  [onClick="HandlerCode"]>
```

Required Attributes:

- ⊕ `TYPE`: Must be set to the string `RADIO`.

- ⊕ `NAME`: The group name by which the radio object will be known. It should be unique to that radio button group within the form.

- ⊕ `VALUE`: If the button is selected, this value is returned with the radio button group name when the form is submitted.

Optional Attributes:

- ⊕ `CHECKED`: Indicates that the button is to appear selected by default.

- ⊕ `onClick`: JavaScript event handler code to be executed when the mouse is clicked on the radio button.

Usage Example:

```
<FORM ACTION="/cgi-bin/order.pl" METHOD="POST" TARGET="frame2">
<INPUT TYPE="RADIO" NAME="food" VALUE="chicken" CHECKED>
```

```
<INPUT TYPE="RADIO" NAME="food" VALUE="fish">
<INPUT TYPE="RADIO" NAME="food" VALUE="salad">
<INPUT TYPE="RADIO" NAME="food" VALUE="burgNfries" onClick=
➥"call911();">
<INPUT TYPE="SUBMIT" NAME="subm" VALUE="Place Order">
</FORM>
```

Parent Object:

Form

Properties:

- name: Corresponds to the HTML attribute NAME.

- value: Corresponds to the HTML attribute VALUE.

- length: The number of elements in the radio button array.

- checked: The Boolean state of the radio button. Assign true to this property to check, or false to uncheck a button.

- defaultChecked: The Boolean default (reset) state of the radio button. This corresponds to the HTML CHECKED attribute.

Methods:

- click: Simulates clicking the button.

Event Handlers:

onClick: Executes when the checkbox is clicked.

Examples:

Example 1: Check and print the nutritional information for the selected food:

```
<HTML>
<HEAD>
<SCRIPT LANGUAGE="JavaScript">
<!— Radio Button example 1
```

```
function makeInfo() {
  this.chicken   = "Chicken is high in protein and potassium.";
  this.fish      = "Fish is low in fat and cholesterol.";
  this.salad     = "Salad is high in fiber and vitamins.";
  this.burgNfries = "Heaven help you, your veins are about to
➥seize.";
}

// Create info message array
infoArray = new makeInfo();

/*
** info() — Show information about selected food
*/
function info() {
  w = window.open("", "outputWin7_17", "width=500,height=200");
  w.document.open("text/plain");

  w.document.writeln("Here's a little info about the food you
➥chose:");

  if (document.eats.food[0].checked) {        // Chicken?
    w.document.writeln(infoArray.chicken);
  } else if (document.eats.food[1].checked) {  // Fish?
    w.document.writeln(infoArray.fish);
  } else if (document.eats.food[2].checked) {  // Salad?
    w.document.writeln(infoArray.salad);
  } else if (document.eats.food[3].checked) {  // Burger?
    w.document.writeln(infoArray.burgNfries);
  } else {
    w.document.writeln("Air is not fattening at all.");
  }

  w.document.close();
}

// –>
</SCRIPT>
</HEAD>
<BODY>
<FORM NAME="eats">
<INPUT TYPE="RADIO" NAME="food" VALUE="chicken" CHECKED>
Chicken<BR>
<INPUT TYPE="RADIO" NAME="food" VALUE="fish"> Fish<BR>
```

```
<INPUT TYPE="RADIO" NAME="food" VALUE="salad"> Salad<BR>
<INPUT TYPE="RADIO" NAME="food" VALUE="burgNfries" onClick=
➥"alert('Call 911');">
Burger and Fries<BR>
<INPUT TYPE="BUTTON" NAME="submit" VALUE="Place Order" onClick=
➥"info();">
</FORM>
</BODY>
</HTML>
```

Example 2: The previous example is improved to make the radio button selection more general:

```
<HTML>
<HEAD>
<SCRIPT LANGUAGE="JavaScript">
<!— Radio Button example 2

function makeInfo() {
   this.chicken   = "Chicken is high in protein and potassium.";
   this.fish      = "Fish is low in fat and cholesterol.";
   this.salad     = "Salad is high in fiber and vitamins.";
   this.burgNfries = "Heaven help you, your veins are about to
➥seize.";
}

/*
** radioval(radiobuttonName)
** — Searches through a radio button group for the checked element,
**    returning the value of that element, 0 if none checked.
*/
function radioval(rb) {
    for (var i=0; i < rb.length; i++) {
        if (rb[i].checked) {
            return(parseInt(rb[i].value));
        }
    }
```

```
        return(0);          // No checked buttons found
    }

    // Create info message array
    infoArray = new makeInfo();

    /*
    ** info() — Show information about selected food
    */
    function info() {
        w = window.open("", "outputWin7_18", "width=500,height=200");
        w.document.open("text/plain");

        w.document.writeln("Here's a little info about the food you
    ➡chose:");
        w.document.writeln(infoArray[radioval(document.eats.food)]);

        w.document.close();
    }

    // —>
    </SCRIPT>
    </HEAD>
    <BODY>
    <FORM NAME="eats">
    <INPUT TYPE="RADIO" NAME="food" VALUE="chicken"
    CHECKED>Chicken<BR>
    <INPUT TYPE="RADIO" NAME="food" VALUE="fish"> Fish<BR>
    <INPUT TYPE="RADIO" NAME="food" VALUE="salad"> Salad<BR>
    <INPUT TYPE="RADIO" NAME="food" VALUE="burgNfries"
    onClick="alert('Call 911');">
    Burger and Fries<BR>
    <INPUT TYPE="BUTTON" NAME="submit" VALUE="Place Order"
    onClick="info();">
    </FORM>
    </BODY>
    </HTML>
```

See Also:

The other form elements: Button, Checkbox, Hidden, Password, Reset, Select, Submit, Text, **and** Textarea.

Reset Object

The Reset button object creates a reset pushbutton widget in an HTML form with a given label. When the user clicks the Reset button, the form data is reset to its default state.

The Reset button object can exist only within an HTML form. If the programmer specifies event handler code by using the onClick attribute, that code will be executed when the button is pressed.

As with all form elements, the Reset button is accessible both via its name and the form's Elements array. Please note that changing the Value property of the reset button after it has been rendered by the browser will not modify its appearance on the screen but will change the value of the Value property.

Syntax:

```
<INPUT
    TYPE="RESET"
    NAME="ResetButtonName"
    VALUE="ResetButtonLabel"
    [onClick="HandlerCode"]>
```

Required Attributes:

- TYPE: Must be set to the string RESET.

- NAME: The name by which the Reset button object will be known. It should be unique among form elements.

- VALUE: The label text to be printed on the face of the button.

Optional Attributes:

- onClick: JavaScript event handler code to be executed when the mouse is clicked on the button.

Usage Example:

```
<INPUT TYPE="RESET" NAME="res1" VALUE="Defaults" onClick=
➡"alert('Reset done');">
```

Parent Object:

form

Properties:

- name: Corresponds to the HTML attribute NAME.

- value: Corresponds to the HTML attribute VALUE.

Methods:

- click: Simulates clicking the button.

Event Handlers:

- onClick: Executes the indicated JavaScript code when the button is clicked. Note that the onClick handler cannot prevent the form from being reset. Use a regular button with a validate routine as its onClick event handler, and then reset to defaults with a JavaScript loop through the form's Elements array.

Example:

Validate and submit a service request form:

```
<HTML>
<SCRIPT LANGUAGE="JavaScript">

/*
** checkComplete(form) -- Assure the critical information was
➥entered
*/
function checkComplete(theform) {
  if ((theform.uname.value == "") || (theform.roomno.value ==
➥"")) {
    alert("Hey! Some information was missing.\n" +
      "You should have given both your name and room number.");
  } else {
    alert("Information sent. Your data looked good to me!");
  }
}
```

```
</SCRIPT
<BODY>
<FORM NAME="wiringRequest" ACTION="/cgi-bin/wr.pl" METHOD="POST">
<INPUT TYPE="TEXT" NAME="uname" SIZE="25"> Name <BR>
<INPUT TYPE="TEXT" NAME="roomno" SIZE="25"> Room Number
<BR>
<INPUT TYPE="RADIO" NAME="type" CHECKED> Telephone
<INPUT TYPE="RADIO" NAME="type"> Electrical
<BR>

<INPUT TYPE="RESET" NAME="res" VALUE="Reset To Defaults"
    onClick="alert('Form Reset to Defaults');">
<INPUT TYPE="SUBMIT" NAME="sbm" VALUE="Send Request"
    onClick="checkComplete(this.form);">
</FORM>

</BODY>
</HTML>
```

See Also:

The other form elements: Checkbox, Button, Hidden, Password, Radio, Select, Submit, Text, and Textarea.

Select and *Options* Objects

The Select pulldown and scrolling list object is an object created with the HTML form element <SELECT> block. It's similar in purpose to a group of radio buttons in that it's intended to allow the user to choose a single selection from a range of choices. Instead of buttons, the Select object offers a pulldown selection list widget appropriate to the platform. In an alternate mode activated by the MULTIPLE HTML attribute, the Select object presents a scrolling list. This list allows the user to choose any and all selections, much like a set of checkboxes.

The Select object can exist only within an HTML form. If the programmer specifies event handler code by using the onFocus, onBlur or onChange attributes, that code will be executed when the Select object obtains or loses keyboard focus or is changed.

As with all form elements, the select pulldown is accessible both via its name and the form's Elements array. Its programming interface is different from that of the radio button, however. Where the radio button has a separate entry in the Elements array for each button in the radio button group, the select pulldown has just one entry for the entire select object.

Additionally, where the radio button has the CHECKED HTML attribute and the corresponding defaultChecked and checked properties, the select options has the SELECTED HTML attribute and the corresponding defaultSelected and selected properties.

The Select object automatically creates an array called Options, corresponding to each <OPTION> element of the Select object.

Please note that changing the Text property of the Select object after it has been rendered by the browser will not modify its appearance on the screen but will change the Text property's value.

Syntax:

```
<SELECT
  NAME="SelectName"
  [SIZE="number"]
  [MULTIPLE]
  [onBlur="HandlerCode"]
  [onChange="HandlerCode"]
  [onFocus="HandlerCode"]>
  <OPTION VALUE="OptionValue" [SELECTED]> SelectLabel
  [<OPTION VALUE="OptionValue" [SELECTED]> SelectLabel ...]
</SELECT>
```

```
document.form[n].SelectName.property
document.form[n].SelectName.method()
document.form[n].elements[m].property
document.form[n].elements[m].method()
```

```
document.form[n].SelectName.options[i].property
document.form[n].elements[m].options[i].property
```

Required Attributes:

- ⊙ NAME: The name by which the Select object will be known. It should be unique within the form.

Optional Attributes:

- `SIZE`: The number of entries that should be shown at once. If this number is set to other than 1, the list will appear as a scrolling list rather than a pulldown selector.

- `MULTIPLE`: Causes the `Select` to be displayed as a scrolling list, allowing multiple elements of the list to be selected.

- `onFocus`: Specifies the JavaScript event handler for the `Focus` event.

- `onBlur`: Specifies the JavaScript event handler for the `Blur` event.

- `onChange`: Specifies the JavaScript event handler for the `Change` event.

- `OPTION`: The HTML `<OPTION>` tag delimits the start of a selectable option, including an optional `VALUE` attribute. The text following the `<OPTION>` tag will be displayed in the selection pulldown corresponding to that option.

- `VALUE`: In HTML `<OPTION>` tag, this sets the value of the `Value` attribute of that option. By default, this string is blank.

Parent Object:

`form`

Properties of the `Select` Object:

- `length`: The number of elements in the `Options` array.

- `name`: Corresponds to the select object's `NAME` HTML attribute.

- `selectedIndex`: Indicates the index of the selected option. If `MULTIPLE` is used, it indicates the first index selected.

Properties of the `Options` Array:

- `defaultSelected`: A Boolean value (true or false) indicating if an option was selected by default.

- `index`: An option's index (array subscript).

- `length`: The number of elements in the `Options` array.

- name: Corresponds to the select object's NAME HTML attribute.

- selected: An option's Boolean selection status.

- selectedIndex: Indicates the index of the selected option. If MULTIPLE is used, it indicates the first index selected.

- text: An option's SelectLabel from the HTML code after the <OPTION> tag.

- value: An option's VALUE HTML attribute value.

Methods:

- focus: Directs keyboard focus to the Select object.

- blur: Removes keyboard focus from the Select object.

Event Handlers:

- onFocus: JavaScript event handler code to be executed when the keyboard focus is directed at the password input box.

- onBlur: JavaScript event handler code to be executed when the keyboard focus is removed from the password input box.

- onChange: JavaScript event handler code to be executed when the contents of the text input box are changed by the user.

Examples:

This is an adaptation of the Checkbox object burger selector example used previously in this chapter. When the following form for ordering at Burger Czar is submitted, the order is printed out on the browser window. Note that the form elements may be accessed via the Document object or via the Form object passed from the onSubmit event handler using the this keyword. This is shown in the cheese and pickles checkbox objects:

```
<HTML>
<HEAD>
<SCRIPT LANGUAGE="JavaScript">
function processform(theform) {
    w = window.open("", "outputWin7_20", "width=500,height=200");
    w.document.open("text/plain");
```

YOUR COMMENTS

Send Us

Dear Reader:

Thank you for buying this book. In order to offer you more quality books on the topics **you** would like to see, we need your input. At Prima Publishing, we pride ourselves on timely responsiveness to our readers' needs. If you complete and return this brief questionnaire, **we will listen!**

Name (First) _____ (M.I.) _____ (Last) _____

Company _____ Type of business _____

Address _____ City _____ State ____ ZIP ____

Phone _____ Fax _____ E-mail address: _____

May we contact you for research purposes? ❑ Yes ❑ No

(If you participate in a research project, we will supply you with the Prima computer book of your choice.)

❶ How would you rate this book, overall?

❑ Excellent ❑ Fair
❑ Very good ❑ Below average
❑ Good ❑ Poor

❷ Why did you buy this book?

❑ Price of book ❑ Content
❑ Author's reputation ❑ Prima's reputation
❑ CD-ROM/disk included with book
❑ Information highlighted on cover
❑ Other (please specify):_____

❸ How did you discover this book?

❑ Found it on bookstore shelf
❑ Saw it in Prima Publishing catalog
❑ Recommended by store personnel
❑ Recommended by friend or colleague
❑ Saw an advertisement in:_____
❑ Read book review in:_____
❑ Saw it on Web site:_____
❑ Other (please specify):_____

❹ Where did you buy this book?

❑ Bookstore (name):_____
❑ Computer store (name):_____
❑ Electronics store (name):_____
❑ Wholesale club (name):_____
❑ Mail order (name):_____
❑ Direct from Prima Publishing
❑ Other (please specify):_____

❺ Which computer periodicals do you read regularly?_____
_____
_____
_____

❻ Would you like to see your name in print?

May we use your name and quote you in future Prima Publishing books or promotional materials?

❑ Yes ❑ No

❼ Comments & suggestions: _____
_____
_____

8 **I am interested in seeing more computer books on these topics**

❏ Word processing   ❏ Databases/spreadsheets   ❏ Networking   ❏ Programming

❏ Desktop publishing   ❏ Web site development   ❏ Internetworking   ❏ Intranetworking

9 **How do you rate your level of computer skills?**   **10** **What is your age?**

❏ Beginner

❏ Intermediate

❏ Advanced

❏ Under 18   ❏ 40–49

❏ 18–29   ❏ 50–59

❏ 30–39   ❏ 60–over

SAVE A STAMP

Visit our Web site at **http://www.primapublishing.com**

and simply fill out one of our online response forms.

PRIMA PUBLISHING
Computer Products Division
701 Congressional Blvd., Suite 350
Carmel, IN 46032

```
    w.document.write("You have ordered two tofu patties, ");
    if (document.burger.condiments.options.selectedIndex == 0)
        w.document.write("special sauce, ");
    if (document.burger.condiments.options[1].selected)
        w.document.write("lettuce, ");
    if (theform.condiments.options[2].selected)
        w.document.write("cheese, ");
    if (theform.condiments.options[3].selected)
        w.document.write("pickles, ");
    if (document.burger.condiments.options[4].selected)
        w.document.write("onions, ");
    w.document.write("on a sesame seed bun.");

    w.document.close();

    return true;
}
</SCRIPT>
</HEAD>
<BODY>
<FORM NAME="burger" ACTION="/cgi-bin/kitchensel.pl" METHOD="POST"
    onSubmit="return processform(this);">
What would you like on your Burger Czar Tofu Burger:
<CENTER>
<SELECT NAME="condiments" MULTIPLE
        onFocus="alert('Yo man— Try the Special Sauce! Eh!');">
<OPTION VALUE="Yow"> Special Sauce
<OPTION> Lettuce
<OPTION> Cheese
<OPTION> Pickles
<OPTION> Onions
</SELECT>
</CENTER>
<BR>
<INPUT TYPE="SUBMIT" NAME="sbm" VALUE="Process Form">
</FORM>
</BODY>
</HTML>
</HTML>
```

See Also:

The other form elements: Checkbox, Button, Hidden, Password, Radio, Reset, Submit, Text, **and** Textarea.

String Object

The String object is a built-in data type object that serves to provide access to string handling and manipulation methods and to the length of the String property for *strings*, which are sequences of characters. All strings are String objects and can use any String property or method.

All methods use their String objects for input but do not modify them; they simply return a new string value.

Syntax:

stringObject.method(params)

stringObject.length

Parent Object:

None.

Properties:

- ☻ length: The integer number of characters in the string.

Methods:

- ☻ anchor: Add HTML to make string an anchor (NAME).

- ☻ big: Add HTML to make string display in large font.

- ☻ blink: Add HTML to make string blink.

- ☻ bold: Add HTML to make string display in bold font.

- ☻ charAt: Extract the single character at a given offset from the string.

- ☻ fixed: Add HTML to make string display in fixed-width font.

- ☻ fontcolor: Add HTML to make string display in the specified color text.

- ☻ fontsize: Add HTML to make string display in the given size font.

- ☻ indexOf: Search through the string for a given substring beginning at a given point in the string.

- ◈ **italics:** Add HTML to make string display in italics font.

- ◈ **lastIndexOf:** Search backward through the string for a given sub-string beginning at a given point in the string.

- ◈ **link:** Add HTML to make string a link (HREF).

- ◈ **small:** Add HTML to make string display in small font.

- ◈ **strike:** Add HTML to make string display in strike-out font.

- ◈ **sub:** Add HTML to make string display as subscript.

- ◈ **substring:** Extract a substring from the string given a starting and ending offset.

- ◈ **sup:** Add HTML to make string display as superscript.

- ◈ **toLowerCase:** Convert the string to lowercase and return.

- ◈ **toUpperCase:** Convert the string to uppercase and return.

Event Handlers:

None.

Examples:

Example 1:

```
myCapName = myName.toUpperCase();
document.writeln("This should appear blinking, in bold!".blink().
➥bold());
MyString = "I want to extract THIS word";
extractedWord = MyString.substring(18, 22);
```

Example 2: This is a library routine that parses the QUERY_STRING (location search property) and creates a new object with properties corresponding to the CGI encoded values:

```
/*
**          JavaScript CGI Processing Library
**
** Function    Description
```

```
** --------      ------------------------
** object()     Dummy function for creating empty objects
** CGIdecode(qs)  Decode a CGI encoded string of the QUERY_STRING
➥type
** CGItrans(s)   Translate escaped characters according to the
➥CGI standard
**
*/



/*
** object() -- Dummy function for creating empty objects
*/
function object() { }



/*
** CGIdecode(QUERY_SRTING) -- Decode a CGI encoded string of the
➥form
**   ?myvar=value&dohnuts=123%2B456&FullName=Paul+T.+Kooros
** Returns an object with subscripts/keys having corresponding
➥values:
**   pairs[myvar] = "value";
**   pairs[dohnuts] = "123+456";
**   pairs[FullName] = "Paul T. Kooros";
*/
function CGIdecode(query) {
  var left=1;   // Marks the left end of a pair
  var right=0;    // Marks the right end + 1 of a pair
  var eqpos=0;    // Marks the position of the '=' sign
  var key="";   // Holds the CGI variable name, left of '='
  var value="";    // Holds the CGI variable value, right of '='
  var pairs=null;    // The pairs associative array

  // Sanity check
  if ((query.length == 0) || ((query.indexOf("?", 0)) != 0)) {
   return null;
  }
```

```
    // Divide query into "variablename=value" string pairs
    pairs = new object();
    while ((right=query.indexOf("&", left)) != -1) {
     eqpos = query.indexOf("=", left);

      // Skip if null variable name
      if (eqpos <= 0)
        continue;

      // Translate CGI data encoding format, "+"=>" ", "%NN"=>"X"
      value = CGItrans(query.substring(eqpos+1, right));
      key = query.substring(left, eqpos);
      if (key.length > 0)
        pairs[key] = value;

      // Position left marker
      left = right + 1;
     }
    eqpos = query.indexOf("=", left);
    key = query.substring(left, eqpos);
    value = CGItrans(query.substring(eqpos+1, query.length));
    if (key.length > 0)
     pairs[key] = value;

    return pairs;
}


/*
** CGItrans(s) -- Translate escaped characters according to the
➥CGI standard
**      '+' -> ' '
**      '%NN' -> 'X' X is character with ASCII value hex(NN)
*/
function CGItrans(s) {
  var i=0;

  // Null case
```

```
    if (s.length == 0)
     return s;

    // Translate '+' -> ' '
    while ((i = s.indexOf("+", 0)) >= 0) {
     s = s.substring(0, i) + " " + s.substring(i+1, s.length);
    }

    // Translate '%NN' -> 'X'  where NN is ASCII hex, and X is
➥ASCII
     i = 0;
    while ((i < s.length-2) && ((i = s.indexOf('%', i)) >= 0)) {
     if (i >= s.length-2)
        break;

     // Generate unescaped version of '%NN'
     ss = unescape(s.substring(i, i+3));
     s = s.substring(0, i) + ss + s.substring(i+3, s.length);
     i++;    // Skip past %NN
    }

    return s;
}
```

Submit Object

The Submit button object creates a Submit pushbutton widget in an HTML form with a given label. When the user clicks the Submit button, the form data is transmitted to the URL indicated in the <FORM> tag's ACTION attribute.

The Submit object can exist only within an HTML form. If the programmer specifies event handler code by using the onClick attribute, that code will be executed when the button is pressed. The user may also specify a Submit event handler with the <FORM> tag's onSubmit attribute, to be executed when the Submit button is clicked but before the data has been transmitted to the URL. The onSubmit event handler may be used to validate the form data and, if necessary, abort the transmission.

As with all form elements, the Submit button is accessible both via its name and the form's Elements array.

Please note that changing the `Value` property of the Submit button after it has been rendered by the browser will not modify its appearance on the screen but will change the `Value` property's value.

Syntax:

```
<INPUT
  TYPE="SUBMIT"
  NAME="SubmitButtonName"
  VALUE="SubmitButtonLabel"
  [onClick="HandlerCode"]>
```

Required Attributes:

- `TYPE`: Must be set to the string `SUBMIT`.

- `NAME`: The name by which the `Submit` button object will be known. It should be unique among form elements.

- `VALUE`: The label text to be printed on the face of the button.

Optional Attributes:

- **onClick:** JavaScript event handler code to be executed when the mouse is clicked on the button.

Usage Example:

```
<INPUT TYPE="SUBMIT" NAME="sub1" VALUE="Send In" onClick=
➥"validate(this.form);">
```

Parent Object:

`form`

Properties:

- `name`: Corresponds to the HTML attribute NAME.

- `value`: Corresponds to the HTML attribute `VALUE`.

Methods:

- `click`: Simulates clicking the button.

Event Handlers:

🌀 `onClick`: Executes the indicated JavaScript code when the button is clicked. Note that the `onClick` handler cannot prevent the form from being submitted. Use the `<FORM>` tag's `onSubmit` instead.

Example:

Validate and submit a service request form:

```
<HTML>
<SCRIPT LANGUAGE="JavaScript">

/*
** checkComplete(form) -- Assure the critical information was
➥entered
*/
function checkComplete(theform) {
  if ((theform.uname.value == "") || (theform.roomno.value ==
➥"")) {
    alert("Hey! Some information was missing.\n" +
      "You should have given both your name and room number.");
  } else {
    alert("Information sent. Your data looked good to me!");
  }
}

</SCRIPT
<BODY>
<FORM NAME="wiringRequest" ACTION="/cgi-bin/wr.pl" METHOD="POST">
<INPUT TYPE="TEXT" NAME="uname" SIZE="25"> Name <BR>
<INPUT TYPE="TEXT" NAME="roomno" SIZE="25"> Room Number
<BR>
<INPUT TYPE="RADIO" NAME="type" CHECKED> Telephone
<INPUT TYPE="RADIO" NAME="type"> Electrical
<BR>

<INPUT TYPE="SUBMIT" NAME="sbm" VALUE="Send Request"
   onClick="checkComplete(this.form);">
</FORM>
```

```
</BODY>
</HTML>
```

See Also:

The other form elements: Checkbox, Button, Hidden, Password, Radio, Reset, Select, Text, and Textarea.

Text **Object**

The Text object creates a scrollable text input box in an HTML form. The Text input box object can exist only within an HTML form.

Specifying a Text object in HTML creates a new property, named according to its HTML NAME attribute, in the enclosing Form object.

If the programmer specifies event handler code by using the onFocus, onBlur, onChange, or onSelect HTML attributes, that code will be executed respectively when focus is obtained, lost, or text is changed or selected by clicking and dragging the mouse.

As with all form elements, the Text object is accessible as a property of its enclosing Form object both via its name and the form's Elements array.

Syntax:

```
<INPUT
   TYPE="TEXT"
   NAME="TextInputName"
   [VALUE="InitialText"]
   [SIZE="number"]
   [MAXLENGTH="number"]
   [onFocus="HandlerCode"]
   [onBlur="HandlerCode"]
   [onChange="HandlerCode"]
   [onSelect="HandlerCode"]>
```

Required Attributes:

- TYPE: Must be set to the string TEXT.

- NAME: The name by which the Text object will be known. It should be unique within the form.

Optional Attributes:

- ◑ VALUE: This is the initial contents of the text input box.

- ◑ SIZE: The number of characters width the text input box should be. Defaults to 20 characters if you do not specify SIZE.

- ◑ MAXLENGTH: The maximum limit to the number of characters that may be typed into the text input box.

- ◑ onFocus: Specifies the JavaScript event handler for the Focus event.

- ◑ onBlur: Specifies the JavaScript event handler for the Blur event.

- ◑ onChange: Specifies the JavaScript event handler for the Change event.

- ◑ onSelect: Specifies the JavaScript event handler for the Select event.

Usage Example:

```
<INPUT TYPE="TEXT" NAME="luggage" SIZE="40" MAXLENGTH="40">
➥Luggage Description <BR>
```

Parent Object:

form

Properties:

- ◑ name: Corresponds to the HTML attribute NAME.

- ◑ value: Corresponds to the HTML attribute VALUE.

- ◑ defaultValue: The default (reset) state contents of the text input box. This corresponds to the HTML VALUE attribute.

Methods:

- ◑ focus: Directs keyboard focus to the text input box.

- ◑ blur: Removes keyboard focus from the text input box.

- ◑ select: Selects the text contents of the text input box.

Event Handlers:

- ⊙ onFocus: JavaScript event handler code to be executed when the keyboard focus is directed at the text input box.

- ⊙ onBlur: JavaScript event handler code to be executed when the keyboard focus is removed from the text input box.

- ⊙ onChange: JavaScript event handler code to be executed when the contents of the text input box are changed by the user.

- ⊙ onSelect: JavaScript event handler code to be executed when the contents of the text input box are selected with the mouse.

Example:

```
<HTML>
<HEAD>
<SCRIPT LANGUAGE="JavaScript">

function checkout(theform) {
    w = window.open("", "outputWin7_23", "width=500,height=200");
    w.document.open();

    w.document.writeln("<PRE>");
    w.document.writeln("Your username:   " + theform.uname.value);
    w.document.writeln("Your real name:" + theform.FullName.value);
    w.document.writeln("Your favorite color: " + ➥theform.favCol.value);
    w.document.writeln("</PRE>");

    w.document.close();
}
// ->
</SCRIPT>
</HEAD>
<BODY>

Please fill in the following vital information:
<FORM ACTION="javascript:checkout(document.forms[0]);" METHOD="POST">
<INPUT TYPE="TEXT" NAME="uname" VALUE="root" MAXLENGTH="8">
<INPUT TYPE="TEXT" NAME="shell" VALUE="/bin/csh"> Login Shell <BR>
<INPUT TYPE="TEXT" NAME="favCol" onBlur="alert('Choose colors
➥wisely...');">
    Favorite Color.<BR>
```

```
<INPUT TYPE="SUBMIT" NAME="subm" VALUE="Register Now">
</FORM>
</BODY>
</HTML>
```

See Also:

The other form elements: Checkbox, Button, Hidden, Password, Radio, Reset, Select, Submit, and Textarea.

Textarea **Object**

The *Textarea* object creates a multi-line scrollable, wrappable text input box in an HTML form. The Textarea object can exist only within an HTML form.

Specifying a Textarea object in HTML creates a new property, named according to its HTML NAME attribute, in the enclosing Form object.

If the programmer specifies event handler code by using the onFocus, onBlur, onChange, or onSelect HTML attributes, that code will be executed respectively when focus is obtained, lost, or text is changed or selected by clicking and dragging the mouse.

As with all form elements, the Textarea object is accessible as a property of its enclosing Form object both via its name and the form's Elements array.

Syntax:

```
<TEXTAREA
    NAME="TextInputName"
    [ROWS="number"]
    [COLS="number"]
    [WRAP="OFF"|"VIRTUAL"|"PHYSICAL"]
    [onFocus="HandlerCode"]
    [onBlur="HandlerCode"]
    [onChange="HandlerCode"]
    [onSelect="HandlerCode"]>
Initial Text
</TEXTAREA>
```

Required Attributes:

- TYPE: Must be set to the string TEXT.

- NAME: The name by which the TextArea object will be known. It should be unique within the form.

Optional Attributes:

- VALUE: The initial contents of the text input box.

- ROWS: The number of lines high the textarea box should be. Defaults to 1 line if you do not specify ROWS.

- COLS: The number of characters width the textarea box should be. Defaults to 20 characters if you do not specify COLS.

- WRAP: Controls the type of end-of-line wrapping behavior. OFF is the default, where lines appear and are transmitted exactly as they were typed in. VIRTUAL automatically wraps the lines at textarea boundaries but transmits lines to the server exactly as they were typed in. PHYSICAL causes line breaks (CR-LF) to actually be inserted into the text if it reaches the textarea boundary.

- MAXLENGTH: The maximum limit to the number of characters that may be typed into the text input box.

- onFocus: Specifies the JavaScript event handler for the Focus event.

- onBlur: Specifies the JavaScript event handler for the Blur event.

- onChange: Specifies the JavaScript event handler for the Change event.

- onSelect: Specifies the JavaScript event handler for the Select event.

Usage Example:

```
<FORM ACTION="http:/www.missmanners.org/cgi-bin/protocol.pl"
➥METHOD="GET">
Please type your comments here:
<TEXTAREA NAME="comments" ROWS="10" COLS="40" WRAP="PHYSICAL
   onChange="this.form.submit();"> Dear Miss Manners: </TEXTAREA>
</FORM>
```

Parent Object:

```
form
```

Properties:

- ◑ `name`: Corresponds to the HTML attribute NAME.

- ◑ `value`: Corresponds to the HTML attribute VALUE.

- ◑ `defaultValue`: The default (reset) state contents of the textarea. This corresponds to the text between the HTML tags `<TEXTAREA>` and `</TEXTAREA>`.

Methods:

- ◑ `focus`: Directs keyboard focus to the textarea.

- ◑ `blur`: Removes keyboard focus from the textarea.

- ◑ `select`: Selects the text contents of the textarea.

Event Handlers:

- ◑ `onFocus`: JavaScript event handler code to be executed when the keyboard focus is directed at the textarea.

- ◑ `onBlur`: JavaScript event handler code to be executed when the keyboard focus is removed from the textarea.

- ◑ `onChange`: JavaScript event handler code to be executed when the contents of the textarea are changed by the user.

- ◑ `onSelect`: JavaScript event handler code to be executed when the contents of the textarea are selected with the mouse.

Example:

A program that allows the user to type in a JavaScript statement or program and view the output in a textarea:

```
<HTML>
<BODY>

<FORM NAME="prg">
```

```
Type in a JavaScript statement here:
<INPUT TYPE="text" NAME="expr" SIZE="60">
<INPUT TYPE="button" NAME="evl2" VALUE="<<== eval"
  onClick="document.prg.outp.value = eval(document.prg.expr.
➥value)">

<BR>
Or type in a JavaScript program here:
<TEXTAREA NAME="program" ROWS=10 COLS=60>
</TEXTAREA>
<INPUT TYPE="button" NAME="evl" VALUE="<<== eval"
  onClick="document.prg.outp.value = eval(document.prg.program.
➥value)">

<BR>
Output appears here:<BR>
<TEXTAREA NAME="outp" ROWS=14 COLS=70>
</TEXTAREA>

</FORM>
</BODY>
</HTML>
```

The other form elements: Checkbox, Button, Hidden, Password, Radio, Reset, Select, Submit, and Text.

Window Object

The JavaScript Window object is the top-level object for Document, Location, and History objects. All other objects are hierarchically below the Window object.

The Window object is the implicit object for all object references. It is assumed in all references, so it may be omitted when setting any of its properties or calling its methods. The only exception to this is using Window Open and Close methods within event handlers. See the Window Open and Close methods for details on this. The Window object is the parent object of subwindow objects called *frames*.

Syntax:

```
window.property
```

```
window.method(parameters)
```

```
winName.property
```

```
winName.method(parameters)
```

Parent Object:

None.

Properties:

- defaultStatus: The message to be displayed in the window's status bar when other messages are not being displayed.

- document: A link to the document residing at the topmost level within the window. See Document object.

- frames: An array whose entries correspond to all the frames declared in a window using a <FRAMESET> HTML tag. See Frame object.

- length: The number of frames in the window's frames array.

- location: The location object, allowing knowledge of the document's current URL location and extraction of its various components.

- name: The name of the window.

- parent: Normally this is used by frames to access their parent frames. However, to the application's top-level window, this is a synonym for itself.

- self: A synonym for the current top-level window.

- status: The message to be displayed in the status bar of the browser window.

- top: Normally this is used by frames to access the top-level frame, but to windows, this is a synonym for the application window.

- window: This is a synonym for the current application window.

Methods:

- alert: Brings up a pop-up window with a message.

- close: Closes the given window.

- ◔ `confirm`: Brings up a pop-up window with a message, requesting an "OK" or "Cancel" action, returning the result.

- ◔ `open`: Opens the window given a URL, a window name, and possibly a specification for various window parameters and decorations.

- ◔ `prompt`: Brings up a pop-up window with a message requesting an input, returning the string typed in as its result.

- ◔ `setTimeout`: Schedule a timer event, giving JavaScript code to be executed should the timer expire without being disabled.

- ◔ `clearTimeout`: Cancel a previously scheduled timer event.

Event Handlers:

- ◔ `onLoad`: JavaScript event handler code to be executed after the current document has been loaded in its entirety.

- ◔ `onUnload`: JavaScript event handler code to be executed when the user departs from current document.

Examples:

Example 1: Open another window and display a given URL:

```
winvar = window.open("http://www.xyz.com", "myWind", "status=1,
➥width=200,height=50");
```

Example 2: Open another browser window, with a status bar and menu bar, for the display of quotations. Every five seconds, update the document showing in the browser to show a different quotation:

```
<HTML>
<HEAD>
<SCRIPT LANGUAGE="JavaScript">

/*
** State Variables
*/
var quoteNum=0;


/*
** makeQuotes() -- Constructor function for the quotes array.
```

```
*/
function makeQuotes() {
   this[0] = "The Walrus and the Carpenter\nwere walking close at
➥hand,";
   this[1] = "They wept like anything to see\nsuch quantities of
➥sand.";
   this[2] = '"If this were to all to be cleared away"\n';
   this[3] = 'they said "it would be grand!"';
   this[4] = '"If seven maids with seven mops\nswept for half a
➥year,"';
   this[5] = '"do you suppose," the Walrus said';
   this[6] = '"that they could get it clear?"';
   this[7] = '"I doubt it," said the Carpenter';
   this[8] = '"and shed a bitter tear."';
   this.length = 9;
}


/*
** showNextQuote(w) -- Display quotation, and schedule the next
➥quotation.
**              Quote is displayed in window w.
*/
function showNextQuote() {
   w.document.clear();     // Clear the document frame
   w.document.open("text/plain");    // Begin display of document
   w.document.writeln(quotes[quoteNum]); // Display quote
   w.document.close();     // End, flush output and display
   quoteNum++;

   // If there are more quotes to display, schedule another in 5
➥sec.
   if (quoteNum < quotes.length)
    setTimeout("showNextQuote()", 5000);
}

// Initialize quotes array
quotes = new makeQuotes();
```

```
// Open a new, empty window for output
w = window.open("", "quoteWin", "status=1,menubar=1");

// Show first quote:
showNextQuote();

</SCRIPT>
</HEAD>
</HTML>
```

See Also:

frame, document

Chapter 8

JavaScript Methods

Methods are yet another example of the modularity and encapsulation of JavaScript as an object-based language. They provide a way to perform specific operations on objects. Each object has its own set of methods. Remember that *methods* are functions associated with an object. Objects are discussed in Chapter 7, "JavaScript Objects."

The JavaScript methods in this chapter are supplied by JavaScript. JavaScript has methods for date, math, string manipulation, document, window control, and keeping track of history. The following table contains a list of all methods in alphabetical order and their associated objects. Look to the appropriate object section for a complete description of the method. Also, every method has at least one example showing its usage.

Method	Object
abs	Math
acos	Math
alert	window
anchor	string
asin	Math
atan	Math
back	history
big	string
blink	string
blur	password, select, text, textarea
bold	string
ceil	Math
charAt	string
clear	document
clearTimeout	frame, window
click	button, checkbox, radio, reset, submit
close (document)	document
close (window)	window
confirm	window
cos	Math
exp	Math
fixed	string
floor	Math
focus	password, select, text, textarea
fontcolor	string
fontsize	string
forward	history
getDate	Date
getDay	Date
getHours	Date
getMinutes	Date
getMonth	Date
getSeconds	Date

Method	Object
getTime	Date
getTimezoneOffset	Date
getYear	Date
go	history
indexOf	string
italics	string
lastIndexOf	string
link	string
log	Math
max	Math
min	Math
open (document)	document
open (window)	window
parse	Date
pow	Math
prompt	window
random	Math
round	Math
select	password, text, textarea
setDate	Date
setHours	Date
setMinutes	Date
setMonth	Date
setSeconds	Date
setTime	Date
setTimeout	frame, window
setYear	Date
sin	Math
small	string
sqrt	Math
strike	string
sub	string
submit	form

Method	Object
substring	string
sup	string
tan	Math
toGMTString	Date
toLocaleString	Date
toLowerCase	string
toUpperCase	string
UTC	Date
write	document
writeln	document

 ## Math Methods

JavaScript supplies mathematical methods for use in programs. The basic syntax of Math methods is

```
Math.methodname(argument);
```

Methods supplied cover all of the functions usually found on calculator buttons. They also include a random number generator and rounding functions. A description of the method, its syntax, and an example of usage is included.

Method *abs*

abs returns the absolute value of a number. abs is useful in situations in which the program cannot tolerate a negative or floating-point number. This method may be called to precheck the value input by a user.

Sometimes Math.abs() is useful for testing for near-equality. There are often very small differences between floating-point numbers because of rounding of least significant bits, and a loss of accuracy that occurs when converting from a decimal form into the computer's internal binary format. For example, if the test of two numbers is

```
a = 0.6;
b = 0.2;
if (a/b == 3.0) {
// statements
}.
```

more than likely a/b will be just a teensy bit off, such as 2.99999999999999936, in which case the computer will conclude not equal. Instead, this test can be rewritten as

```
a = 0.6;
b = 0.2;
if (Math.abs(a/b - 3.0) < 0.000000001) {
// statements
}
```

The problem can then be avoided:

```
a = 60;
b = 20;
if ((a/b < 3.0000000001) && (a/b > 2.9999999) ) {
// statements
}
```

Syntax:

```
Math.abs(number);
```

number is any numeric expression or property of an object.

Example:

```
Math.sqrt(Math.abs(x1 - x2));
```

Method *acos*

acos returns the arc (inverse) cosine, in radians, of a number. This method always returns a numeric value between 0 and pi radians. The *number* used as an argument to acos must be between –1 and 1. Return value is 0 if the argument is outside the range of –1 and 1.

acos is related to asin, atan, cos, sin, and tan methods.

Syntax:

```
Math.acos(number);
```

number is a numeric expression or property of an existing object with a value of between –1 and 1.

Example:

```
elev_angle = Math.acos(distance / projectionDist);
theta = Math.acos(x / r);
```

Method *asin*

asin returns the arc (inverse) sine, in radians, of a number. This method returns a numeric value between –pi/2 and pi/2 radians. The *number* used as an argument to asin must be between –1 and 1, or the return value is always 0.

Syntax:

```
Math.asin(number);
```

number is a numeric expression or a property of an existing object with a value between –1 and 1.

Example:

```
elevAngle = Math.asin(mountain.elevation / observer.radius);
theta = Math.asin(y / r);
```

Method *atan*

atan returns the arc (inverse) tangent, in radians, of a number. This method returns a numeric value between -pi/2 and pi/2 radians. The *number* argument passed to the method is the tangent of an angle.

Syntax:

```
Math.atan(number);
```

number is a numeric expression or a property of an existing object containing the value of the tangent of an angle.

Example:

```
elev_angle = Math.atan(mountain.elevation / distance);
elev_angle = Math.atan(rise / run);
```

Method *ceil*

ceil returns the next integer greater than or equal to a number. While abs truncates a floating-point number, ceil rounds up. If the value to be tested is 37.3, abs returns 37.3 while ceil returns 38.

See also methods *floor* and *round*.

Syntax:

```
Math.ceil(number);
```

number is any numeric expression or property of an existing object.

Example:

```
piesToOrder = Math.ceil(party.people * piesPerPerson);
```

Method *cos*

cos returns the cosine of a number. The argument passed to the method is the size of an angle in radians. cos returns a numeric value between –1 and 1.

See also methods *sin*, *tan*, *acos*, *asin*, and *atan*.

Syntax:

```
Math.cos(number);
```

number is a numeric expression or property of an existing object with the value of the size of an angle in radians.

Example:

Math.cos() can be used to convert polar coordinates (r, θ) into Cartesian (rectangular) coordinates (x, y):

```
x = r * Math.cos(theta);
y = r * Math.sin(theta);
```

Method *exp*

exp returns e to the power of its argument. e, the base, is Euler's constant. Euler's constant is the base of natural logarithms, approximately 2.71828. exp is the inverse of method log. To compute another base raised to a power, use the method pow.

Syntax:

```
Math.exp(number);
```

number is any numeric expression of property of an existing object with a numeric value.

Example:

```
populationNow = 231500;
growthRate = 0.034;        // 3.4% growth
years = 4;
populationAfter = populationNow * Math.exp(growthRate * years);

v = v0 * Math.exp(-k*t);    // Exponential decay
```

Method *floor*

floor returns the next-lower or equal-to integer of a floating-point number. This is the opposite of ceil, which returns the next-greater integer. The floor of 37.3 is 37, while the ceil is 38. The floor of –37.3 is –38, while the ceil is –37.

Syntax:

```
Math.floor(number);
```

number is any numeric expression or property of an existing object with a numeric value.

Example:

```
piesCompletelyEaten = Math.floor(party.people * piesPerPerson);
```

Method *log*

log (the inverse of exp) returns the natural logarithm (base *e*) of a number. The value returned for out-of-range expressions is –1.797693134862316e+308, the largest possible negative double. log is related to methods exp and pow.

See also methods *exp* and *pow*.

Syntax:

```
Math.log(number);
```

number is any positive numeric expression or property of an existing object.

Example:

```
populationBefore = 185300;
populationNow = 231500;
```

```
years = 4;
growthRate = Math.log(populationNow/populationBefore) /years;
yearsForPopulationToTriple = growthRate / Math.log(3.0);
```

To take the log base a of n:

```
logBaseAOfN = Math.log(n) / Math.log(a);
```

Method *max*

max returns the greater of two numbers.

See also method *min*.

Syntax:

```
Math.max(number1, number2);
```

number1 and *number2* are any numeric expressions or the properties of existing objects.

Example:

Example 1: setting a lower limit:

```
i = Math.max(3, i);
```

If i is less than 3, it will be set to 3.

Example 2: Find the largest value in an array, arr:

```
big = arr[0];
for (var i=1; i < arr.length; i++) {
   big = Math.max(big, arr[i]);
}
```

Method *min*

min returns the lessor of two numbers.

See also method *max*.

Syntax:

```
Math.min(number1, number2);
```

`number1` and `number2` are any numeric expressions or properties of existing objects.

Example:

Example 1: setting an upper limit:

```
sandwiches = Math.min(4, sandwichesRequested);
```

If `i` is less than 3, it will be set to 3.

Example 2: Find the smallest value in an array, `arr`:

```
small = arr[0];
for (var i=1; i < arr.length; i++) {
  small = Math.min(small, arr[i]);
}
```

Method *pow*

`pow` returns a value equal to the *base* raised to the *exponent* power. The base and exponent are sent as arguments to the method. If the numbers would result in an imaginary number, such as when the base is negative, it returns a value of zero.

See also methods *exp* and *log*.

Syntax:

```
Math.pow(base, exponent);
```

`base` is any numeric expression or property of an existing object with a numeric value.

`exponent` is any numeric expression or property of an existing object with a numeric value.

Example:

Cube root of x:

```
crx = pow(x, 1.0/3);
```

Take *n*th root of x:

```
nthRootOfX = pow(x, 1.0/n);
```

Print out the number of grains of rice for the mythical inventor of the game of chess:

```
document.writeln("<pre>Square#  Number of Grains");
for (var i=0; i < 64; i++) {
    n = Math.pow(2, i);
    document.writeln(" " + i + " " + n);
}
document.writeln("Total grains: " + Math.pow(2, 64));
```

Method *random*

random returns a pseudo-random number between zero and one. random is specific to UNIX platforms.

Syntax:

```
Math.random()
```

Example:

Print a random greeting phrase:

```
function makePhraseArray() {
    this[0] = "Greetings, your excellency!";
    this[1] = "Howdy, pardner!";
    this[2] = "Hey, Yo!";
    this[3] = "Ciao.";
    this[4] = "Hi, hows it going.";
    this.length = 5;
}
phrases = new makePhraseArray();
document.write(phrases[Math.floor(Math.random() * 5)]);
```

Method *round*

round returns the value of a number passed as an argument rounded to the nearest integer. A value of .5 or greater is rounded to the next highest integer. Less than .5 returns the next lowest integer. This is different from methods ceil and floor, which always move to the next higher or lower integer if the argument is not a whole number.

See also methods *floor* and *ceil*.

Syntax:

```
Math.round(number);
```

number is any numeric expression or property of an existing object with a numeric value.

Example:

```
piesToBuy = Math.round(averagePiesEatenAtPastParties);
```

Method *sin*

sin returns the sine of an angle. The return value is between –1 and 1.

Syntax:

```
Math.sin(number)
```

number is a numeric expression representing the size of an angle in radians.

Example:

Math.sin() can be used to convert polar coordinates (r, θ) into Cartesian (rectangular) coordinates (x, y):

```
x = r * Math.cos(theta);
y = r * Math.sin(theta);
```

Method *sqrt*

sqrt returns the square root of a number. The method returns a zero if the value of the argument is outside the range, as in a negative number.

For other roots, see method *pow.*

Syntax:

```
Math.sqrt(number)
```

number is any non-negative expression or property of an existing object with a numeric value.

Example:

Calculate the length of the hypotenuse of a right triangle by using the Pythagorean theorem:

```
hypotenuse = Math.sqrt(x*x + y*y);
```

Calculate the two roots of the quadratic equation:

```
xRoot1 = (-b + Math.sqrt(b*b * 4 * a * c)) / (2 * a);
xRoot2 = (-b - Math.sqrt(b*b * 4 * a * c)) / (2 * a);
```

Method *tan*

tan, along with methods acos, asin, atan, cos, and sin, is used in trigonometric functions. tan returns the tangent of an angle in radians.

Syntax:

```
Math.tan(number)
```

number is a numeric expression representing the size of an angle in radians.

Example:

Math.tan computes the trigonometric tangent, the slope (rise/run), of the hypotenuse of a right triangle, given the measure of its angle in radians.

```
mountain.slope = Math.tan(theta);
jet.climbRate = Math.tan(jet.climbAngle) * jet.velocity
```

Window Methods

Window methods provide ways to manipulate window objects. Window objects include browser windows, which the programmer may open, close, and manipulate by name, and more incidental pop-up window objects.

Method *alert*

alert displays a dialog box with a message and an OK button. This box is informational only and does not require any other user action than to click on the OK button. JavaScript program execution is not delayed by an alert; it continues to execute. The alert's string argument may be made longer than one line by putting newline characters (\n) in the string.

Syntax:

```
alert("message");
```

message is any string or property of an existing object with a string value.

Example:

Alerts are often used for debugging purposes to examine variables.

Example 1:

```
str = "The first value is " + myobj.val1;
str += "\nThe second value is " + myobj.val1;
alert(str);
```

Example 2 shows the use of newline:

```
alert("You may request at most 4 sandwiches.\nTry again.");
```

This is an HTML form that displays an alert if the form is submitted without a string in the input box firstname.

Example 3:

```
<HTML>
<HEAD>
<SCRIPT LANGUAGE="JavaScript">
// Check for valid (non-null) input data in theform.firstname
function checkvalid(theform) {
  if (theform.firstname.value == "") {
    // Nothing was input --fail
    alert("Hey, you didn't input anything! Try again.");
    return false;
  } else {
    // Something was input
    return true;
  }
}
</SCRIPT>
</HEAD>
```

```
<BODY>
<FORM NAME="nameform" ACTION="/cgi-bin/nameform.pl" METHOD="GET"
onSubmit="checkvalid(this);">
Please input your first name:
<INPUT TYPE="TEXT" NAME="firstname">
<INPUT TYPE="SUBMIT" NAME="submit" VALUE="Submit First Name">
</FORM>
</BODY>
</HTML>
```

Method close (Window Object)

close used in relation to a window closes the specified window. Without a window specified, close closes the current window by default. close is related to the method open.

See also method open.

window.close() must be specified in use with event handlers. A call to close() in this situation is evaluated to document.close().

The current window is closed by any of these statements:

```
window.close();
```

```
self.close();
```

```
close();
```

Syntax:

```
windowReference.close()
```

Example:

This example displays program output in a new window, then closes the window when the user clicks the Close button:

```
<HTML>
<HEAD>
<SCRIPT LANGUAGE="JavaScript">
// Create new window
yoyo = window.open("", "yoyowindow");
// Output table of values to new window
```

```
yoyo.document.write("<pre>Angle sine of angle\n");
for (var theta=0; theta < (Math.PI/2); theta += 0.1) {
   yoyo.document.write(" "+theta+" "+Math.sin(theta)+"\n");
}
yoyo.document.write("</pre>\n");
yoyo.document.write("<FORM><INPUT TYPE=BUTTON VALUE='Close
➥Window' ");
yoyo.document.write("onClick="'self.close();></FORM>\n");

// Automatically close the window after 60 seconds, anyway.
setTimeout("self.close()", 60000);
</SCRIPT>
</HEAD>
</HTML>
```

Method *confirm*

confirm displays a dialog box with a specified message, as well as OK
and Cancel buttons. Information about the choice is given to the user
through the message sent as an argument to the method. Execution of
the JavaScript program is delayed until the user presses one of the buttons. This is different from alert, which does not stop processing. confirm returns true on a choice of OK and false on a choice of Cancel.

See also methods *alert* and *prompt*.

Syntax:

```
confirm("message");
```
message is any string or property of an existing object with a
➥string value.

Example:

This example pops up a confirmation window asking for a user flavor
preference to which the user replies OK (Yes) or Cancel (No). The program then creates a new window to display output according to the
user's selection.

```
<HTML>
<HEAD>
<SCRIPT LANGUAGE="JavaScript">
if (confirm("Press OK if you prefer Peach pie over Apple.")) {
```

```
    flavor = "Peach";
} else {
    flavor = "Apple";
}
// Create new window
pieWin = window.open("", "piewindow");
pieWin.document.open();
pieWin.document.writeln("<HTML><BODY><B><I>");
pieWin.document.writeln("Here's " + flavor + " pie in your
eye!\n");
pieWin.document.writeln("</I></B></BODY></HTML>");
pieWin.document.close();
</SCRIPT>
</HEAD>
</HTML>
```

Method *open* (Window Object)

open opens a new Web browser window on the client. A call to open() without an object name defaults to document.open() in event handlers.

The object can be either a URL argument representing the address of the window to be opened or an empty string. A new, empty window is created when an empty string URL is the argument.

There are optional window features available to liven up the window. These features are separated by commas in the calling argument to window.open(). All Boolean features are true by default if windowFeatures are specified without values. They are true if specified as yes or 1. They are also true if windowName does not specify an existing window and windowFeatures are not specified. Finally, if *any* features are specified in windowFeatures, then all other Boolean features are false unless otherwise specified. The Boolean features are noted in the following table with a "(B)":

Feature Name	Function Creates
toolbar	Standard Navigator toolbar (B)
location	Location entry field (B)
directories	Standard Navigator directory buttons (B)
status	Status bar at bottom of window (B)

continues

Feature Name	Function Creates
menubar	Menu at top of window (B)
scrollbars	Horizontal and vertical scrollbars if doc. is larger than window (B)
resizable	Allows a user to resize the window (B)
width	Width of the window in pixels
height	Height of the window in pixels

Syntax:

```
[windowVar = ][window].open("URL", "windowName",
➥["windowFeatures"]);
```

windowVar is the name of the new window.

URL is the URL to open in the new window.

windowName is the window name to use in the TARGET attribute of a
<FORM> or <A> tag.

windowFeatures is a comma-separated list of display features
described earlier.

Example:

This example opens three new windows from the current browser
page: one with the current page displayed, one that displays the
Netscape home page, and one that is blank to write program output
to.

```
<HTML>
<HEAD>
<SCRIPT LANGUAGE="JavaScript">
// Create a new browser window viewing the current page
// when the form below's button is clicked
function btnclicked() {
   newSameWin = window.open(document.location, "newsame");
}
// Create a new browser window NOT viewing any page, for output:
newWin = window.open("", "newOutputWindow");
newWin.document.write("<HTML><BODY>Hi there! This is newWin");
```

```
// Create another new browser window viewing netscape's home
➡page.
// The window should have a status bar and tool bar only.
window.open("http://home.netscape.com/", "nshp", "status=1,
➡toolbar=1");
</SCRIPT>
</HEAD>
<BODY>
<FORM>
<INPUT TYPE="BUTTON" VALUE="New Window" onClick="btnclicked();">
</FORM>
</BODY>
</HTML>
```

Method *prompt*

prompt creates a dialog box that allows user input. This is different from alert and confirm, which only allow a user to click on a button. The prompt dialog box displays a message and, optionally, has an input field for the user's input. The string <undefined> is displayed if no inputDefault is specified. The message and variable name of the input field are sent as arguments to prompt. This method delays processing until the user responds appropriately. This is similar to confirm but the opposite of alert, which does not delay processing.

Syntax:

```
prompt(message, [inputDefault]);
```

message is any string or property of an existing object with a sting value.

inputDefault is a string, integer, or property of an existing object that represents the default value of the input field.

Example:

This example prompts the user for name and zodiac sign with separate pop-up prompt boxes:

```
<HTML>
<HEAD>
<SCRIPT LANGUAGE="JavaScript">
yourname = prompt("What's your name?", "");
```

```
// Prompt with a default value
yoursign = prompt("What's your sign?", "Capricorn")
document.write("Hey "+yourname+", I think "+yoursign+"is
➥groovy.");
</SCRIPT>
</HEAD>
</HTML>
```

 String Methods

String methods provide functionality to String objects. Strings, or String objects, are a fundamental type in JavaScript. The programmer may create a literal string simply by enclosing a sequence of characters between a pair of single or double quotation marks. Variables can also hold strings.

The following methods can operate on any string object, either as a variable or as a literal. They allow manipulation of the appearance of a display string, including font style, color, and size. String methods also allow manipulation of string contents. Finally, some string methods allow search and extraction of portions of a string.

Method *anchor*

anchor creates an HTML anchor that is used as a hypertext target. This method, along with write or writeln, creates and displays an anchor in a document. These anchors become elements in the anchors array. The anchors array is administered by the anchor object. The following is the correct sequence of events to create and display an anchor:

```
windowName = window.open("","displayWindow")
windowName.document.writeln(stringName.anchor("anchorName"))
windowName.document.close()
```

See also method *link*.

Syntax:

```
text.anchor(nameAttribute);
```

text is a string or property of an existing object with a string value.

nameAttribute is also a string or string property.

Example:

This example produces a page that outputs a table and produces a link that allows the user to skip past the table:

```
<HTML>
<HEAD>
<SCRIPT LANGUAGE="JavaScript">
document.writeln("<HTML><BODY>");
document.writeln("<A href='#aftertable'>Go to after the
➥table</A>");
// Output table of values
document.write("<pre>\nAngle cosine of angle\n");
for (var theta=0; theta < (Math.PI/2); theta += 0.1) {
   document.write(" "+theta+" "+Math.cos(theta)+"\n");
}
var text = "This is the Part after the Table";
document.write("</PRE>" + text.anchor("aftertable"));
</SCRIPT>
</HEAD>
</HTML>
```

Method *big*

`big` displays a string in large font. This is the same as using the HTML <BIG> tag. `big` is used in conjunction with `write` or `writeln` methods to display a string in a document in large fontsize.

See also methods *fontsize* and *small*.

Syntax:

```
stringname.big();
```

stringname is any string or a property of an existing object which has a string value.

Example:

The following two JavaScript program fragments produce identical results, text output in an enlarged size font:

```
var text = "The rain in Spain falls mainly on the plain.";
document.write(text.big());
```

and

```
document.write("<BIG>The rain in Spain falls mainly on the
plain.</BIG>");
```

Method *blink*

blink displays a string that blinks. This is the same as the HTML tag <BLINK>. blink is used in conjunction with write or writeln methods to format and display a string in a document.

See also methods *bold*, *italics*, and *strike*.

Syntax:

```
stringname.blink();
```

stringname is any string or a property of an existing object with a string value.

Example:

The following two JavaScript program fragments produce identical results:

```
var text = "Chocolate On Sale NOW!";
document.write(text.blink());
```

and

```
document.write("<BLINK>Chocolate On Sale NOW!</BLINK>");
```

Keep in mind that many users consider blinking text to be annoying.

Method *bold*

bold displays a string in bold text. This is the same as the HTML <B> tag. bold is used in conjunction with the write or writeln methods to format and display a string in a document.

bold is related to methods *blink*, *italics*, and *strike*.

Syntax:

```
stringname.bold();
```

stringname is any string or a property of an existing object with a string value.

Example:

The following two JavaScript program fragments produce identical results:

```
var text = "Caution!";
document.write(text.bold() + " This page will self-destruct in 5
➥seconds");
setTimeout("window.close()", 5000);
```

and

```
document.write("<B>Caution!</B> This page will self-destruct in 5
➥seconds");
setTimeout("window.close()", 5000);
```

Method *charAt*

charAt returns a character in a given position from a string. Positions in the string are referenced from left to right, with positions 0 to stringname.length. The last character in the string is equivalent to stringname.length -1. JavaScript returns an empty string when an out-of-range request is made.

See also methods *indexOf* and *lastIndexOf*.

Syntax:

```
stringname.charAt(index);
```

stringname is any string or property of an existing object with a string value.

index is any integer which points to the position of the character in the string.

Example:

Example 1: Print the third letter of a word:

```
var word = "Abracadabra";
// Letters start with number 0,
// so letter number 2 is the third letter.
document.write(word.charAt(2));
```

Example 2: Print positions 7 through 16 of a string:

```
var mystring = "The hail in Vail falls mainly by the pail."
for (var i=12; i <= 21; i++) {
  document.write(mystring.charAt(i));
}
```

Example 3: Print a string backward:

```
var backwardstring = "Was it a Bar or a Bat I saw?";
for (var i=backwardstring.length-1; i >= 0; i++) {
  document.write(backwardstring.charAt(i));
}
```

Example 4: A function to reverse a string, which is then used to print the string backward:

```
function reverse(str) {
  var revStr = "";
  for (var i=str.length-1; i >= 0; i++) {
   revstr += str.charAt(i));
  }
  return(revStr);
}
document.write(reverse("Able was I ere I saw Elba"));
```

Method *fixed*

fixed is equivalent to the HTML tag <TT>. It causes a string to be displayed in a fixed-pitch font. fixed is used with the write or writeln methods to format and display a string in a document.

Syntax:

```
stringname.fixed()
```

stringname is any string or property of an existing object with a string value.

Example:

Example 1: The following two JavaScript program fragments produce identical results:

```
var text = "Fixed width typewriter font!";
document.write(text.fixed());
```

and

```
document.write("<TT>Fixed width typewriter font</TT>");
```

Example 2: Displays a crude graphics sine curve on the browser. The fixed-width font allows the display to be rectangular:

```
var browserWidth = 60;
for (var theta = 0.0; theta < (2 * Math.PI); theta += 0.1) {
  str = "";
  n = (1.0 + Math.sin(theta)) * browserWidth / 2;
  // Add 'n' periods on to str
  for (var i=0; i < n; i++) {
    str += ".";
  }
str += "X<br>";
document.writeln(str.fixed());
}
```

Method *fontcolor*

fontcolor is equivalent to the HTML tag `<FONT COLOR=color>`. fontcolor is used with the write or writeln methods to format and display a string in a document. Color may be expressed as either one of the string literals listed in the Color Values section of the JavaScript documentation or as a hexadecimal RGB triplet. See Appendix A, "Colors," for further information on specifying colors.

Syntax:

```
stringname.fontcolor(color);
```

stringname is any string or a property of an existing object with a string value.

color is a string which designates color as a hexadecimal or named literal.

Example:

Display important information in a red font color:

```
var text = "Important";
document.write("It is " + text.fontcolor("red") + " to floss
➥daily!");
```

The color can also be specified by using a hexadecimal color specifier:

```
var text = "Important";
document.write("It is "+text.fontcolor("FF0000")+" to floss
➥daily!");
```

The two preceding examples produce output identical to this HTML:

```
document.write("It is <FONT COLOR="red">Important</FONT> to floss
➥daily!");
```

Method *fontsize*

`fontsize` is equivalent to the HTML tag `<FONTSIZE=`*size*`>`. `fontsize` is used with `write` and `writeln` methods to format and display a string in a document.

JavaScript has seven defined font sizes. The argument of the method `size` can be an integer between 1 and 7, which corresponds to a preset font size. 1 is the smallest font size, and 7 is the largest. `size` may also be a negative number, which adjusts the font size relative to the size set in the `<BASEFONT>` tag. Negative numbers such as –1 decrease the font size by one relative to the current font size.

Font size and color changes are local only. They apply only to the string text they operate on and do not effect any text that comes after them.

See also methods *big* and *small*.

Syntax:

```
stringname.fontsize(size);
```

stringname is any string or property of an existing string with a string value.

size is an integer between one and seven or a signed integer between one and seven.

Example:

Example 1: Display important information in a large sized font, specifying absolute size:

```
var text = "Important";
document.write("Its " + text.fontsize(6) + " to floss daily!");
```

The preceding produces output identical to this HTML:

```
document.write("Its <FONT SIZE='6'>Important</FONT> to floss
➥daily!");
```

Example 2: Display important information in a large sized font, specifying relative font size. It is important to note that the argument to `fontsize()` must be a string if relative font sizing is to be used.

```
var text = "Important";
document.write("Its " + text.fontsize("+2") + " to floss
➥daily!");
```

The preceding produces output identical to this JavaScript/HTML:

```
document.write("Its <FONT SIZE='+2'>Important</FONT> to floss
➥daily!");
```

Example 3: Display incidental information in a smaller font specifying relative font size:

```
var text = "Brought to you by GasBeGone";
document.write("Dining in Pasadena" + text.fontsize('-3'));
```

The preceding produces output identical to this JavaScript/HTML:

```
document.write("Dining in Pasadena ");
document.write("<FONT SIZE='-3' Brought to you by GasBeGone
➥</FONT>");
```

Method *indexOf*

`indexOf` is used along with methods `charAt` and `lastIndexOf` to locate characters or groups of characters within a string. The location is returned as an integer greater than zero, if found. `-1` is returned if no match is made. Indexing starts from zero for the leftmost character.

It is also possible to start the search from other than the leftmost character by adding a second argument. Zero, or the leftmost character, is the default.

Syntax:

```
stringname.indexOf(searchValue, [fromIndex]);
```

stringname is any string or a property of an existing object with a string value.

searchValue is a string or a property of an existing object, represent-ing the match string.

fromIndex is the location within the calling string to begin the search. The default is zero. It can be any integer from 0 up to the length of the object –1.

Example:

Example 1: Finds the first occurrence of the sequence of letters abc in a string.

```
var text = "The abc quick abc fox abc jumped over the lazy
➥dogs";
var find = "abc";
pos = text.indexOf(find, 0);
if (pos == -1) {
  document.write(find + " not found in string.");
} else {
  document.write(find + " found at position " + pos);
}
```

Example 2: A function to count the number of non-overlapping occurrences of a word in a string:

```
<HTML>
<HEAD>
<SCRIPT LANGUAGE="JavaScript">
// return the number of occurences of "word" in str
function countwords(str, word) {
  var count=0;   // Number of matches found
  var pos=0;     // Position within string to search from
  while ((n=str.indexOf(word, pos)) >=0) {
   count++;
   // The next search starts after the current one
   pos = n + str.length;
  }
return(count);
}
```

```
function tellWords(myform) {
  numFound = countwords(myform.sentence, myform.word);
  alert("Number found = " + numFound);
}
</SCRIPT>
</HEAD>
<BODY>
<FORM NAME="WordForm">
<INPUT TYPE="TEXT" NAME="sentence">
<INPUT TYPE="TEXT" NAME="word">
<INPUT TYPE="BUTTON" NAME="pressMe" onClick="tellWords
➥(this.form);">
</FORM>
</BODY>
</HTML>
```

Note that the while loop condition repeats as long as indexOf() reports other than -1, meaning pattern not found.

Method *italics*

italics is equivalent to the HTML tag <I>. italics produces an italicized string for output to the screen. It is used in conjunction with the write or writeln methods to format a string in a document.

Syntax:

```
stringname.italics();
```

stringname is any string or property of an existing string with a string value.

Example:

The following two JavaScript program fragments produce identical results:

```
var text = "Watch out";
document.write(text.italics() + " for wild animals.");
```

and

```
document.write("<I>Watch out</I> for wild animals.");
```

Method *lastIndexOf*

lastIndexOf, along with methods charAt and indexOf, is a string search method. lastIndexOf returns the index of the last occurrence of the specified character or group of characters. The calling string is searched backward, starting at the index specified in the calling argument. The default is to start searching with the last character in the string. Characters are indexed from left to right, starting with zero. Therefore, the default to start searching is the length of string −1.

Syntax:

```
stringname.lastIndexOf(searchValue, [fromIndex]);
```

stringname is any string or a property of an existing object with a string value.

searchValue is a string or a property of an existing object, representing the match string.

fromIndex is the location within the calling string to begin the search. The default is length of the object −1. It can be any integer up to the length of the object −1.

Example:

Example 1: Finds the last occurrence of the sequence of letters abc in a string:

```
var text = "The abc quick abc fox abc jumped over the lazy
➥dogs";
var find = "abc";
pos = text.lastIndexOf(find, text.length - 1);
if (pos == -1) {
  document.write(find + " not found in string.");
} else {
  document.write(find + " found at position " + pos);
}
```

Example 2: A function to count the number of non-overlapping occurrences of a word in a string, counting backward:

```
<HTML>
<HEAD>
```

```
<SCRIPT LANGUAGE="JavaScript">
// return the number of occurences of "word" in str
function countwords(str, word) {
   var count=0;          // Number of matches found
   var pos=str.length-1;  // Position in string to search from
   while ((n=str.lastIndexOf(word, pos)) >=0) {
    count++;
    // The next search starts after the current one
    pos = n - str.length;
    }
   return(count);
}
function tellWords(myform) {
   numFound = countwords(myform.sentence, myform.word);
   alert("Number found = " + numFound);
}
</SCRIPT>
</HEAD>
<BODY>
<FORM NAME="WordForm">
<INPUT TYPE="TEXT" NAME="sentence">
<INPUT TYPE="TEXT" NAME="word">
<INPUT TYPE="BUTTON" NAME="pressMe"
onClick="tellWords(this.form);">
</FORM>
</BODY>
</HTML>
```

Note that the while loop condition repeats as long as indexOf() reports other than -1, meaning pattern not found.

Method *link*

link is similar to method anchor in that it is used to create an HTML hypertext link. Where anchor defines a named anchor within a document, link creates a hypertext reference link to somewhere else. link is used in conjunction with write and writeln methods to create and display a hypertext link in a document. link creates the link, which is then displayed in a document by the write or writeln.

Syntax:

```
linkText.link(hrefAttribute);
```

linktext is any string or property of an existing object.

hrefAttribute is a string or property of an existing object with a URL string value.

Example:

Example 1: Displays a page with a link to another site and a link back to the page that brought the user here. The link is not displayed if the user typed a location directly into the location window rather than clicking on an anchor to lead the user here.

```
<HTML>
<HEAD>
<SCRIPT LANGUAGE="JavaScript">
var text = "Sun HomePage";
document.writeln("Go to the " +
text.link("http://www.sun.com/"));
// Show a link back to the referring document, if there is one.
if (document.referrer != "") {
  text = "previous page";
  document.writeln(" or Go to the ");
  document.writeln(text.link(document.referrer));
}
</SCRIPT>
</HEAD>
```

Example 2: The preceding example for the anchor method can be improved slightly by building the link with the `link` method rather than in HTML:

```
<HTML>
<HEAD>
<SCRIPT LANGUAGE="JavaScript">
document.writeln("<HTML><BODY>");
var text = "Go to after the table";
document.writeln(text.link("#aftertable"));
```

```
// Output table of values
document.write("<pre>\nAngle cosine of angle\n");
for (var theta=0; theta < (Math.PI/2); theta += 0.1) {
   document.write(" "+theta+" "+Math.cos(theta)+"\n");
}
var text = "This is the Part after the Table";
document.write("</PRE>" + text.anchor("aftertable"));
</SCRIPT>
</HEAD>
```

Example 3: Given an array of URL strings, create a listing of the links where the text and the URL are the same on the current page:

```
for (var i in listOlinks) {
// link text ----\\\\\\\\\\\\     ////////////---HREF
document.writeln(listOlinks[i].link(listOlinks[i])+"<BR>");
}
```

Method *small*

small is equivalent to the HTML tag <SMALL>. This method is used in conjunction with the methods write or writeln to display a string in small font.

Syntax:

```
stringname.small()
```

stringname is any string or property of an existing object.

Example:

The following two JavaScript program fragments produce identical results, text output in a reduced sized font:

```
var text = "The sleet in Crete falls mainly on your feet.";
document.write(text.small());
```

and

```
document.write("<SMALL>The sleet in Crete falls mainly on your
➥feet.</SMALL>");
```

Method *strike*

strike, along with methods blink, bold, and italics, is used to manipulate display strings. It is equivalent to the HTML tag <STRIKE>. strike is used in conjunction with methods write or writeln to format and display a string in a document.

Syntax:

```
stringname.strike()
```

stringname is any string or property of an existing object with a string value.

Example:

The following two JavaScript program fragments produce identical results, stricken out text, used mostly in legal documents:

```
var text = "The snow in Moscow falls mainly way down low.";
document.write(text.strike());
```

and

```
document.write("<STRIKE>The snow in Moscow falls mainly way down
➥low.</STRIKE>");
```

Method *sub*

sub is equivalent to the HTML tag <SUB>. It formats a string to be displayed as a subscript. sub is used in conjunction with methods write and writeln to format and display a string in a document. sub is the opposite of sup, which is superscript.

Syntax:

```
stringname.sub()
```

stringname is any string or property of an existing object.

Example:

Example 1: The following two JavaScript program fragments produce identical results, subscripted text, convenient for Chemistry and Mathematics:

```
var subtext = "4";
document.write("KMnO" + subtext.sub());
```

and

```
document.write("KMnO<SUB>4</SUB>");
```

Example 2:

```
document.write("C" + "2".sub() + "H" + "5".sub() + "OH");
```

Method *substring*

substring returns a portion of a string as indicated by the arguments sent to the method. Indexing of the string starts with zero at the left-most character. The last character is the length of the string –1.

The substring is extracted starting at position indexA and ending at the character before the position of indexB, if indexA is less than indexB. If indexB is less than indexA, then the substring begins with the character at position indexB and goes to the character at position indexA-1. An empty string is returned when indexA and indexB are equal.

Syntax:

```
stringname.substring(indexA, indexB)
```

stringname is any string or property of an existing object with a string value.

indexA and *indexB* are any integer from 0 to the length of the string –1.

Example:

Example 1: Given a form input box where the user's first and last names will be entered in the same box, separate and extract each of them:

```
<HTML>
<HEAD>
<SCRIPT LANGUAGE="JavaScript">
function getfirst(str) {
   pos = str.indexOf(" ");
   // Return everything up to,
   // but not including, the space
```

```
      return(str.substring(0, pos));
  }
  function getlast(str) {
    pos = str.lastIndexOf(" ");
    // Return everything from after the space thru the end
    return(str.substring(pos+1, str.length));
  }
  function alertname(fullname) {
    alert("First name: " + getfirst(fullname) + "\n"
    + "Last name: " + getlast(fullname));
  }
</SCRIPT>
</HEAD>
<BODY>
<FORM>
Please enter your full name, separating your first and last
name only with a space:<BR>
<INPUT TYPE="TEXT" NAME="fullname"
onBlur="alertname(this.value);">
</FORM>
</BODY>
</HTML>
```

Example 2: Given a string, construct a new string, delete all characters before and including the first X, and delete all characters after and including the last X. If the original string is "blah foo zomXbeeblebroX the wierdXblahooey mix mop", the resulting string is "beeblebroX the wierd".

```
var text = "blah foo zomXbeeblebroX the wierdXblahooey mix mop";
function cleanup(str) {
  leftpos = str.indexOf("X") + 1;
  rightpos = str.lastIndexOf("X");
  return(str.substring(leftpos, rightpos));
}
document.writeln(cleanup(text));
```

Method *sup*

sup is equivalent to the HTML tag <SUP>. sup formats and displays a string as a superscript. It is used in conjunction with methods write or `writeln`. This is the opposite of `sub`, which causes a string to be displayed as a subscript.

Syntax:

```
stringname.sup()
```

stringname is any string or property of an existing object with a string value.

Example:

Example 1: The following two JavaScript program fragments produce identical results, superscripted text, useful in mathematics and footnoting:

```
var suptext = "-kt";
var subtext = "0";
document.write("N = N" + subtext.sub() + " e" + suptext.sup());
```

and

```
document.write("N = N<SUB>0</SUB> e<SUP>-kt</SUP>");
```

Example 2:

```
// Pythagorean Theorem:
document.write("x"+"2".sup()+" + y"+"2".sup()+" = r"+"2".sup());
```

Method *toLowerCase*

`toLowerCase` returns the value of the string in which all letters have been converted to lowercase. The calling string itself is not converted. `toLowerCase` is used in conjunction with `write` or `writeln` to display the lowercase value. This is the opposite of method `toUpperCase`, which returns a display string of uppercase. Lowercase is often used to put user input into a standard lowercase form for comparison or storage.

Syntax:

```
stringname.toLowerCase()
```

stringname is any string or a property of an existing object with a string value.

Example:

Check to see if the user has typed the string "tomatoes" in the form
input text box, regardless of the case of letters typed:

```
<HTML>
<HEAD>
<SCRIPT LANGUAGE="JavaScript">
function caseInsensitiveCompare(str1, str2) {
  if (str1.toLowerCase() == str2.toLowerCase()){
   return true;
   } else {
   return false;
   }
}
function alerttomatoes(str) {
  if (caseInsensitiveCompare(str, "tomatoes")) {
   alert("Tomatoes FOUND");
   } else {
   alert("Tomatoes NOT found");
   }
}
</SCRIPT>
</HEAD>
<BODY>
<FORM>
Please enter a vegetable name:
<INPUT TYPE="TEXT" NAME="vegie"
onBlur="alerttomatoes(this.value);">
</FORM>
</BODY>
</HTML>
```

Method *toUpperCase*

toUpperCase returns the value of the calling string converted to
uppercase. The calling string itself is not converted. toUpperCase is
used in conjunction with write or writeln to display the lowercase
value. This is the opposite of method toLowerCase, which returns a
display string of lowercase.

Syntax:

stringname.toUpperCase()

stringname is any string or a property of an existing object with a string value.

Example:

Example 1: Generates an error alert pop-up if a form does not have method GET or POST:

```
<HTML>
<HEAD>
<SCRIPT LANGUAGE="JavaScript">
formMethod = nameform.method.toUpperCase();
if ((formMethod != "GET") && (formMethod != "POST")) {
   alert("Error: form has invalid method: neither GET nor POST");
}
</SCRIPT>
</HEAD>
<BODY>
<FORM NAME="nameform" ACTION="/cgi-bin/nameform.pl" METHOD="GET"
<INPUT TYPE="TEXT" NAME="fnord">
</FORM>
</BODY>
</HTML>
```

Example 2: Check to see if the user has typed the string "garbonzo" in the form input text box, regardless of the case of letters typed:

```
<HTML>
<HEAD>
<SCRIPT LANGUAGE="JavaScript">
function caseInsensitiveCompare(str1, str2) {
   if (str1.toUpperCase() == str2.toUpperCase()){
    return true;
   } else {
    return false;
   }
}
```

```
function alertgarbonzo(str) {
  if (caseInsensitiveCompare(str, "garbonzo")) {
   alert("Garbonzo FOUND");
  } else {
   alert("Garbonzo NOT found");
  }
}
</SCRIPT>
</HEAD>
<BODY>
<FORM>
Please enter a legume name:
<INPUT TYPE="TEXT" NAME="legume"
onBlur="alertgarbonzo(this.value);">
</FORM>
</BODY>
</HTML>
```

History Methods

History methods allow basic access to the browser's history mechanism, which is the browser's recollection of URLs it has visited. Regrettably, access to the browser's history is limited to directing the browser to load a page in its history. The programmer cannot access the contents of the URLs. Users can do only the equivalent of clicking on the Forward or Back buttons, or selecting a URL from the GO pulldown menu on the browser.

Method *back*

back is similar to choosing the Back button in the Navigator. It reloads the previous URL in the history list. back is equivalent to history.go (-1). The previous page is not kept in memory; only the URL is kept in the History array.

See also methods *forward* and *go*.

Syntax:

```
history.back()
```

Example:

Example 1: Pops up an alert window and returns to the page the user just came from if the search part of the location is null:

```
<HTML>
<HEAD>
<SCRIPT LANGUAGE="JavaScript">
if (document.location.search == "") {
  alert("You must fill in the form before submitting it.");
  history.back();
}
</SCRIPT>
</HEAD>
</HTML>
```

The search part of the location is known as the QUERY_STRING to CGI programmers. It consists of any characters typed after a ? in the URL. It is automatically appended to the end of the URL specified in a FORM's ACTION attribute if its METHOD is GET. All the data entered into the form elements are encoded according to the CGI standard and appended to the URL.

```
history.back();
```

is identical to

```
history.go(-1);
```

Remember that once the browser moves to a different page using the history mechanism, the current page's JavaScript program transfers control of the browser to the new page and stops running. Thus, use of the history mechanism makes the most sense when used to jump between pages in a sequence designed by the JavaScript programmer.

Example 2: A form that sends the browser back to the previous page if the user presses a button:

```
<HTML>
<BODY>
<FORM>
<INPUT TYPE="BUTTON" NAME="mybutton" VALUE="Go to Previous Page"
➥onClick="history.back();">
```

```
</FORM>
</BODY>
</HTML>
```

Method *forward*

forward is the same as choosing the Forward button in the
Navigator. It is also the same as history.go(1). forward loads the
next URL in the history list.

forward is related to methods *back* and *go*.

Syntax:

```
history.forward();
```

Example:

A form that sends the browser forward to the next page if the user
presses a button:

```
<HTML>
<BODY>
<FORM>
<INPUT TYPE="BUTTON" NAME="mybutton" VALUE="Go to Next Page"
➥onClick="history.forward();">
</FORM>
</BODY>
</HTML>
```

The JavaScript code

```
history.forward();
```

is identical to

```
history.go(1);
```

Method *go*

go uses the browser history mechanism to move to another page. The
arguments passed to go may be a delta to move forward or backward
from the current page. This is noted by a positive or negative integer.
A positive integer moves forward the number of pages indicated in
the history list to get to the desired URL. A negative integer moves
backward in the list. A value of zero reloads the current page.

The arguments may also be a string containing the desired URL or a substring from the history list. The substring match does not have to be exact. The browser makes an attempt to find a match closest to the current page in history. The page located by the URL is then loaded.

Syntax:

```
history.go(delta);
```

delta is the negative or positive integer which represents a relative position in the history list.

```
history.go("location");
```

location is a string or a property of an existing object which contains all or part of a URL in the history list.

Example:

Example 1: A form button that goes 2 pages forward in the browser history:

```
<HTML>
<BODY>
<FORM>
<INPUT TYPE="BUTTON" NAME="mybutton" VALUE="Resume filling out
➥form"
onClick="history.go(2);">
</FORM>
</BODY>
</HTML>
```

Example 2: A form button that goes 3 pages backward in the browser history:

```
<HTML>
<BODY>
<FORM>
<INPUT TYPE="BUTTON" NAME="mybutton" VALUE="Go back to Main Page"
onClick="history.go(-3);">
</FORM>
</BODY>
</HTML>
```

Example 3: A form button that reloads the current page:

```
<HTML>
<BODY>
<FORM>
<INPUT TYPE="BUTTON" NAME="mybutton" VALUE="Reload Current Page"
➥onClick="history.go(0);">
</FORM>
</BODY>
</HTML>
```

Example 4: A form button that loads the last page in the browser history having "moose" in its URL:

```
<HTML>
<BODY>
<FORM>
<INPUT TYPE="BUTTON" NAME="mybutton" VALUE="Go to Moose Page"
onClick="history.go("moose");">
</FORM>
</BODY>
</HTML>
```

This string comparison is not case sensitive. JavaScript searches for the closest match in the browser history, both forward and back.

Document Methods

The following sections discuss the Document methods.

Method *clear*

clear deletes the document in a window. The window is cleared regardless of the method used to paint the window.

Syntax:

```
document.clear();
```

Example:

```
document.clear();
```

Method *close* (Document Object)

close is the method used to stop the "metero shower" in the Netscape icon and display Document: Done in the status bar. close does this by closing the stream that was opened by the document.open() method. close forces the content of the stream to be displayed in the window if the stream was opened to layout.

close is not the only method that forces the input layout buffer to flush to the screen. big and <CENTER> also force the display.

Syntax:

```
document.close();
```

Example:

```
document.close();
```

Method *open* (Document Object)

open opens a document that will later be closed by the document.close() method. This open is document specific.

This method opens a stream to receive output from methods write or writeln. Output is opened to a layout if it is text or an image. All other forms of output are opened to a plug-in. (*Plug-ins* are add-on program modules that dynamically extend the capability of Netscape Navigator. By using plug-ins, Web authors can seamlessly integrate new content within Web pages.) The open method clears a target window if the document already exists in the window. text/html is the default.

Input is displayed in the target window after the stream is ended by the call to document.close. Additional window update streams are created by another call to document.open.

The allowable mimeType output types are:

mimeType	Document Description
text/html	ASCII text with HTML formatting
text/plan	plain ASCII text with end-of-line delimiters
image/gif	GIF header and pixel data encoded bytes
image/jpeg	JPEG header and pixel data encoded bytes

continues

mimeType	Document Description
image/x-bitmap	bitmap header and pixel data encoded bytes
plugIn	loads plug-in as destination for `write` **or** `writeln` methods

Syntax:

```
document.open(["mimeType"]);
```

mimeType is any of the above document types. *plugIn* must be Netscape supportable.

Example:

```
document.Open("text")
```

Method *write*

`write` displays expressions in an open document window. These expressions include numerics, strings, or logicals. `write` displays the output to the screen but does not append a newline character, as does method `writeln`.

`write` is used within the HTML tag `<SCRIPT>` or within an event handler. The document is usually opened using `document.open()`. Event handlers perform their duties after the document opened by `document.open()` is closed by `document.close()`. In this situation, a new document window is automatically opened, and the `write` contents are displayed.

`write` is used in conjunction with many of the string formatting methods, such as `italics` and `bold`, for string displays.

Syntax:

```
document.write(expression1 [,expression2] [,expressionN])
```

expression1 through *expressionN* are any JavaScript expressions or the properties of any existing objects.

Example:

```
document.write("You have ordered two tofu patties ");
```

Method *writeln*

writeln is the same as write except that it appends a newline character to the end of the display. The newline character is ignored by HTML in most situations. HTML tag <PRE> forces the newline character to be displayed.

writeln displays an unlimited number of JavaScript expressions. These expressions include numerics, strings, and logicals.

writeln is used within the HTML tag <SCRIPT> or within an event handler. The document is usually opened by using document.open(). Event handlers perform their duties after the document opened by document.open() is closed by document.close(). In this situation, a new document window is automatically opened, and the writeln contents are displayed.

writeln is used in conjunction with many of the string formatting methods, such as italics and bold, for string displays.

Syntax:

document.writeln(expression1 [,expression2] [,expressionN])

expression1 through *expressionN* are any JavaScript expressions or the properties of any existing objects.

Example:

document.writeln("You are in JavaScript ");

Date Methods

Date methods provide a multitude of ways to query and manipulate time information. JavaScript resolves time down to the millisecond and accepts three representations of date information. One representation is in the verbose (IETF) string format Sat, 30 Mar 1996 13:54:00 MST. The second representation is the number of milliseconds since 1 Jan 1970 00:00:00. The third representation is as a list of integers: 96,30,2,13,54,0.

Date methods are also used to perform timezone conversion.

Method *getDate*

getDate returns the day of the month for the specified date. The date is returned as an integer between 1 and 31. getDate is a read-only value computed from other date properties.

Syntax:

```
dateObjectName.getDate();
```

dateObjectName is the name of a date object or a property of an existing object.

Example:

Example 1: A user's homepage that pops up a reminder to pay the rent if today is the first of the month:

```
<HTML>
<HEAD>
<SCRIPT LANGUAGE="JavaScript">
now = new Date();
if (now.getDate() == 1) {
  alert("Don't forget to pay the rent today!");
}
</SCRIPT>
</HEAD>
</HTML>
```

Example 2: A user's homepage that pops up a reminder that today is April 15th, deadline to file tax returns:

```
<HTML>
<HEAD>
<SCRIPT LANGUAGE="JavaScript">
now = new Date();
if ((now.getDate() == 15) && (now.getMonth == 3)) {
  alert("Today is Tax Day! Aaaaieee!");
}
</SCRIPT>
</HEAD>
</HTML>
```

Method *getDay*

getDay returns the day of the week for the specified date. This day is in the form of an integer representing the day of the week. 0 is Sunday, 1 is Monday, and so on.

Syntax:

```
dateObjectName.getDay();
```

dateObjectName is either the name of a date object or a property of an existing object.

Example:

Example 1: A user's homepage that pops up a reminder to go vote in the election if today is the second Tuesday in November:

```
<HTML>
<HEAD>
<SCRIPT LANGUAGE="JavaScript">
now = new Date();
if ((now.getDay==2) && (now.getDate()>=8) && (now.getDate()<=14))
➥{
  alert("Don't forget to GO VOTE today!");
}
</SCRIPT>
</HEAD>
</HTML>
```

Example 2: An improved version of the JavaScript program on the user's homepage, which pops up a reminder that today is April 15th, the deadline to file tax returns. If today is Sunday, indicate that tomorrow is the real deadline.

```
<HTML>
<HEAD>
<SCRIPT LANGUAGE="JavaScript">
now = new Date();
if ((now.getDate() == 15) && (now.getMonth == 3)) {
  if (now.getDay() == 0) {
    alert("Tomorrow is Tax Day! One more day to go!");
  } else {
    alert("Today is Tax Day! Aaaaieee!");
  }
}
```

```
</SCRIPT>

</HEAD>

</HTML>
```

Example 3: An even further improved version of the preceding example. If today is Sunday, April 15th or April 14th (any day but Saturday), indicate that tomorrow is the filing deadline. If today is Monday, April 16th or April 15th (any day but Sunday), indicate that today is the day.

```
<HTML>

<HEAD>

<SCRIPT LANGUAGE="JavaScript">

now = new Date();

// If 4/15 Sunday, OR 4/14 NOT Saturday

if (((now.getDate()==15) && (now.getMonth==3) &&
➥(now.getDay()==0))

   || ((now.getDate()==14) && (now.getMonth==3) &&
➥(now.getDay()!=6)))

   {

   alert("Tomorrow is Tax Day! One more day to go!");

}

// If 4/16 Monday, OR 4/15 NOT Sunday

if (((now.getDate()==16) && (now.getMonth==3) &&
➥(now.getDay()==1))

   || ((now.getDate()==15) && (now.getMonth==3) &&
➥(now.getDay()!=0)))

   {

   alert("Today is Tax Day! Aaaaieee!");

}

</SCRIPT>

</HEAD>

</HTML>
```

Method *getHours*

getHours returns the hour for the specified date. The value returned is an integer between 0 and 23. getHours ignores any minutes associated with the date.

Syntax:

```
dateObjectName.getHours();
```

dateObjectName is either the name of a date object or a property of an existing object.

Example:

An amusement page on a server at work. During working hours, 9:00 a.m. to noon, and 1:00 p.m. to 5:00 p.m. on weekdays, the page admonishes the user to get back to work.

```
<HTML>
<HEAD>
<SCRIPT LANGUAGE="JavaScript">
now = new Date();
// Check for weekday first (NOT Saturday and NOT Sunday)
if ((now.getDay() != 6) && (now.getDay != 0)) {
  // Work hours? (9:00am to 11:59am, and 1:00pm to 4:59pm)
  if (((now.getHours() >= 9) && (now.getHours() <= 11))
  || ((now.getHours() >= 13) && (now.getHours() <= 4 ))) {
  alert("Slacker! Get back to work!");
  history.back();
}
</SCRIPT>
</HEAD>
<BODY>
<H1>Joke of the day</H1>
</BODY>
</HTML>
```

Method *getMinutes*

getMinutes returns the minutes in the specified date. getMinutes is an integer between 0 and 59.

Syntax:

```
dateObjectName.getMinutes()
```

dateObjectName is either the name of a date object or a property of an existing object.

Example:

Display a 24-hour time-of-day clock in a form element. The displayed time updates every 10 seconds.

```
<HTML>
<HEAD>
<SCRIPT LANGUAGE="JavaScript">
function nextOne() {
  now = new Date();
  hrs = now.getHours();
  mins = now.getMinutes();
  // In case minutes has only one digit, add a 0,
  // ...so 7 past 9 displays as "9:07", not "9:7"
  if (mins < 10) {
   time = "" + hrs + ":0" + mins;
  } else {
   time = "" + hrs + ":" + mins;
  }
  // Write the time into the form text box
  document.timeform.timeclock.value = time;
  // Delay 10000ms (10 seconds)
  setTimeout("nextOne();", 10000);
}
setTimeout("nextOne();", 10000);
</SCRIPT>
</HEAD>
<BODY>
<FORM NAME="timeform">
Current time:
<INPUT TYPE="TEXT" NAME="timeclock" SIZE="5">
</FORM>
</BODY>
</HTML>
```

Method *getMonth*

getMonth returns the month in the specified date. The value returned by getMonth is an integer between 0 and 11. 0 is January, 1 is February, and so on.

Syntax:

```
dateObjectName.getMonth();
```

dateObjectName is either the name of a date object or a property of an existing object.

Example:

Play a harmless April fool's trick on the user (heh, heh, heh...):

```
<HTML>
<HEAD>
<SCRIPT LANGUAGE="JavaScript">
if ((Date.getDate()==1) && (Date.getMonth==3)) {
  document.write("<H2>File not found: Severe Error 276</H2>");
  while (true) {
  // Delay 5 seconds, then show a further pop up alert
  setTimeout("alert('Finished deleting all files');", 5000);
  // And repeat until the user has the sense to leave this page
  }
}
</SCRIPT>
</HEAD>
</HTML>
```

Method *getSeconds*

getSeconds returns the seconds in the specified time or date. The value of getSeconds that is returned is an integer between 0 and 59.

Syntax:

```
dateObjectName.getSeconds();
```

dateObjectName is either the name of a date object or a property of an existing object.

Example:

An improved version of the clock example from Date.getMinutes(), earlier. Displays a 24-hour time-of-day clock in a form element, also including seconds. The time displayed updates every second.

```
<HTML>
<HEAD>
<SCRIPT LANGUAGE="JavaScript">
function nextOne() {
  now = new Date();
  hrs = now.getHours();
  mins = now.getMinutes();
  secs = now.getSeconds();
  // In case minutes has only one digit, add a 0.
  if (mins < 10) {
   time = "" + hrs + ":0" + mins;
  } else {
   time = "" + hrs + ":" + mins;
  }
  // In case minutes has only one digit, add a 0.
  if (secs < 10) {
   time += ":0" + secs;
  } else {
   time += ":" + secs;
  }
  // Write the time into the form text box
  document.timeform.timeclock.value = time;
  // Delay 1000ms (1 second)
  setTimeout("nextOne();", 1000);   // Schedule next display
}
setTimeout("nextOne();", 5000);     // Schedule first display
</SCRIPT>
</HEAD>
<BODY>
<FORM NAME="timeform">
Current time:
<INPUT TYPE="TEXT" NAME="timeclock" SIZE="5">
</FORM>
</BODY>
</HTML>
```

Method *getTime*

getTime returns the numeric value of the time for the specified date.
This value is in number of milliseconds since 1 January 1970 00:00:00.

Syntax:

```
dateObjectName.getTime();
```

dateObjectName is either the name of a date object or a property of an existing object.

Example:

A simple stopwatch. Pressing one button sets a mark; pressing another button displays the number of elapsed milliseconds since the mark.

```
<HTML>
<HEAD>
<SCRIPT LANGUAGE="JavaScript">
var marktime = 0;
// Set mark: Make a note of the time.
function mark() {
  now = new Date();
  marktime = now.getTime();
}
// Measure the number of milliseconds since the mark was set
function measure() {
  now = new Date();
  difference = now.getTime() - marktime;
  // Write the difference in time into the form text box
  document.timeform. msecs.value = difference;
}
</SCRIPT>
</HEAD>
<BODY>
<FORM NAME="timeform">
<INPUT TYPE="BUTTON" NAME="btn1" VALUE="Set Mark"
onClick="mark();">
<INPUT TYPE="BUTTON" NAME="btn2" VALUE="Measure" onClick=
➥"measure();">
<BR>
Milliseconds elapsed:
<INPUT TYPE="TEXT" NAME="msecs" SIZE="10">
</FORM>
```

```
</BODY>
</HTML>
```

Method *getTimezoneOffset*

getTimezoneOffset returns the time zone offset in minutes for the current locale. The offset is between Greenwich Mean Time and the local time. Local time is derived from the Date() method.

Syntax:

dateObjectName.getTimezoneOffset();

dateObjectName is either the name of a date object or a property of an existing object.

Example:

Example 1: Prints the current timezone's number of hours difference from Greenwich Mean Time:

```
<HTML>
<HEAD>
<SCRIPT LANGUAGE="JavaScript">
// Compute the number of hours different from GMT
now = new Date();                // Create dummy Date
minutes = now.getTimezoneOffset();
hours = Math.floor(minutes / 60);     // Round down to hour
// Print timezone
document.writeln("You are <B>" + hours + "</B> different from
➥GMT.");
</SCRIPT>
</HEAD>
</HTML>
```

Example 2: Prints a symbolic representation of the current timezone (disregarding daylight savings time):

```
<HTML>
<HEAD>
<SCRIPT LANGUAGE="JavaScript">
function makeTZarray() {
  this[0] = "GMT+0 London";
  this[1] = "GMT+1 Paris";
```

```
        this[2] = "GMT+2 Vienna";
        this[3] = "GMT+3 Moscow";
        this[4] = "GMT+4 Gorki";
        this[5] = "GMT+5 Karachi";
        this[6] = "GMT+6 Tashkent";
        this[7] = "GMT+7 Djakarta";
        this[8] = "GMT+8 Irkutsk";
        this[9] = "GMT+9 Tokyo";
        this[10] = "GMT+10 Vladivostok";
        this[11] = "GMT+11 Magadan";
        this[12] = "GMT+12 Aukland";
        this[13] = "GMT-11 Gilbert Islands";
        this[14] = "GMT-10 Honolulu";
        this[15] = "GMT-9 Anchorage";
        this[16] = "GMT-8 Los Angeles";
        this[17] = "GMT-7 Denver";
        this[18] = "GMT-6 Chicago";
        this[19] = "GMT-5 New York";
        this[20] = "GMT-4 Grenada";
        this[21] = "GMT-3 Greenland";
        this[22] = "GMT-2 Cape Verde";
        this[23] = "GMT-1 Guinnea Bissau";
        this.length = 24;
}
tzarr = new makeTZarray();
// Compute the number of hours different from GMT
now = new Date();     // Create dummy Date
minutes = now.getTimezoneOffset();
hours = Math.floor(minutes / 60);     // Round down to hour
// Normalize hours to the range 0 thru 23
hours = (hours + 24) % 24;
// Print timezone
document.writeln("You are in the <B>" + tzarr[hours] + "</B>
➥zone");
</SCRIPT>
</HEAD>
</HTML>
```

Method *getYear*

getYear returns the year in the specified date. The value of getYear is the year minus 1900. For example, if the year is 1996, the value returned is 96.

Syntax:

```
dateObjectName.getYear();
```

dateObjectName is either the name of a date object or a property of an existing object.

Example:

Example 1: Compute and print a person's age in years:

```
<HTML>
<HEAD>
<SCRIPT LANGUAGE="JavaScript">
now = new Date();
year = 1900 + now.getYear();
function showage(yob) {
age = year - yob;
alert("You would seem to be " + age + " years old now.");
}
</SCRIPT>
</HEAD>
<BODY>
<FORM>
Please enter the year of your birth:
<INPUT TYPE="TEXT" NAME="yob" onChange="showage(this);">
</FORM>
</BODY>
</HTML>
```

Example 2: Improve on the previous example by taking into account the month and date of birth. Output is also in the form itself, instead of popping up the alert window:

```
<HTML>
<HEAD>
```

```
<SCRIPT LANGUAGE="JavaScript">
now = new Date();
year = 1900 + now.getYear();
function showage(ageform) {
  month = ageform.mob.value - 1;
  date = ageform.dob.value;
  age = year - ageform.yob.value;
  // Decrease age by 1 if a full year has not elapsed
  if (now.getMonth() < month) {
    --age;
  } else if ((now.getMonth() == month)
   && (now.getDate() < date)) {
    --age;
  }
  ageform.result.value = "You are " + age + " years old now.");
}
</SCRIPT>
</HEAD>
<BODY>
<FORM>
Please enter the day of the month you were born:
<INPUT TYPE="TEXT" NAME="mob"><br>
Please enter the month number you were born:
<INPUT TYPE="TEXT" NAME="dob"><br>
Please enter the year you were born:
<INPUT TYPE="TEXT" NAME="yob"><br>
<INPUT TYPE="BUTTON" NAME="btn1" VALUE="Compute" onClick=
➥"showage(this.form);"><br>
<INPUT TYPE="TEXT" SIZE=40 NAME="result">
</FORM>
</BODY>
</HTML>
```

Method *parse*

parse returns the number of milliseconds in a date string since 1 January 1970 00:00:00. parse assumes local time but it's possible to use U.S. time zone abbreviations in the argument or time zone offsets. For example, parse understands Sat, 30 Mar 1996 13:54:00

MST. This could also be expressed in the argument as Sat, 30 Mar 1996 13:54:00 GMT+7.

Syntax:

Date.parse(*dateString*);

dateString is a string or an existing object with a date value.

Example:

Example 1: Compute and print the age in years of a person, improving on the example from dateObj.getYear() by allowing the user to type his or her birthdate as a string like July 31, 1974. Remember, Date doesn't work for dates before 1970:

```
<HTML>
<HEAD>
<SCRIPT LANGUAGE="JavaScript">
now = new Date();
year = 1900 + now.getYear();
function showage(ageform) {
  then = new Date();
  then.setTime(Date.parse(ageform.dateofbirth.value));
  month = then.getMonth();
  date = then.getDate();
  age = year - then.getYear();
  // Decrease age by 1 if a full year has not elapsed
  if (now.getMonth() < month) {
    --age;
  } else if ((now.getMonth() == month)
   && (now.getDate() < date)) {
    --age;
  }
  ageform.result.value = "You are " + age + " years old now.");
}
</SCRIPT>
</HEAD>
<BODY>
<FORM>
Please enter your birthdate (e.g. "July 31, 1974"):
```

```
<INPUT TYPE="TEXT" NAME="dateofbirth"><br>
<INPUT TYPE="BUTTON" NAME="btn1" VALUE="Compute" onClick=
➥"showage(this.form);"><br>
<INPUT TYPE="TEXT" SIZE=40 NAME="result">
</FORM>
</BODY>
</HTML>
```

Example 2: Compute and print the age in years of a person, simplifying the previous example by using the numeric time directly, instead of breaking the example up into year, month, and date:

```
<HTML>
<HEAD>
<SCRIPT LANGUAGE="JavaScript">
now = new Date();
nowms = now.getTime();
function showage(ageform) {
   thenms = Date.parse(ageform.dateofbirth.value);
   secondsPerYear = 60 * 60 * 24 * 365.24;
   // Round down to integer year
   age = Math.floor(nowms - thenms) / secondsPerYear);
   ageform.result.value = "You are " + age + " years old now.");
}
</SCRIPT>
</HEAD>
<BODY>
<FORM>
Please enter your birthdate (e.g. "July 31, 1974"):
<INPUT TYPE="TEXT" NAME="dateofbirth"><br>
<INPUT TYPE="BUTTON" NAME="btn1" VALUE="Compute"
onClick="showage(this.form);"><br>
<INPUT TYPE="TEXT" SIZE=40 NAME="result">
</FORM>
</BODY>
</HTML>
```

Method *setDate*

setDate changes or sets the day of the month for a specified date. This method sets the day to an integer between 1 and 31.

Syntax:

dateObjectName.setDate(dayValue)

dateObjectName is either the name of a date object or a property of an existing object.

dayValue is an integer from 1 to 31.

Example:

Print the first day of the current month on the current page, as a freshness date for hypothetical data that is pointed to by the page:

```
<HTML>
<HEAD>
<SCRIPT LANGUAGE="JavaScript">
mydate = new Date();
mydate.setDate(1);
document.write("This data should have been last updated on ");
document.write(mydate.toLocaleString());
</SCRIPT>
</HEAD>
<BODY>
This month's <A HREF="/data/current.html">data set</A> is
➥available.
</BODY>
</HTML>
```

Method *setHours*

setHours changes or sets the hours for a specified date. The argument is an integer between 0 and 23, representing the hour of a date.

Syntax:

dateObjectName.setHours(hoursValue)

dateObjectName is either the name of a date object or a property of an existing object.

hoursValue is an integer between 0 and 23.

Example:

There is a long examination form to be filled out by the user. Set an alarm for one hour from now, when an alert pop-up should appear:

```
<HTML>
<HEAD>
<SCRIPT LANGUAGE="JavaScript">
mydate = new Date();
if (mydate.getHours() < 23) {
  mydate.setHours(mydate.getHours() + 1);
} else {
  mydate.setDate(mydate.getDate() + 1);
  mydate.setHours(0);
}
now = new Date();
// Compute the delay in milliseconds
delay = mydate.getTime() - now.getTime();
// Check for a negative delay time
if (delay < 0) {
  alert("Problem setting alarm --bailing out");
} else {
  setTimeout("alert('Ding! -- Time is up.');", delay);
}
</SCRIPT>
</HEAD>
<BODY>
<H1>Examination Alert!</H1>
You have one hour to answer all the questions in the form below.
A pop-up alert box will notify you when you are out of time.
</BODY>
</HTML>
```

Method *setMinutes*

setMinutes changes or sets the minutes for a specified date. The value of the argument is between 0 and 59.

Syntax:

```
dateObjectName.setMinutes(minutesValue)
```

dateObjectName is either the name of a date object or a property of an existing object.

minutesValue is an integer between 0 and 59.

Example:

Set an alarm for one minute before midnight tonight, then pop up an alert:

```
<HTML>
<HEAD>
<SCRIPT LANGUAGE="JavaScript">
mydate = new Date();
mydate.setHours(23);
mydate.setMinutes(59);
mydate.setSeconds(0);
now = new Date();
// Compute the delay in milliseconds
delay = mydate.getTime() - now.getTime();
setTimeout("alert('It is one minute to midnight!');", delay);
</SCRIPT>
</HEAD>
<BODY>
...
</BODY>
</HTML>
```

Method *setMonth*

setMonth changes or sets the month for a specified date. The argument values are between 0, representing January, and 11, representing December.

Syntax:

dateObjectName.setMonth(monthValue)

dateObjectName is either the name of a date object or a property of an existing object.

monthValue is an integer between 0 and 11.

Example:

Report the "Julian day," the day number this year. January first is
Julian day 1, February first is Julian day 32, and so on:

```
<HTML>
<HEAD>
<SCRIPT LANGUAGE="JavaScript">
// Determine Julian Day by counting the number of
// 24 hour periods since Jan 1 of this year
today = new Date();
today.setHours(0);
today.setMinutes(0);
today.setSeconds(0);
jan1st = new Date();
jan1st.setMonth(0);
jan1st.setDate(1);
jan1st.setHours(0);
jan1st.setMinutes(0);
jan1st.setSeconds(0);
// Compute milliseconds since Jan 1st
elapsedms = today.getTime() - jan1st.getTime();
// Convert milliseconds to days
elapseddays = elapsedms / (1000 * 60 * 60 * 24);
// Add one to adjust for Jan 1st being day 1, not day 0
jd = elapseddays + 1;
document.writeln("Today is Julian Day " + jd);
</SCRIPT>
</HEAD>
</HTML>
```

Method *setSeconds*

setSeconds changes or sets the seconds for a specified date. The
value of the argument is an integer between 0 and 59.

Syntax:

dateObjectName.setSeconds(*secondsValue*)

dateObjectName is either the name of a date object or a property
of an existing object.

secondsValue is an integer between 0 and 59.

Example:

Compute the number of seconds remaining until 5 p.m. today:

```
<HTML>
<HEAD>
<SCRIPT LANGUAGE="JavaScript">
timeat5pm = new Date();
timeat5pm.setHours(17);
timeat5pm.setMinutes(0);
timeat5pm.setSeconds(0);
now = new Date();
// Compute milliseconds until 5pm
// A negative number will be after 5pm
remaining = timeat5pm.getTime() - now.getTime();
// Convert milliseconds to seconds
remaining /= 1000;
if (remaining >= 0) {
  document.writeln("Seconds until 5pm: " + remaining);
} else {
  document.writeln("Seconds since 5pm: " + remaining);
}
</SCRIPT>
</HEAD>
</HTML>
```

Method *setTime*

setTime sets or changes the value of a date object. This method sets the time in milliseconds since 1 January 1970 00:00:00 and translates the milliseconds into recognizable time features.

Syntax:

```
dateObjectName.setTime(timevalue)
```

dateObjectName is either the name of a date object or a property of an existing object.

timevalue is an integer representing the number of milliseconds since 1 January 1970 00:00:00 GMT.

Example:

Determine if the current year is a leap year:

```
<HTML>
<HEAD>
<SCRIPT LANGUAGE="JavaScript">
// Time just before March 1, OR Feb. 29 (if its a leap year)
time = new Date();
time.setMonth(1);      // February
time.setDate(29);      // 29th
time.setHours(23);     // at 11:59:59 PM
time.setMinutes(59);
time.setSeconds(59);
// Add one second to make it the next day
time.setTime(time.getTime() + 1000);
if (time.getMonth() == 1) {
  document.writeln("This IS a leap year");
} else {
  document.writeln("This is NOT a leap year");
}
</SCRIPT>
</HEAD>
</HTML>
```

Method *setYear*

setYear changes or sets the year for a specified date. The value of the argument is an integer of the appropriate year minus 1900. For example, 1996 is passed to the method as 96.

Syntax:

```
dateObjectName.setYear(yearValue)
```

dateObjectName is either the name of a date object or a property of an existing object.

yearValue is an integer representing the appropriate year minus 1900.

Example:

Determine if a February 29th (of a leap year) lies between now and one year from now:

```
<HTML>
<HEAD>
<SCRIPT LANGUAGE="JavaScript">
now = new Date();
nextyear = new Date();
nextyear.setYear(nextyear.getYear() + 1);
// Compute elapsed time
elapsed = nextyear.getTime() - now.getTime();
// Convert milliseconds to days
edays = elapsed / (1000 * 60 * 60 * 24);
// Is the elapsed time 365 or 366 days?
if (Math.round(edays) == 366) {
  document.writeln("There IS");
} else {
  document.writeln("There is NOT");
}
document.writeln(" a leap year between now and this time next
➥year.");
</SCRIPT>
</HEAD>
</HTML>
```

Method *toGMTString*

toGMTString converts a date to a string. The exact format of the date is platform specific. The conversion uses the Internet GMT conventions. toGMTString relies on the operating system's time zone offset.

Syntax:

dateObjectName.toGMTString()

dateObjectName is either the name of a date object or a property of an existing object with a date value.

Example:

Print the current GMT (Greenwich Mean Time) time on the page. GMT is also known as UTC (Universal Coordinated Time):

```
<HTML>
<HEAD>
<SCRIPT LANGUAGE="JavaScript">
now = new Date();
document.writeln("The current UTC time is " + now.toGMTString());
</SCRIPT>
</HEAD>
</HTML>
```

Method *toLocaleString*

toLocaleString converts a date to a string. It is different from toGMTString in that the date is converted to the local convention's form. This form is platform and locale specific. If the returned string is to be manipulated further, it is recommended that getHours, getMinutes, and getSeconds be used for more predictable results.

Syntax:

dateObjectName.toLocaleString()

dateObjectName is either the name of a date object or a property of an existing object with a date value.

Example:

Print the current local time, in the local customary format, on the page:

```
<HTML>
<HEAD>
<SCRIPT LANGUAGE="JavaScript">
now = new Date();
document.writeln("The current time is " + now.toLocaleString());
</SCRIPT>
</HEAD>
</HTML>
```

Method *UTC*

UTC returns a date in milliseconds since 1 January 1970 00:00:00. Universal Coordinated Time (UTC) is equivalent to Greenwich Mean Time (GMT). UTC is a static method, which means that it is always invoked as Date.UTC(*argumentList*).

Syntax:

Date.UTC(year, month, day [,*hour*] [,*minutes*] [,*seconds*])

year is a date minus 1900.

month is a month between 0 and 11, 0 being January and 11 being December.

day is a day of the month between 1 and 31.

hour is hours between 0 and 23.

minutes is minutes between 0 and 59.

seconds is seconds between 0 and 59.

Example:

Determine the time zone the computer is operating in by comparing local time to GMT:

```
<HTML>
<HEAD>
<SCRIPT LANGUAGE="JavaScript">
localdate = new Date( Date.parse("Feb 9, 1990"));
gmtdate  = new Date( Date.UTC(90, 1, 9));
// Hours and Minutes difference from GMT
hrdiff = localdate.getHours()  - gmtdate.getHours();
mindiff = localdate.getMinutes() - gmtdate.getMinutes();
if ((hrdiff < 0) || (mindiff < 0)) {
  // East of Greenwich
  document.write("You are " + Math.abs(hrdiff) + " hours and "
  + Math.abs(mindiff) + "Minutes East of Greenwich");
} else {
  // West of Greenwich
```

```
    document.write("You are " + hrdiff + " hours and " + mindiff +
➥"Minutes West of Greenwich");
}
</SCRIPT>
</HEAD>
</HTML>
```

Form Methods

This section discusses an important method of the form object: the submit method.

Method *submit*

submit sets data back to an http server. This method submits the specific form using either GET or POST, as specified in the method property. submit is equivalent in action to the Submit button.

Syntax:

formName.submit()

formName is the name of any form or an element in the forms array.

Example :

theform.submit()

Methods Used by Multiple Objects

Some JavaScript methods, like blur, that are described in this section are used by multiple objects.

Method *blur*

blur removes focus from a specified form element. These form elements may be a password object, a select object, a text object, or a textarea object. blur, along with methods focus and select, operates on form elements. The objects may be accessed by the elements array.

Method of:

password, select, text, and textarea

Syntax:

passwordName.blur()

or

```
selectName.blur()
```

or

```
textName.blur()
```

or

```
textareaName.blur
```

`passwordName` is the value of the NAME attribute of a password object.

`selectName` is the value of the NAME attribute of a select object.

`textName` is the value of the NAME attribute of a text object.

`textareaName` is the value of the NAME attribute of a textarea object.

Example:

```
someText.blur()
```

assuming that `someText` is defined as

```
<input type="text" name="someText">
```

Method *clearTimeout*

`clearTimeout` cancels a timeout that was set with the `setTimeout` method. The argument to `clearTimeout` is the identifier set by `setTimeout`. `setTimeout` evaluates an expression after a specified number of milliseconds has elapsed. Whatever event is scheduled is canceled with `clearTimeout`.

Method of:

```
frame, window
```

Syntax:

```
clearTimeout(timeoutID)
```

timeoutID is the identifier set by *setTimeout*.

Property of:

`document`

Example:

The following example sets the color to yellow:

`document.alinkColor="yellow"`

See Also:

bgColor, *fgColor*, *linkColor*, and *vlinkColor*

Property *anchors*

Anchors is an array of all defined anchors in the current document.

Syntax:

`document.anchors[index]`

Property of:

`anchor` array

Example:

The following represents the second anchor array in a document:

`document.anchors[2]`

Property *appCodeName*

`appCodeName` is a read-only property. `appCodeName` returns a read-only string specifying the code name of the browser. This is different from `appName`, which returns the name of the browser.

Syntax:

`navigator.appCodeName`

Property of:

`navigator`

Example:

```
document.write("The code name of the browser you are using is "
➥+ navigator.appCodeName)
```

See Also:

appName, appVersion, userAgent

Property *appName*

appName is a read-only property. appName returns a string specifying the name of the browser. This is different from appCodeName, which returns the code name of the browser.

Syntax:

```
navigator.appName
```

Property of:

```
navigator
```

Example:

```
document.write("The application name is "  + navigator.appName)
```

See Also:

appCodeName, appVersion, userAgent

Property *appVersion*

appVersion is a read-only property that returns the version information for the Navigator. The version is returned in the format *releaseNumber* (*platform; country*). *releaseNumber* is the version number of the Navigator. *platform* is the platform currently running the Navigator. *country* is either I for the international release or U for U.S. release.

Syntax:

```
navigator.appVersion
```

Property of:

```
navigator
```

Example:

```
document.write("The version information of your browser is " +
➥navigator.appVersion)
```

See Also:

appName, *appCodeName*, *userAgent*

Property *bgColor*

bgColor manipulates the background color of the document. This property is the JavaScript equivalent to the HTML tag <BODY> and its attribute BGCOLOR.

bgColor may be set as either a hexadecimal RGB triplet or by a string literal. The string literal must be one of the accepted COLOR values. See Appendix A, "Colors," for a complete list of JavaScript color literals.

Syntax:

```
document.bgColor=colorLiteral
```

or

```
document.bgColor=RGBValue
```

colorliteral is the string value for the desired color.

RGBValue is the string value representing the hexadecimal RGB
➥color triplet.

Property of:

document

Example:

```
document.bColor := "darkcyan"
```

See Also:

alinkColor, *fgColor*, *linkColor*, and *vlinkColor*

Property *checked*

checked has a Boolean value reflecting the state of a checkbox or radio button object. If the button is selected, it is true; if not, it is false. checked can be set at any time. Setting a radio button or checkbox to true immediately updates its display.

Syntax:

```
checkboxName.checked
radioName[index].checked
```

checkboxName is the name of the checkbox object or an element in the `elements` array. The name of the checkbox object should be the same as the `NAME` attribute.

radioName is the value of the `NAME` attribute of a radio object.

index is an integer representing a radio button in a radio object.

Property of:

`checkbox, radio`

Example:

```
form.square.checked
```

See Also:

Property *defaultChecked*

Property *cookie*

The `cookie` property stores the string value of a cookie. A *cookie* is information stored by the Navigator in cookies.txt. String methods such as `substring`, `charAt`, `indexOf`, and `lastIndexOf` are used to extract the string stored in the cookie. The cookie property can be set at any time.

Syntax:

```
document.cookie
```

Property of:

`document`

Example:

To create a third cookie in a document:

```
document.cookie := "cookie3=Third_cookie";
```

See Also:

hidden object

Property *defaultChecked*

defaultChecked has a Boolean value reflecting the default state of a checkbox or radio button object. If the button is selected by default, it is true; if not, it is false. defaultChecked can be set at any time. defaultChecked is true if the CHECKED attribute is used within an <INPUT> tag. defaultChecked overrides the CHECKED attribute.

Setting a radio button or checkbox does not update its display, as happens with checked.

Syntax:

checkboxName.defaultChecked
radioName[*index*].defaultChecked

checkboxName is the name of the checkbox object or an element in the elements array. The name of the checkbox object should be the same as the NAME attribute.

radioName is the value of the NAME attribute of a radio object.

index is an integer representing a radio button in a radio object.

Property of:

checkbox, radio

Example:

examples.options[1].defaultSelected = true

See Also:

Property *checked*

Property *defaultSelected*

defaultSelected receives its initial value from the SELECTED attribute of an <OPTION> tag. defaultSelected has a Boolean value based upon whether or not a Select object is selected by default. If so, the value is true. If not, the value is false.

defaultSelected may be set at any time. Setting it overrides the value of the SELECTED attribute. The display of the object does not update as it does with the selected or selectedIndex properties.

Select objects created with the MULTIPLE attribute do not have their default selections affected by the use of defaultSelected. Select objects created without the MULTIPLE attribute lose their single default selection when defaultSelected is used.

Syntax:

selectName.options[index].defaultSelected

selectName is the value of the NAME attribute of a select object or an element in the elements array.

index is an integer representing an option in a select object.

Property of:

options array

Example:

examples.options[0].defaultSelected = true

See Also:

Properties index, selected, selectedIndex

Property *defaultStatus*

defaultStatus creates a default message to display in the status bar at the bottom of the window. The status property is different from defaultStatus in that status is an event-driven message that over-writes the default message.

defaultStatus may be set at any time. A return value of true must be used to set the defaultStatus property in the onMouseOver event handler.

Syntax:

windowReference.defaultStatus

windowReference is a valid way of referring to a window.

Property of:

```
window
```

Example:

```
window.defaultStatus = "Welcome to this JavaScript generated
➥page"
```

See Also:

Property *status*

Property *defaultValue*

`defaultValue` is the default value of a `password`, `text`, or `textarea` object. It is a string variable. The initial setting of the object is overridden when `defaultValue` is set. The new value is returned when queried. However, the display value of the object does not change as it does with the `value` property. The `defaultValue` can be set at any time.

`defaultValue` gets its initial value from its partner HTML attribute associated with the object. The following table shows the initial value of `defaultValue` and its object:

Object	*defaultValue* **Original Value**
text	**VALUE attribute**
textarea	**value specified between <TEXTAREA> and </TEXTAREA>**
password	**null, even if VALUE has been set**

Syntax:

passwordName.defaultValue
textName.defaultValue
textareaName.defaultValue

passwordName is either the value of the NAME attribute of a password object or an element in the elements array.

textName is either the value of the NAME attribute of a text object of an element in the elements array.

textareaName is either the value of the NAME attribute of a textarea object or an element in the elements array.

Property of:

password, text, textarea

Example:

document.Write(mypass.defaultvalue)

See Also:

Property *value*

Property *E*

The *E* property is Euler's constant. It is a read-only Math property, the base of natural logarithms. E's value is approximately 2.718.

Syntax:

Math.E

Property of:

Math

Example:

document.write(math.E)

See Also:

Properties *LN2, LN10, LOG2E, LOG10E, PI,* and *SQRT1_2*

Property *encoding*

encoding is a string that contains the value of the MIME encoding of the form. If *encoding* has not been set, then the value is the ENCTYPE attribute of the <FORM> tag. Setting the value of *encoding* overrides this attribute. *encoding* can be set at any time.

Syntax:

formName.encoding

formName is the name of a form or an element in the *forms* array.

Property of:

```
form
```

Example:

```
document.wtite(theform.encoding)
```

See Also:

Properties *action*, *method*, and *target*

Property *fgColor*

fgColor is the color of the document text. The color is a string that contains either the RGB triplet or a string literal contained in the color list in Appendix A.

The default value of fgColor is set by the user on the Colors tab of the Preferences dialog box. The default fgColor can be overridden by either setting the COLOR attribute of the <FONT> tag or by using the fontcolor method. This property cannot be set after the HTML source has been through layout.

Syntax:

```
document.fgcolor = "green"
```

Property of:

```
document
```

Example:

```
document.fgcolor = "green"
```

See Also:

Properties *alinkColor*, *bgColor*, *linkColor*, and *vlinkColor*

Method *fontcolor*

Property *hash*

hash is a string that specifies an anchor name in the URL. It must begin with a hash mark (#). It is generally better to use the property href to change a location. See RFC 1738 for complete information about this part of the URL.

Syntax:

```
links[index].hash
location.hash
```

index is an integer representing a link object.

Property of:

```
link, location
```

Example:

```
document.write("hash = "+ location.hash)
```

See Also:

Properties *host*, *hostname*, *href*, *pathname*, *port*, *protocol*, and *search*

Property *host*

host specifies a concatenation of the hostname and port properties of a URL. These are separated by a colon. The host property is the same as the hostname property when the port property is null.

It is preferable to use the href property when changing a location. host may be set at any time. An error is returned if the specified host cannot be found. See section 3.1 of RFC 1738 for complete information about the hostname and port properties.

Syntax:

```
links[index].host
location.host
```

index is an integer representing a link object.

Property of:

```
link, location
```

Example:

```
document.write("host is " + location.host)
```

See Also:

Properties *hash*, *hostname*, *href*, *pathname*, *port*, *protocol*, and *search*

Property *hostname*

hostname is a substring of the host property. host consists of the hostname and port properties. hostname is the first part of the host property, from the beginning to the colon.

Syntax:

```
links[index].hostname
location.hostname
```

index is an integer representing a link object.

Property of:

link, location

Example:

```
document.write("hostname = " + location.hostname)
```

See Also:

Properties *hash*, *host*, *href*, *pathname*, *port*, *protocol*, and *search*.

Property *href*

href is a string that contains the full URL. The other location properties, host, hostname, and port, are substrings of href. href can be set at any time.

Syntax:

```
links[index].href
location.href
```

index is an integer representing a link object.

Property of:

link, location

Example:

```
document.wtite("href= "+location.href)
```

See Also:

Properties *hash*, *host*, *hostname*, *pathname*, *port*, *protocol*, and *search*

Property *index*

index is an integer that represents the index of an option in a Select object.

Syntax:

```
selectName.options[indexValue].index
```

selectName is value of the NAME attribute of a select object or an element in the elements array.

indexValue is an integer representing an option in a select object.

Property of:

options array

Example:

```
document.write(document.thisform.elements[index].name)
```

See Also:

Properties *defaultSelected*, *selected*, and *selectedIndex*

Property *lastModified*

lastModified is a string representing the date that a document was last modified. It is a read-only property.

Syntax:

```
document.lastModified
```

Property of:

document

Example:

```
document.write("This page was last modified on " +
➥document.lastModified)
```

Property *length*

length is an integer that is used with many of the objects. Specifically what length measures is dependent on the object. See the following syntax section for a full list of the capabilities of length.

Syntax:

This is the syntax of length used with objects:

```
formName.length
```

formName is either the name of a form or an element in the forms array.

length is the number of elements on a form.

```
frameReference.length
```

frameReference is either the value of the NAME attribute of a frame or an element in the frames array.

length is the number of frames within a frame. A frame that does not load a document containing a <FRAMESET> tag always has a length of 0.

```
history.length
```

length is the number of entries in a history object.

```
radioName.length
```

radioName is either the value of the NAME attribute of a radio object or an element in the elements array.

length is the number of radio buttons in a radio object.

```
selectName.length
```

selectName is either the value of the NAME attribute of a select object or an element in the elements array.

length is the number of options in a select object.

```
stringName.length
```

stringName is any string or a property of an existing object.

length is a the length of a string object.

```
windowReference.length
```

windowReference is a valid way of referring to a window.

length is the number of frames in a parent window.

This is the syntax of length used with array properties:

```
anchors.length
elements.length
forms.length
frameReference.frames.length
windowReference.frames.length
links.length
selectName.options.length
```

length is the number of entries in one of the array properties.

Property of:

Objects frame, history, radio, select, string, and window

Arrays anchors, elements, forms, frames, links, and options

Example:

```
document.write("the length of string str is " + str.length)
```

Property *linkColor*

linkColor is the color of the document hyperlinks. As with all colors in JavaScript, it is either a color string literal or a RGB triplet.

linkColor is the equivalent of the LINK attribute of the <BODY> tag. Users set the default value of linkColor on the Colors tab of the Preferences dialog box. This must be set before the HTML source has been through layout.

Syntax:

```
document.linkColor
```

Property of:

```
document
```

Example:

```
document.linkColor="yellow"
```

See Also:

Properties `alinkColor`, `bgColor`, `fgColor`, and `vlinkColor`

Property *LN2*

LN2 is a Math constant. It is a read-only property. LN2 is the natural logarithm of 2, approximately 0.693.

Syntax:

```
Math.LN2
```

Property of:

```
Math
```

Example:

```
document.write(math.ln2)
```

See Also:

Properties *E, LN10, LOG2E, LOG10E, PI, SQRT1_2,* and *SQRT2*

Property *LN10*

LN10 is a Math constant. It is a read-only property. LN10 is the natural logarithm of 10, approximately 2.302.

Syntax:

```
Math.LN10
```

Property of:

```
Math
```

Example:

```
document.write(math.ln10);
```

See Also:

Properties *E*, *LN2*, *LOG2E*, *LOG10E*, *PI*, *SQRT1_2*, and *SQRT2*

Property *location*

location is a string specifying the complete URL of the document. It is a read-only property of document. This is not the object location.

Syntax:

```
document.location
```

Property of:

```
document
```

Example:

```
document.write("location "+ document.location)
```

See Also:

Object *location*

Property *LOG2E*

LOG2E is a Math constant. It is a read-only property. LOG2E is the base logarithm of e, approximately 1.442.

Syntax:

```
Math.LOG2E
```

Property of:

```
Math
```

Example:

```
document.write(math.log2E)
```

See Also:

Properties *E*, *LN2*, *LN10*, *LOG10E*, *PI*, *SQRT1_2*, and *SQRT2*

Property *LOG10E*

LOG10E is a Math constant. It is a read-only property. LOG10E is the base 10 logarithm of e, approximately 0.434.

Syntax:

```
Math.LOG10E
```

Property of:

```
Math
```

Example:

```
document.write(math.log10E)
```

See Also:

Properties *E*, *LN2*, *LN10*, *LOG2E*, *PI*, *SQRT1_2*, and *SQRT2*

Property *method*

method is a string specifying how form field input information is sent to the server. method is equivalent to the METHOD attribute of the <FORM> tag. method can be set at any time. It should evaluate to either get or post.

See RFC 1867 for more information on specific values of the method property.

Syntax:

```
formName.method
```

formName is either the name of a form or an element in the forms array.

Property of:

```
form
```

Example:

```
document.write("form method" + theform.method)
```

See Also:

Properties *action*, *encoding*, and *target*

Property *name*

`name` is a string specifying the name of an object. Each object uses `name` in a slightly different way. Read the text under the syntax section for more information on the particular way each object deals with `name`.

The `name` property can be set at any time. Also, the `name` property is not used to give a label to a `button`, `reset`, or `submit` object. That is the `value` property. The `name` property is used to reference the objects in question. An array of `name` is created if multiple objects on the same form have the same `NAME` attribute.

Syntax:

```
objectName.name
```

`objectName` is either the value of the `NAME` attribute of any of the objects listed below or an element in the `elements` array.

`name` initially is the value of the `NAME` attribute of the object.

```
frameReference.name
```

`frameReference` is a valid way of referring to a frame.

`name` initially is the value of the `NAME` attribute of the object.

```
frameReference.frames.name
```

`frameReference` is a valid way of referring to a frame.

`name` initially is the value of the `NAME` attribute of the object.

```
radioName[index].name
```

`radioName` is the value of the `NAME` attribute of a radio object.

`index` is any valid integer.

name initially is the value of the NAME attribute of the object.

selectName.options.name

selectName is either the value of the NAME attribute of a select object or an element in the elements array.

name initially is the value of the NAME attribute of the object.

windowReference.name

windowReference is a valid way of referring to a window.

windowReference.frames.name

Property of:

Objects button, checkbox, frame, hidden, password, radio, reset, select, submit, text, textarea, and window

options array

Example:

document.write(name of window is ' + theWindow.name)

See Also:

value property for objects *button*, *reset*, and *submit*

Property *parent*

parent is used to denote the <FRAMESET> window of a frame. parent is a read-only property. It's possible to use parent in the place of the window name when referring to frames at the same level in the hierarchy. Also, a parent.frames array is available for use of accessing frames within a hierarchy.

Syntax:

parent.propertyName

propertyName is the defaultStatus, status, length, name, or parent property when the calling parent refers to a window object.

propertyName is the length, name, or parent property when the calling parent refers to a frame object.

```
parent.methodName
```

`methodName` is any method associated with the window object.

```
parent.frameName
```

`frameName` is any valid frame name.

```
parent.frames[index]
```

`index` is an integer pointing to the frame in the `parent.frames` array.

Property of:

`frame`, `window`

Example:

```
document.write('parent for frame is ' + menuframe.parent)
```

Property *pathname*

`pathname` is a string that contains the value of a portion of the URL. The `pathname` is the path of the specified resource.

`pathname` can be set at any time. It is recommended that `href` is used to change a location. An error occurs if the specified pathname is not found.

Syntax:

```
links[index].pathname
location.pathname
```

`index` is an integer representing a link object.

Property of:

`link`, `location`

Example:

```
document.write('pathname is ' + location.pathname)
```

See Also:

Properties *hash*, *host*, *hostname*, *href*, *port*, *protocol*, and *search*

Property *PI*

PI is a constant, read-only property of Math. It is the ratio of the circumference of a circle to its diameter, approximately 3.14159.

Syntax:

```
Math.PI
```

Property of:

```
Math
```

Example:

```
gamma = Math.PI / 4;
```

See Also:

Properties *E, LN2, LN10, LOG2E, LOG10E, SQRT1_2,* and *SQRT2*

Property *port*

port is a string that contains the value of the communications port used for server communications. port is a portion of the URL, a substring of the host property.

port can be set at any time. It is recommended that the href property be used to change a location. An error occurs if the specified port is not found. The default port property is 80. See Section 3.1 of RFC 1738 for complete information about the port.

Syntax:

```
links[index].port
location.port
```

index is an integer representing a link object.

Property of:

```
link, location
```

Example:

```
document.write('port '+ location.port)
```

See Also:

Properties *hash*, *host*, *hostname*, *href*, *pathname*, *protocol*, and *search*

Property *protocol*

`protocol` is a string that specifies the access method of the URL. For example, a protocol of `"http:"` specifies Hypertext Transfer Protocol. A protocol of `"javascript:"` specifies JavaScript code.

The `protocol` property can be set at any time. It is recommended to use the href property to change a location. An error occurs if the specified protocol cannot be found.

See Section 2.1 of RFC 1738 for more information on the `protocol` schema.

Syntax:

```
links[index].protocol
location.protocol
```

index is an integer representing a link object.

Property of:

```
link, location
```

Example:

```
document.links[0].protocol = "http:"
```

See Also:

Properties *hash*, *host*, *hostname*, *href*, *pathname*, *port*, and *search*

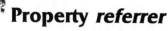

Property *referrer*

`referrer` is the URL of the calling document as evaluated from the destination document. `referrer` receives its value when the user clicks on a link. `referrer` is a read-only property.

Syntax:

```
document.referrer
```

Property of:

```
document
```

Example:

```
document.write("The page from which you came is " +
➥document.referrer)
```

Property *search*

`search` is a string that specifies query information in a URL. It always begins with a question mark. The `search` property may be set at any time, although it is recommended that the `href` property be used to change a location. An error occurs if the specified search cannot be found in the current location. See Section 3.3 of RFC 1738 for complete information about the `search` property.

Syntax:

```
links[index].search
location.search
```

`index` is an integer representing a `link` object.

Property of:

```
link, location
```

Example:

```
window.location.search="?infohere"
```

See Also:

Properties *hash*, *host*, *hostname*, *href*, *pathname*, *port*, and *protocol*

Property *selected*

`selected` is a Boolean value that denotes whether or not an option of a `select` object is selected. If the option is selected, the value is true. If it is not selected, the value is false.

`selected` may be set at any time. The `select` option display updates when `selected` is set.

It is recommended that `selected` be used with `select` objects created with the `MULTIPLE` attribute. It works much better than `selectedIndex` in this situation. Every option in the `options` array can be evaluated with the `selected` property.

Syntax:

`selectName.options[index].selected`

`selectName` is either the value of the `NAME` attribute of a select object or an element in the `elements` array.

`index` is an integer representing an option in a select object.

Property of:

`options` array

Example:

`this.form.meal.options[2].selected=1`

See Also:

Properties `defaultSelected`, `index`, and `selectedIndex`

Property *selectedIndex*

`selectedIndex` is an integer specifying the index of the selected option in a `select` object. `selectedIndex` may be set at any time. The display of the `select` object is updated immediately when set with `selectedIndex`.

Select object options are indexed in the order in which they are defined. The index begins with zero.

It is better to use `selectedIndex` on `select` objects created without the `MULTIPLE` attribute. `selectedIndex` will evaluate only the first option of a multiple `select` object. This is not very useful in that situation.

Syntax:

`selectName.selectedIndex`
`selectName.options.selectedIndex`

selectName is either the value of the NAME attribute of a select object or an element in the elements array.

Property of:

select, options array

Example:

```
document.write("selected index " + thisform.someText.
➥selectedIndex)
```

See Also:

Properties *defaultSelected*, *index*, and *selected*

Property *self*

self is another name for the current window or frame. It is handy to use self to differentiate between windows or frames of the same name.

Syntax:

```
self.propertyName
self.methodName
```

propertyName is the defaultStatus, status, length, or name property when self refers to a window object.

propertyName is the length or name property when self refers to a frame object.

methodName is any method associated with the window object.

Property of:

frame, window

Example:

```
document.write(self.name)
```

See Also:

Property *window*

Property *SQRT1_2*

SQRT1_2 is a constant, read-only Math property. It is the square root of one-half, approximately 0.707.

Syntax:

Math.SQRT1_2

Property of:

Math

Example:

document.write(Math.SQRT1_2)

See Also:

Properties *E*, *LN2*, *LN10*, *LOG2E*, *PI*, and *SQRT2*

Property *SQRT2*

SQRT2 is a constant, read-only Math property. It is the square root of two, approximately 1.414.

Syntax:

Math.SQRT2

Property of:

Math

Example:

MATH.SQRT2

See Also:

Properties *E*, *LN2*, *LN10*, *LOG2E*, *PI*, and *SQRT1_2*

Property *status*

status temporarily overwrites the status bar message at the bottom of the window. It may appear when a mouseOver event occurs over an anchor.

status may be set at any time. status must return true to set the status property in the onMouseOver event handler.

Syntax:

windowReference.status

windowReference is a valid way of referring to a window.

Property of:

window

Example:

Window.Status := 'a sample message for the status bar'

See Also:

Property *defaultStatus*

Property *target*

target is a string that specifies a window name. If it is used as a property of the form object, target specifies the name of the window that receives responses after a form has been submitted. If target is used as a property of a link object, it specifies the name of the window that displays the content of a clicked hypertext link.

target may be set at any time. The target window must be explicitly written. It cannot contain the value of a JavaScript expression or variable.

The initial value of target is equivalent to the TARGET attribute of the <FORM> and <A> tags. Setting target overrides these attributes.

Syntax:

formName.target
links[*index*].target

formName is either the name of a form or an element in the forms array.

index is an integer representing a link object.

Property of:

form, link

Example:

homePage.target = 'http://www.borland.com/"

See Also:

Form Properties *action*, *encoding*, and *method*

Property *text*

text is a string that contains the text that follows an <OPTION> tag in a select object. text receives its initial value from the HTML code. It is possible to overwrite this value, but the displayed value does not change. However, if the value is evaluated, the new value is returned.

Syntax:

selectName.options[index].text

selectName is either the value of the NAME attribute of a select object or an element in the elements array.

index is an integer representing an option in a select object.

Property of:

options array

Example:

document.testform.elements[0].text

Property *title*

title is equivalent to the value within the <TITLE> and </TITLE> tags. title is a read-only property. title is null if the document does not have a title.

Syntax:

document.title

Property of:

document

Example:

document.title = "StopWatch";

Property *top*

top refers to the topmost window that contains frames or nested framesets. Use top as a shorthand for this window. top is a read-only property.

Syntax:

top.propertyName

propertyName is defaultStatus, status, or length.

top.methodName

methodName is any method associated with the window object.

top.frameName
top.frames[*index*]

frameName and frames[*index*] are ways to refer to frames.

Property of:

window

Example:

```
document.write("top is "+ theWindow.top)
```

Property *userAgent*

userAgent is a read-only property that represents the value sent in the user agent header in the HTTP protocol from client to server.

Syntax:

```
navigator.userAgent
```

Property of:

```
navigator
```

Example:

```
document.Write("User agent is "  + navigator.userAgent)
```

See Also:

Properties *appName*, *appVersion*, and *appCodeName*

Appendix A

Colors

JavaScript allows colors to be specified in order to enhance an application. These colors are text color, link color, background color, and so on. Color may be changed from the default.

The two ways of describing a desired color to JavaScript are with a color name or with a special number. Color names must be one of the preset JavaScript color names. These color names are listed later in this appendix.

The numerical representation for colors used by JavaScript comes from the representation used in Netscape 1.1's <BODY> tag. This in turn originated with the notation used by the MIT X Window System. The idea behind using a number is that any color can be described precisely by specifying how much of the primary additive colors red, green, and blue are to be used. If you do not believe this, take a close look at your TV screen with a magnifying glass; the phosphors on the picture tube are red, green, and blue.

A total lack of red, green, and blue all make black. Red, green, and blue all on make white. As you would expect, red on and green and blue off make red. As you might not expect, red and green on and blue off make yellow. It takes a bit of experimentation, but by adjusting the intensities of the red, green, and blue, the RGB value, any desired color may be fabricated.

Because computers store number in bytes, the measure of the RGB intensities is represented as three numbers each in the range 0 through 255. The value 0 represents off, 255 represents full maximum intensity, and 128 is half intensity. For example, the color "coral," a bright red color, has RGB values 255, 127, and 80, respectively.

Unfortunately, these pleasant decimal numbers are not used by the HTML and JavaScript color specification numbers; hexadecimal is used.

Hexadecimal is base 16. Because there are only ten Arabic numeral digits 0 through 9, and because hexadecimal needs 16 different digits, the letters A through F are used to represent the values 10 through 15 (decimal):

A = 10

B = 11

C = 12

D = 13

E = 14

F = 15

The reason many computer people like hexadecimal, *hex* for short, is because it maps very directly and conveniently into binary. Each hex digit corresponds directly to a group of four binary digits, which are called *bits*. Because a *byte* is eight bits, exactly two hex digits are required to represent a one byte value. Hex numbers are often written with a letter *H* appended to signify hex, or with 0x prepended following the C/C++/Java standard notation. In the MIT X Window system and in HTML, hex color values appear in strings prepended by a pound sign (#). In all notations, capitalized or lowercase hex digits A through F may be used. Always use the notation appropriate for the hexadecimal numbers' use.

A hex integer literal in a JavaScript program must be given the prepended 0x format; HTML must be given six hex digits prepended with the # character. Examples of hexadecimal number representations include the following:

0x1eb9

0x0D

9ff0H

FFffE000H

#B8860B

#6495ed

The rightmost hex digit is the "ones" place, with the "sixteens" digit on its left. Decimal numbers less than 255 may be converted into hexadecimal simply by using division. Divide the number by 16, obtaining quotient and remainder. The quotient is the value of the left digit, and the remainder is the value of the right digit.

Example: What is the hexadecimal value of 171 decimal?

```
171 / 16 = 10, remainder 11
171 = ((10) x 16) + 11
    = 0xAB
```

Likewise, hex may be converted to decimal simply using multiplication.

Example: What is the decimal value of 9A hex?

```
The hex digit A = 10
(9 x 16) + 10 =
(9 x 16) + 10 = 154
```

When making HTML color specifications using hex, the three pairs of hex digits are written as a set of six adjacent characters, prepended by a pound sign. For example, the color with Red intensity 44, Green intensity 90, and Blue intensity E0 would have an HTML representation of #4490E0.

The order is always first the Red digits, then Green, then Blue (RGB). This format originates with the MIT X Window system used on UNIX workstations, the historical development platform for most Internetworking tools.

Composing a custom color may be accomplished by choosing a starting point from the following table, then adjusting the Red, Green, and Blue values up or down. You might also choose to use one of the many publicly available color selection Web pages, implemented both in CGI and JavaScript. The CGI sites include:

Thalia color compose:

```
http://www.sci.kun.nl/cgi-bin-thalia/color/compose
```

ColorServe Pro:

```
http://www.biola.edu/cgi-bin/colorpro/colorpro.cgi
```

A very interesting color selection site based on JavaScript is:

hIdaho Color Center:

```
http://www.hIdaho.com/c3/
```

After the user has a color name or #RRGGBB triplet, it may be used to set document-wide colors with the document properties fgColor, bgColor, linkColor, alinkColor, and vlinkColor. It may also be used in the HTML <FONT> tag's COLOR attribute value and the associated String method fontcolor().

The JavaScript program in the following HTML file may be used to create custom colors in decimal numeric form. It does this by converting to hexadecimal from decimal:

```
<HTML>
<HEAD>
<TITLE>Color Selection Example</TITLE>
<SCRIPT LANGUAGE="JavaScript">
<!- Color selection example

function htod(n) {
    return parseint(n, 16);
}


/*
**   dtoh(n)  - Convert Decimal to Hex
**      Use reverse horners method to convert a decimal string to
➥a hex string.
*/
function dtoh(n) {
    var hd = "0123456789ABCDEF";        // Hex digits

    n = parseInt(n);

    if (n < 16) {
        return (hd.charAt(n));
    } else {
        return (dtoh(n / 16) + hd.charAt(parseInt(n % 16)));
    }
}


/*
**   zp(s, n)  - Zero-Pad string 's' to 'n' digits
*/
function zp(s, n) {
  while (s.length < n) {
      s = "0" + s;
  }

    return s;
}
```

```
/*
**   makeRGB(r, g, b)  — Build RGB hex string from values
*/
function makeRGB(r, g, b) {
    return ("#" + zp(dtoh(r), 2) + zp(dtoh(g), 2) + zp(dtoh(b),
➡2));
}


/*
**   colordoc(win, r, g, b)  — Draw (R,G,B) color document in
➡window 'win'
*/
function colordoc(win, r, g, b) {
   win.document.open();
   win.document.title   = "Color Display";
   win.document.writeln("<HTML>");
   win.document.bgColor = makeRGB(r, g, b);
   win.document.writeln("Generated with: "+makeRGB(r, g, b));
   win.document.close();
}



// Open window to display color
win = window.open("", "Cwin", "height=50,width=220,resize=1");

// ->
</SCRIPT>
</HEAD>

<BODY>
<H1>Color Selection</H1>
<FORM>
Red:<BR>
Decimal:<INPUT TYPE="TEXT" NAME="Rdec"
   onChange="this.form.Rhex.value = dtoh(this.value);">
<INPUT TYPE="TEXT" NAME="Rhex"> Hex<BR>
```

```
Green:<BR>
Decimal:<INPUT TYPE="TEXT" NAME="Gdec"
    onChange="this.form.Ghex.value = dtoh(this.value);">
<INPUT TYPE="TEXT" NAME="Ghex"> Hex<BR>
Blue:<BR>
Decimal:<INPUT TYPE="TEXT" NAME="Bdec"
    onChange="this.form.Bhex.value = dtoh(this.value);">
<INPUT TYPE="TEXT" NAME="Bhex"> Hex<BR>

<INPUT TYPE="BUTTON" NAME="rend" VALUE="Render"
onClick="colordoc(win, this.form.Rdec.value,
this.form.Gdec.value,
    this.form.Bdec.value);"><BR>
</FORM>
</BODY>
</HTML>
```

Here is a list of currently known color names and their RGB values:

Table A.1
Color Names and
Their RGB Values.

Color Name	RR	GG	BB
aliceblue	F0	F8	FF
antiquewhite	FA	EB	D7
aqua	00	FF	FF
aquamarine	7F	FF	D4
azure	F0	FF	FF
beige	F5	F5	DC
bisque	FF	E4	C4
black	00	00	00
blanchedalmond	FF	EB	CD
blue	00	00	FF
blueviolet	8A	2B	E2
brown	A5	2A	2A
burlywood	DE	B8	87
cadetblue	5F	9E	A0
chartreuse	7F	FF	00

continues

Color Name	RR	GG	BB
chocolate	D2	69	1E
coral	FF	7F	50
cornflowerblue	64	95	ED
cornsilk	FF	F8	DC
crimson	DC	14	3C
cyan	00	FF	FF
darkblue	00	00	8B
darkcyan	00	8B	8B
darkgoldenrod	B8	86	0B
darkgray	A9	A9	A9
darkgreen	00	64	00
darkkhaki	BD	B7	6B
darkmagenta	8B	00	8B
darkolivegreen	55	6B	2F
darkorange	FF	8C	00
darkorchid	99	32	CC
darkred	8B	00	00
darksalmon	E9	96	7A
darkseagreen	8F	BC	8F
darkslateblue	48	3D	8B
darkslategray	2F	4F	4F
darkturquoise	00	CE	D1
darkviolet	94	00	D3
deeppink	FF	14	93
deepskyblue	00	BF	FF
dimgray	69	69	69
dodgerblue	1E	90	FF
firebrick	B2	22	22
floralwhite	FF	FA	F0
forestgreen	22	8B	22
fuchsia	FF	00	FF
gainsboro	DC	DC	DC
ghostwhite	F8	F8	FF

Color Name	RR	GG	BB
gold	FF	D7	00
goldenrod	DA	A5	20
gray	80	80	80
green	00	80	00
greenyellow	AD	FF	2F
honeydew	F0	FF	F0
hotpink	FF	69	B4
indianred	CD	5C	5C
indigo	4B	00	82
ivory	FF	FF	F0
khaki	F0	E6	8C
lavender	E6	E6	FA
lavenderblush	FF	F0	F5
lawngreen	7C	FC	00
lemonchiffon	FF	FA	CD
lightblue	AD	D8	E6
lightcoral	F0	80	80
lightcyan	E0	FF	FF
lightgoldenrodyellow	FA	FA	D2
lightgreen	90	EE	90
lightgrey	D3	D3	D3
lightpink	FF	B6	C1
lightsalmon	FF	A0	7A
lightseagreen	20	B2	AA
lightskyblue	87	CE	FA
lightslategray	77	88	99
lightsteelblue	B0	C4	DE
lightyellow	FF	FF	E0
lime	00	FF	00
limegreen	32	CD	32
linen	FA	F0	E6
magenta	FF	00	FF

continues

Color Name	RR	GG	BB
maroon	80	00	00
mediumaquamarine	66	CD	AA
mediumblue	00	00	CD
mediumorchid	BA	55	D3
mediumpurple	93	70	DB
mediumseagreen	3C	B3	71
mediumslateblue	7B	68	EE
mediumspringgreen	00	FA	9A
mediumturquoise	48	D1	CC
mediumvioletred	C7	15	85
midnightblue	19	19	70
mintcream	F5	FF	FA
mistyrose	FF	E4	E1
moccasin	FF	E4	B5
navajowhite	FF	DE	AD
navy	00	00	80
oldlace	FD	F5	E6
olive	80	80	00
olivedrab	6B	8E	23
orange	FF	A5	00
orangered	FF	45	00
orchid	DA	70	D6
palegoldenrod	EE	E8	AA
palegreen	98	FB	98
paleturquoise	AF	EE	EE
palevioletred	DB	70	93
papayawhip	FF	EF	D5
peachpuff	FF	DA	B9
peru	CD	85	3F
pink	FF	C0	CB
plum	DD	A0	DD
powderblue	B0	E0	E6
purple	80	00	80

Color Name	RR	GG	BB
red	FF	00	00
rosybrown	BC	8F	8F
royalblue	41	69	E1
saddlebrown	8B	45	13
salmon	FA	80	72
sandybrown	F4	A4	60
seagreen	2E	8B	57
seashell	FF	F5	EE
sienna	A0	52	2D
silver	C0	C0	C0
skyblue	87	CE	EB
slateblue	6A	5A	CD
slategray	70	80	90
snow	FF	FA	FA
springgreen	00	FF	7F
steelblue	46	82	B4
tan	D2	B4	8C
teal	00	80	80
thistle	D8	BF	D8
tomato	FF	63	47
turquoise	40	E0	D0
violet	EE	82	EE
wheat	F5	DE	B3
white	FF	FF	FF
whitesmoke	F5	F5	F5
yellow	FF	FF	00
yellowgreen	9A	CD	32

We hope that you choose to use these colors in your applications. Colors may really jazz up an otherwise mundane application. You, the programmer, have worked hard to create something useful and interesting. Don't use boring colors. Do, however, be aware that the users of your applications have gotten used to the "standard" colors used in most applications on the Web. If your application gets too wild with unexpected colors, it may confuse users.

Glossary

argument   Input data to a function or method. Parameter.

binary   Having two. The binary number system has two digits: 0 and 1. A binary operator operates on two operands. Here the minus sign (-) is a binary operator, subtracting the second operand from the first: `cars = vehicles - trucks;`.

block   A compound statement. Enclosing multiple statements within curly braces (`'{'`, `'}'`) constructs a compound statement that can take the place of a single simple statement anywhere.

Boolean   The logical state "true" or "false." Named after Boole, a British mathematician who worked on expanding the formal understanding of mathematical operations using true/false quantities.

CGI   Common Gateway Interface, a specification of how browsers should encode and send HTML form data to HTTP servers for processing. `http://w3.org/`, `http://ncsa.uiuc.edu/`.

control structure   A language element allowing the alteration of the sequence of program statement execution. These include "if-else" conditionals, and "while" and "for" loops.

cookie   A mechanism for storing state information and data on the client (browser). A server can store and retrieve information of its choosing to and from the browser. JavaScript provides the document.cookie property for the purpose of interacting with this information. See the Netscape specification at http://www.netscape.com/newsref/std/cookie_spec.html.

event   A JavaScript event is some occurrence that triggers an "event handler." These may include page loading and unloading, form submission, form element clicked on, movement of the mouse over a link, and change of keyboard input focus.

event handler   JavaScript code specified to be executed when a certain event occurs. These are usually specified in an HTML attribute, the name of which begins with the letters *on*. For example, the attribute onSubmit specifies JavaScript code to be run when a form is submitted.

focus   A term used to refer to the destination of keystrokes. A form's input box is said to have the keyboard focus if keystrokes appear in the input box. Focus is directed with a mouse click or Tab key. Netscape indicates keyboard focus by activating the cursor within the input box.

form   An HTML form is a mechanism for obtaining user input using a variety of different visual gadgets, including text input boxes, checkboxes, selection pull-down menus, pushbuttons, and others. Form contents were formerly only capable of being processed by server CGI scripts.

frame   A subdivision of a browser window or of another frame. The structure of the subdivision of windows is defined by a *frameset*. A frameset specifies the frames to be loaded into these subwindows and their geometry. A frame is a mini-browser and is capable of displaying most any document.

frameset   A frameset defines the subdivision of a browser window into horizontal or vertical subwindows. Each of these frames may be loaded with an HTML document, or further subdivided with another frameset.

function   A grouping of statements into a block, associating a name to that group of statements by which the block of statements can be executed from elsewhere within the program. Functions may take input data via argument lists (enclosed in parentheses) and return data as a "return value."

HTML   HyperText Markup Language.

HTTP   HyperText Transfer Protocol. A protocol for transferring HTML files, now extended to be capable of carrying any MIME type file.

identifier   A JavaScript name for a variable, function, method, or property. Identifiers must start with a letter, followed by letters or digits. Special: the underscore character (_) is considered to be a letter, for the purpose of identifiers.

IETF   Internet Engineering Task Force. An arm of the Internet Society, a cooperative consensus-oriented multilateral organization made up of volunteers from industry. It helps to guide the development of networking and content-delivery technology by issuing standards documents of variable authority, including RFCs.

method   A function, which is a property of an object. Object-oriented terminology.

MIME   Multipurpose Internet Mail Extensions, defined by RFC-1521 and RFC-1522. MIME defines a standard method of putting a header on the front of data describing its characteristics. Specifications in the MIME header include, among others, those of "content-type" and "content-length."

MIME content-type   A MIME specification with two parts, separated by a /. The first part defines a type of data; the second describes the specific format. For example: `image/gif`, `image/jpeg`, `text/html`, and `text/plain`. Consult RFC-1521 for a full description. `http://www.isi.edu/`, `ftp://nic.ddn.mil/`.

object   A special variable capable of having sub-variables (called *properties*).

`onBlur`   The `onBlur` event occurs when an object loses the keyboard focus when it had the focus previously.

`onFocus`   The `onFocus` event occurs when an object receives the keyboard focus when it did not have the focus previously.

parameter   Input data to a function or method. Argument. There are two official types of parameters: *formal* and *actual*. The formal parameters are the parameters as they are defined with the function definition. The actual parameters are those parameters actually used when the function is called.

property   A characteristic, attribute, or information about an object. Object-oriented terminology.

RFC   Acronym for Request For Comment. RFCs are a numbered sequence of Internet standards documents issued by the IETF and associated technical and standards entities. They are living documents in the sense that they evolve over time and are modified and reissued from time to time as technical needs require. `http://www.isi.edu/`, `ftp://nic.ddn.mil/`.

target   The destination window or frame for a hypertext link or form action. Clicking on a hypertext link normally loads the new page into the same window or frame where the link was. The `TARGET` attribute allows you to specify the name of another frame or window into which the page should be loaded.

`this`   A JavaScript object that refers to the current object. `this` may be used only in constructor functions and within event handlers inside of HTML objects. This allows constructor functions to refer implicitly to the object that has just been created.

unary   Associated with one item. A unary operator operates on a single item. Here the `-` is a unary operator, negating the value of the variable `x`: `new_x = -x * 2;`.

URL   Uniform Resource Locator, vs. URI and URN.

VRML   Virtual Reality Modeling Language.

W3O   The World Wide Web Consortium, a developer of open standards and technology for the World Wide Web community. `http://www.w3.org/`.

window   A graphical user interface (GUI) window object created by the browser and managed by the platform's window manager (such as Windows 95, X, OpenWindows). A window is distinct from a frame in that a frame resides within a window and is *not* under direct control of the platform window manager.

WWW   The World Wide Web, the set of internetworked computers offering to speak hypertext transfer protocol (HTTP).

Index

Other books from Prima Publishing, Computer Products Division

ISBN	Title	Release Date	Price
0-7615-0064-2	Build a Web Site	Available Now	34.95
1-55958-744-X	The Windows 95 Book	Available Now	24.95
0-7615-0383-8	Web Advertising and Marketing	Available Now	34.95
1-55958-747-4	Introduction to Internet Security	Available Now	34.95
0-7615-0063-4	Researching on the Internet	Available Now	29.95
0-7615-0693-4	Internet Information Server	Available Now	40.00
0-7165-0430-3	The Essential Book for Microsoft Office	Available Now	27.99
0-7615-0688-8	Managing with Microsoft Project	Available Now	30.00
0-7615-0678-0	Java Applet Powerpack	Summer 1996	
0-7615-0684-5	VBScript	Summer 1996	
0-7615-0726-4	The Webmaster's Handbook	Summer 1996	
0-7615-0691-8	Netscape FastTrack Server	Summer 1996	
0-7615-0733-7	The Essential Netscape Navigator Gold Book	Summer 1996	
0-7615-0759-0	Professional Web Design	Summer 1996	

FILL IN AND MAIL TODAY

Prima Publishing
P.O. Box 1260BK
Rocklin, CA 95677-1260

USE YOUR VISA/MC AND ORDER BY PHONE:
1-800-632-8676 extension 4444

OR, TO ORDER BOOKS ONLINE:
sales@primapub.com

YOU CAN ALSO VISIT OUR WEB SITE:
www.primapublishing.com

Please send me the following titles:

Quantity	Title	Amount
_____	_____	_____
_____	_____	_____
_____	_____	_____
_____	_____	_____
	Subtotal	$_____
	Postage & Handling ($4.00 for the first book plus $1.00 each additional book)	$_____
	Sales Tax **7.25% Sales Tax (California only)** **8.25% Sales Tax (Tennessee only)** **5.00% Sales Tax (Maryland only)** **7.00% General Service Tax (Canada)**	$_____
	TOTAL (U.S. funds only)	$_____

❏ Check enclosed for $_____ (payable to Prima Publishing)

Charge my ❏ Master Card ❏ Visa

Account No. _____

Exp. Date _____

Signature _____

Your Name _____

Address _____

City/State/Zip _____

Daytime Telephone _____

Satisfaction is guaranteed—or your money back!
Please allow three to four weeks for delivery.
THANK YOU FOR YOUR ORDER

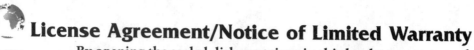

License Agreement/Notice of Limited Warranty

By opening the sealed disk container in this book, you agree to the following terms and conditions. If, upon reading the following license agreement and notice of limited warranty, you cannot agree to the terms and conditions set forth, return the unused book with unopened disk to the place where you purchased it for a refund.

License:

The enclosed software is copyrighted by the copyright holder(s) indicated on the software disk. You are licensed to copy the software onto a single computer for use by a single concurrent user and to a backup disk. You may not reproduce, make copies, or distribute copies or rent or lease the software in whole or in part, except with written permission of the copyright holder(s). You may transfer the enclosed disk only together with this license, and only if you destroy all other copies of the software and the transferee agrees to the terms of the license. You may not decompile, reverse assemble, or reverse engineer the software.

Notice of Limited Warranty:

The enclosed disk is warranted by Prima Publishing to be free of physical defects in materials and workmanship for a period of sixty (60) days from end user's purchase of the book/disk combination. During the sixty-day term of the limited warranty, Prima will provide a replacement disk upon the return of a defective disk.

Limited Liability:

THE SOLE REMEDY FOR BREACH OF THIS LIMITED WARRANTY SHALL CONSIST ENTIRELY OF REPLACEMENT OF THE DEFEC-TIVE DISK. IN NO EVENT SHALL PRIMA OR THE AUTHORS BE LIABLE FOR ANY OTHER DAMAGES, INCLUDING LOSS OR COR-RUPTION OF DATA, CHANGES IN THE FUNCTIONAL CHARAC-TERISTICS OF THE HARDWARE OR OPERATING SYSTEM, DELETE-RIOUS INTERACTION WITH OTHER SOFTWARE, OR ANY OTHER SPECIAL, INCIDENTAL, OR CONSEQUENTIAL DAMAGES THAT MAY ARISE, EVEN IF PRIMA AND/OR THE AUTHORS HAVE PREVI-OUSLY BEEN NOTIFIED THAT THE POSSIBILITY OF SUCH DAM-AGES EXISTS.

Disclaimer of Warranties:

PRIMA AND THE AUTHORS SPECIFICALLY DISCLAIM ANY AND ALL OTHER WARRANTIES, EITHER EXPRESS OR IMPLIED, INCLUDING WARRANTIES OF MERCHANTABILITY, SUITABILITY TO A PARTICULAR TASK OR PURPOSE, OR FREEDOM FROM ERRORS. SOME STATES DO NOT ALLOW FOR EXCLUSION OF IMPLIED WARRANTIES OR LIMITATION OF INCIDENTAL OR CONSEQUENTIAL DAMAGES, SO THESE LIMITATIONS MAY NOT APPLY TO YOU.

Other:

This Agreement is governed by the laws of the State of California with-out regard to choice of law principles. The United Convention of Contracts for the International Sale of Goods is specifically disclaimed. This Agreement constitutes the entire agreement between you and Prima Publishing regarding use of the software.